D1555299

# The Political Philosophy of Hannah Arendt

"This is an incisive, penetrating and clear presentation of some of the major philosophical and political tensions in Hannah Arendt's work. Departing from the usual characterization of Hannah Arendt's political thought as a nostalgic longing for the lost Greek *polis*, d'Entrèves analyzes the persistence and complexity of the problems of modernity in Arendt's thought. It is well written and well argued and will be immensely useful to newcomers as well as more advanced readers of Hannah Arendt's work."

Seyla Benhabib, *Harvard University*

"The conclusions that d'Entrèves draws from Hannah Arendt's work for the implementation of more extended and participatory forms of democracy and citizenship demonstrate the acute contemporary relevance of Arendt's writings for our political thinking after the collapse of totalitarianism. d'Entrèves' writing is distinguished by compelling and clearly articulated argument, and his exposition and assessment of Arendt is of a consistently high quality. This is a sophisticated entrance point to Arendt's political thought."

Simon Critchley, *University of Essex*

"A learned and subtle account of Arendt's work. It offers a fresh and needed perspective."

George Kateb, *Princeton University*

Hannah Arendt is recognized as one of the seminal thinkers of the twentieth century. This book provides a systematic reconstruction of four major concepts underpinning her work: modernity, action, judgment, and citizenship. Taking each concept in turn, d'Entrèves offers an original assessment of Arendt's conception of modernity, identifies two distinct models of political action as well as two distinct conceptions of judgment, and shows the relevance of her political theory to contemporary debates on the nature and scope of democratic citizenship. D'Entrèves argues that Arendt's conception of active citizenship and democratic deliberation provides the best framework for rethinking the nature of political agency and for the reactivation of public life in the modern world. *The Political Philosophy of Hannah Arendt* is an ideal text for students of Arendt, as it provides a novel and systematic account of her political theory and offers a fresh perspective from which to evaluate her work.

# The Political Philosophy of Hannah Arendt

Maurizio Passerin d'Entrèves

London and New York

First published 1994
by Routledge
11 New Fetter Lane, London EC4P 4EE

# 27768123

Simultaneously published in the USA and Canada
by Routledge
29 West 35th Street, New York, NY 10001

© 1994 Maurizio Passerin d'Entrèves

Typeset in 10 on 12 point Palatino by
Megaron, Cardiff, Wales
Printed and bound in Great Britain by
Clays, St Ives plc

*British Library Cataloguing in Publication Data*
A catalogue record for this book is available from the British Library.

*Library of Congress Cataloging in Publication Data*
Passerin d'Entrèves, Maurizio
  The political philosophy of Hannah Arendt/Maurizio Passerin
d'Entrèves.
    p.  cm.
  Includes bibliographical references and index.
  1.  Arendt, Hannah – Contributions in political
science.  2.  Arendt, Hannah – Philosophy.  I.  Title.
JC251.A74P39 1993
320.5–dc20  93-18492

ISBN 0–415–08790–2 (hbk)
ISBN 0–415–08791–0 (pbk)

# Contents

# Acknowledgments

The writing of a book, although conducted in the solitude of one's study, is always the product of a collective dialogue. During the years in which this work took shape, I had the privilege of learning from and conversing with a number of generous and supportive scholars. I would first like to thank Seyla Benhabib, who has been my principal source of inspiration and support. If this book has taken the shape that it has, it is due to her vision, her example, and her generous advice. I would also like to thank James Schmidt for the unfailing care and attention he gave to an earlier version of this work. He has been a careful reader, a learned commentator, and a most constructive critic. I also owe a great debt to George Kateb, who gave me crucially supportive comments at various stages and whose deep and nuanced understanding of Arendt's thought was a model for my own (different) reading of her. I also want to thank him for having introduced me to the works of Emerson, Thoreau, and Whitman, and for his fine defense of the value of democratic individuality. At the opposite side of the theoretical spectrum, I wish to thank Michael Sandel for drawing my attention to the neglected dimensions of agency and community in liberal thought. To Thomas McCarthy I owe my gratitude for having clarified and deepened my understanding of Habermas, and for his lively conversations. During the two years spent in Italy, I had the fortune of attending the seminars of Steven Lukes and John Pocock. To Steven I owe my thanks for keeping my intellectual project on course. To John Pocock, whose *Machiavellian Moment* was crucial for my understanding of Arendt (and for much else beside), I owe my deepest thanks for his generous comments and constructive support during a difficult phase of my life. It was also a great pleasure to witness a scholar at work. Finally, I wish to thank my friend William Falcetano for the many conversations we have had in the last ten years, for exemplifying the idea of vocation, and for having sustained my commitment when it truly mattered.

I would like to thank Adrian Driscoll at Routledge for his interest in my work and for his unfailing competence in seeing it through.

This book is dedicated to Laura and Niccolò, who know best.

I wish to thank the editors of *Praxis International*, *Philosophy and Social Criticism*, and *Thesis Eleven*, where earlier versions of portions of this book were published.

# Introduction

Hannah Arendt was one of the seminal political thinkers of the twentieth century. The power and originality of her thinking was evident in works such as *The Origins of Totalitarianism*, *The Human Condition*, *On Revolution* and *The Life of the Mind*. In these works and in numerous essays she grappled with the most crucial political events of our century, trying to grasp their meaning and historical import, and showing how they affected our categories of moral and political judgment. What was required, in her view, was a new framework that could enable us to come to terms with the twin horrors of the twentieth century, Nazism and Stalinism. She provided such framework in her book on totalitarianism, and went on to develop a new set of categories that could illuminate the human condition and provide a fresh perspective on political life.

Although some of her works now belong to the classics of the Western tradition of political thought, she has always remained difficult to classify. Her political philosophy cannot be characterized in terms of the traditional categories of conservatism, liberalism, and socialism. Nor can her thinking be assimilated to the recent revival of communitarian political thought, to be found, for example, in the writings of A. MacIntyre, M. Sandel, C. Taylor, and M. Walzer. Her name has been invoked by some of the communitarian critics, on the grounds that she presented a vision of politics radically at odds with the principles of liberalism. There are many strands of Arendt's thought that could justify such a claim, in particular, her critique of representative democracy, her stress on civic engagement and political deliberation, her separation of morality from politics, and her praise of the revolutionary tradition. To place Arendt's thought within the growing chorus of communitarian objections against liberalism would, however, be a mistake. Arendt was in fact a stern defender of constitutionalism and the rule of law, an advocate of fundamental human rights (among which she included not only the right to life, liberty, and freedom of expression, but also the right to action and to opinion), and a critic of all forms of political community based on traditional ties and customs, as well as those based on religious, ethnic, or racial identity.

Arendt's political thought cannot, in this sense, be identified either with the liberal tradition or with the claims advanced by a number of communitarian critics. Arendt did not conceive of politics as a means for the satisfaction of individual preferences, nor as a way to integrate individuals around a single or transcendent conception of the good. Her conception of politics is based instead on the idea of *active citizenship*, that is, on the value and importance of civic engagement and collective deliberation about all matters affecting the political community. If there is a tradition of thought with which Arendt can be identified, it is the classical tradition of civic republicanism originating in Aristotle and embodied in the writings of Machiavelli, Montesquieu, Jefferson, and Tocqueville. According to this tradition politics finds its authentic expression whenever citizens gather together in a public space to deliberate and decide about matters of collective concern. Political activity is valued not because it may lead to agreement or to a shared conception of the good, but because it enables each citizen to exercise his or her powers of agency, to develop the capacities for judgment, and to attain by concerted action some measure of political efficacy.

Arendt's conception of politics, with its stress on civic engagement and unconstrained political deliberation, is clearly indebted to this tradition of thought. Her conception of action and political discourse is aimed, in fact, at the reactivation of political agency and efficacy, and articulates the conditions for the exercise of active citizenship and democratic self-determination.

In this book I reconstruct and critically evaluate Arendt's political philosophy with respect to four major themes. In the first chapter I examine her conception of modernity, in the second her theory of action, in the third her theory of judgment, and in the fourth her conception of citizenship. Throughout these chapters I attempt to provide a reading of Arendt that highlights her contribution to a theory of participatory democracy based on the principles of freedom, plurality, equality, and solidarity.

# CHAPTER 1: HANNAH ARENDT'S CONCEPTION OF MODERNITY

In this chapter I examine Arendt's conception of modernity and her critique of modern forms of social and political life. For Arendt modernity is characterized by the "loss of the world," by which she means the restriction or elimination of the public sphere of action and speech in favor of the private world of introspection and the private pursuit of economic interests. Modernity is the age of mass society, of the rise of the "social" out of a previous distinction between the public and the private, and of the victory of *animal laborans* over both contemplation and action. It is the age of bureaucratic administration and anonymous labor, rather than politics and action, of elite domination and the manipulation of public opinion. It is the age when totalitarian forms of government, such as Nazism and Stalinism, have emerged as a result of the institutionalization of terror and violence. It is the age where history as a "natural process" has replaced history as a fabric of actions and events, where homogeneity and conformity have replaced plurality and freedom, and where isolation and loneliness have eroded human solidarity and all spontaneous forms of living together. Modernity is the age where the past no longer carries any certainty of evaluation, where individuals, having lost their traditional standards and values, must search for new grounds of human community as such.

This is Arendt's vision of modernity, a vision so stark and unredeeming as to offer at first sight little room for alternative accounts or different characterizations. In the first part of the chapter, however, I argue that Arendt's negative appraisal of modernity was shaped by her experience of totalitarianism in the twentieth century, and that her work provides a number of important insights that may help us to address certain problematic features of the modern age. In her political writings, and especially in *The Origins of Totalitarianism*, Arendt claimed that the phenomenon of totalitarianism has broken the continuity of Occidental history, and has rendered meaningless most of our moral and political categories. The break in our tradition has become irrevocable after the tragic events of our century and the triumph of totalitarian movements in East and West. In the form of Stalinism and Nazism, totalitarianism has exploded the established categories of political thought and the accepted standards of moral judgment, and has thereby broken the continuity of our history. Faced with the tragic events of the Holocaust and the Gulag, we can no longer go back to traditional concepts and values, so as to explain the unprecedented by means of precedents, or to understand the monstrous by means of the familiar. The burden of our time must be faced without the aid of tradition, or as Arendt once put it, "without a bannister." Our inherited concepts and criteria for judgment have been dissolved under the impact of modern political events, and the task now is to re-establish the meaning of the past outside the framework of any tradition, since none has retained its original validity. It is the past, then, and not tradition, that Arendt attempts to preserve from the rupture in modern time-consciousness. Only by reappropriating the past by means of what Arendt called "the deadly impact of new thoughts" can we hope to restore meaning to the present and throw some light on the contemporary situation.

The hermeneutic strategy that Arendt employed to re-establish a link with the past is indebted to both Benjamin and Heidegger. From Benjamin she took the idea of a fragmentary historiography, one that seeks to identify the moments of rupture, displacement, and dislocation in history. Such fragmentary historiography enables one to recover the lost potentials of the past in the hope that they may find actualization in the present. From Heidegger she took the idea of a deconstructive reading of the Western philosophical tradition, one that seeks to uncover the original meaning of our categories and to liberate them from the distorting incrustations of tradition. Such deconstructive hermeneutics enables one to recover those primordial experiences (*Urphaenomene*) which have been occluded or forgotten by the philosophical tradition, and thereby to recover the lost origins of our philosophical concepts and categories.

By relying on these two hermeneutic strategies Arendt hopes to redeem from the past its lost or "forgotten treasure," that is, those fragments from the past that might still be of significance to us. In her view it is no longer possible, after the collapse of tradition, to save the past as a whole; the task, rather, is to redeem from oblivion those elements of the past that are still able to illuminate our situation. To re-establish a linkage with the past is not an antiquarian exercise; on the contrary, without the critical reappropriation of the past, our temporal horizon becomes disrupted, our experience precarious, and our identity more fragile. In Arendt's view, then, it is necessary to redeem from the past those moments worth preserving, to save those fragments from past treasures that are significant for us. Only by means of this critical reappropriation can we discover the past anew, endow it with relevance and meaning for the present, and make it a source of inspiration for the future.

This critical reappropriation is facilitated, in part, by the fact that after the rupture in modern time-consciousness the past may "open up to us with unexpected freshness and tell us things no one has yet had ears to hear." The breakdown of tradition may in fact provide the great chance to look upon the past "with eyes undistorted by any tradition, with a directness which has disappeared from Occidental reading and hearing ever since Roman civilization submitted to the authority of Greek thought." Arendt's return to the original experience of the Greek *polis* represents, in this sense, an attempt to break the fetters of a worn-out tradition and to rediscover a past over which tradition no longer has a claim. Against tradition Arendt sets the criterion of genuineness, against the authoritative that which is forgotten, concealed, or displaced at the margins of history. Only by operating against the grain of traditionalism and the claims of conventional historiography can the past be made meaningful again, provide sources of illumination for the present, and yield its treasures to those who search for them with "new thoughts" and saving acts of remembrance.

In the second part of the chapter I go on to examine the key features of Arendt's conception of modernity; these are world alienation, earth alienation, the rise of the social, and the victory of *animal laborans*. World alienation refers to the loss of an intersubjectively constituted world of experience and action by means of which we establish our self-identity and an adequate sense of reality. Earth alienation refers to the attempt to escape from the confines of the earth; spurred by modern science and technology, we have searched for ways to overcome our earth-bound condition by setting out on the exploration of space, by attempting to recreate life under laboratory conditions, and by trying to extend our given life-span. The rise of the social refers to the expansion of the market economy from the early modern period and the ever-increasing accumulation of capital and social wealth. With the rise of the social everything has become an object of production and consumption, of acquisition and exchange; moreover, its constant expansion has resulted in the blurring of the distinction between the private and the public. The victory of *animal laborans* refers to the triumph of the values of labor over those of *homo faber* and of man as *zoon politikon*. All the values characteristic of the world of fabrication – permanence, stability, durability – as well as those characteristic of the world of action and speech – freedom, plurality, solidarity – are sacrificed in favor of the values of life, productivity, and abundance.

Arendt identifies two main stages in the emergence of modernity: the first, from the sixteenth to the nineteenth century, corresponds to world alienation and the rise of the social, the second, from the beginning of our century, corresponds to earth alienation and the victory of *animal laborans*. She also identifies a number of causes: the discovery of America and the corresponding shrinking of the earth, the waves of expropriation started during the Reformation, the invention of the telescope challenging the adequacy of the senses, the rise of modern science and philosophy and subsequently of a conception of man as part of a process of Nature and History, and the expansion of the realm of the economy, of the production and accumulation of social wealth.

Having examined the key features, the main stages, and the principal causes of the emergence of modernity, I turn in the third part of the chapter to a critique of Arendt's interpretation of modernity. In particular, I focus on three categories employed by Arendt, those of *nature*, of *process*, and of the *social*. With respect to the category of nature, I argue that Arendt oscillated between two contrasting accounts. According to the first account, the modern age, by elevating labor, the most natural of human activities, to the highest position within the *vita activa*, has brought us too close to nature. Instead of building and preserving the human artifice and creating public spaces for action and deliberation, we are reduced to engage in the activity of sheer survival and in the production of things that are by definition perishable. According to the second account, however, the modern age is characterized by a growing artificiality, by the rejection of anything that is not man-made. Arendt cites the fact that natural processes, including that of life itself, have been recreated artificially by means of scientific experiment, that our natural environment has been extensively transformed and in some instances entirely replaced by technology, and that we have searched for ways to overcome our natural condition as earth-bound creatures by setting out on the exploration of space and envisaging the possibility of inhabiting other planets. All this leads to a situation where nothing around us will be a naturally given event, object, or process, but will instead be the product of our instruments and the will to refashion the world in our image. I argue that these two accounts are difficult to reconcile, since in the former we have nature intruding upon and even destroying the human artifice, while in the latter we have art (i.e., *techne*) expanding upon and replacing everything natural or merely given. The result is to endow nature with an ambiguous status, since in the former case the victory of *animal laborans* indicates our subjection to natural processes, while in the latter case the expansion of scientific knowledge and of technological mastery indicates the overcoming of all natural limits. The modern world would thus appear to be too natural and too artificial, too much under the dominance of labor and the life-process of the species, as well as too much under the dominance of *techne*.

With respect to the second category, that of process, I argue that Arendt exhibited a deep ambivalence towards it. On the one hand, she claimed that the modern age was characterized by the subsumption of Nature and History under the category of process, and that the break with contemplation and the elevation of labor to the highest position within the *vita activa* resulted from the introduction of the concept of process into making. On the other hand, she claimed that processes are the inevitable result of human action, and that action itself has a process-like character. This claim is surprising, since for Arendt one of the principal features of action is to introduce the unexpected, the novel, the unpredictable, and thus to break the automatism associated with the idea of process. The greater puzzle, however, is the fact that Arendt identifies some of the worst features of modernity (in particular, the understanding of history and nature as all-encompassing processes, and our willingness to "act into nature") with the consequences of that capacity for action which is held to be the highest and most valuable of all human capacities. How can the capacity to act, to begin something new (i.e., freedom), be reconciled with the automatism of its consequences (i.e., necessity)? How do we reconcile the negative assessment of those features of modernity associated with the idea of process with the acknowledgment that action is responsible for initiating processes? What Arendt said of Marx – that his attitude toward labor never ceased to be equivocal – can be said of Arendt too: her attitude toward process is characterized by a deep ambivalence, an ambivalence which affected her assessment of modernity and her understanding of the relation between freedom and necessity.

I conclude the chapter with a critique of Arendt's concept of the social. Arendt identifies the social with all those activities formerly restricted to the private sphere of the household and having to do with the necessities of life. Her claim is that with the tremendous expansion of the economy from the end of the eighteenth century, all such activities have taken over the public realm and transformed it into a sphere for the satisfaction of our material needs. Society has thus invaded and conquered the public realm, turning it into a function of what previously were private needs and concerns, and has thereby destroyed the boundary separating the public and the private. Arendt also claims that with the expansion of the social realm the tripartite division of human activities has been undermined to the point of becoming meaningless. In her view, once the social realm has established its monopoly, the distinction between labor, work, and action is lost, since every effort is now expended on reproducing our material conditions of existence. Obsessed with life, productivity, and consumption, we have turned into a society of laborers and job-holders who no longer appreciate the values associated with work, nor those associated with action.

From this brief account it is clear that Arendt's concept of the social plays a crucial role in her assessment of modernity. I argue, however, that it blinds her to many important issues and leads her to a series of questionable judgments. In the first place, Arendt's characterization of the social is overly restricted. She claims that the social is the realm of labor, of biological and material necessity, of the reproduction of our condition of existence. She also claims that the rise of the social coincides with the expansion of the economy from the end of the eighteenth century. I argue, however, that having identified the social with the growth of the economy in the past two centuries, Arendt cannot characterize it in terms of a subsistence model of simple reproduction. In the second place, Arendt's identification of the social with the activities of the household is responsible for a major shortcoming in her analysis of the economy. She is, in fact, unable to acknowledge that a modern capitalist economy constitutes a structure of power with a highly asymmetric distribution of costs and rewards. By relying on the misleading analogy of the household, she maintains that all questions pertaining to the economy are pre-political, and thus ignores the crucial question of economic power and exploitation. Finally, by insisting on a strict separation between the private and the public, and between the social and the political, she is unable to account for the essential connection between these spheres and the struggles to redraw their boundaries. Today many so-called private issues have become public concerns, and the struggle for justice and equal rights has extended into many spheres. I conclude, therefore, that by insulating the political sphere from the concerns of the social, and maintaining a strict distinction between the public and the private, Arendt is unable to account for some of the most important achievements of modernity – the extension of justice and equal rights, and the redrawing of the boundaries between the public and the private.

## CHAPTER 2: HANNAH ARENDT'S THEORY OF ACTION

In this chapter I examine Arendt's theory of action and defend the claim that Arendt's revival of the ancient notion of *praxis* represents her most original attempt to respond to the aporias of the modern age. By distinguishing action (*praxis*) from fabrication (*poiesis*), by linking it to freedom and plurality, and by showing its connection to speech and remembrance, Arendt is able to articulate a conception of politics in which questions of meaning, identity, and value can be addressed in a pertinent manner. Moreover, by viewing action as a mode of human togetherness based on equality and solidarity, Arendt is able to offer a conception of participatory democracy that stands in direct contrast to the bureaucratized and elitist forms of political representation so characteristic of the modern epoch.

In the first part of the chapter I provide a reconstruction of Arendt's theory of action, focusing on its principal components, such as freedom, natality, plurality, and disclosure. I then show the links between action and narrative, between action and remembrance, and the importance of what I call "communities of memory." I then examine the connection between action, power, and the space of appearance. Lastly, I look at the remedies for the unpredictability and irreversibility of action, namely, the power of promise and the power to forgive.

In the second part I examine and respond to a number of criticisms that have been made of her theory. I argue that these criticisms are only partially valid, since they fail to account for the complexity and the tensions of Arendt's theory of action. I look at the most significant critiques, namely, those advanced by M. Jay, G. Kateb, M. Canovan, B. Parekh, P. Fuss, and J. Habermas. These critiques differ considerably both in substance and in terms of the implications that are drawn with respect to the validity of Arendt's theory. Jay and Kateb are concerned with the apparent lack of a normative or moral dimension in Arendt's theory of action, and maintain that this seriously impairs its validity. Canovan, Parekh, and Fuss, on the other hand, are more concerned with the political feasibility of her theory, and argue that it contains a tension between two different visions of politics, an elitist and a democratic one in the case of Canovan, a heroic and participatory one in the case of Parekh, and an agonal and accommodational one in the case of Fuss. Habermas, finally, thinks that Arendt remains bound to the constellation of classical Greek philosophy and is unable for this reason to conceptualize adequately the phenomenon of power in modern capitalist societies.

My response to these critiques is to show that Arendt's theory of action incorporates two models, an expressive and a communicative one, and that her critics (with the exception of Habermas) have concentrated almost exclusively on the expressive model of action at the expense of the communicative one. I also argue, however, that Arendt was never able to integrate these two models in a satisfactory manner, and that this inability affected her theory of action as well as her conception of politics.

My argument is developed as follows. On the one hand, Arendt conceives action as that mode of human activity in which individuals are able to disclose their unique identities, their distinctive "who" as against their shared "what," and to overcome the futility and mortality of their lives through the performance of exemplary deeds. Both the disclosure of one's identity and the attainment of earthly immortality depend, in turn, upon a community of interpreters who are able to ascertain and to preserve for posterity the unique identity of the actors. Although a communicative dimension is present in this conception of action, it is clear that the emphasis is on the expressive dimension, that is, on the articulation and confirmation of the unique qualities and capacities of actors. On the other hand, Arendt articulates a conception of action as a mode of human togetherness in which individuals are able to establish relations of reciprocity and solidarity. In this conception what matters is not so much the disclosure of the uniqueness of the self, or the overcoming of one's mortality, but the establishment of communicative relations based on mutuality, symmetry, and persuasion. Here action is characterized by the sharing of words and deeds, by processes of collective deliberation and mutual accommodation, rather than by the striving for glory and immortality.

I argue that there is a tension between these two conceptions of action, and that Arendt was prone, especially in her earlier writings, to emphasize the expressive conception at the expense of the communicative one. I also argue that the tension between these two conceptions affects not just her theory of action but also her understanding of politics. As Fuss and Parekh point out, Arendt put forward two models of politics, the first of which can be characterized as agonal or heroic, the second as accommodational or participatory; they argue that she never managed to integrate the two in a satisfactory manner. While accepting this charge, I go on to show that the tension between these two models of politics corresponds rather closely to the tension between the two conceptions of action. When action is conceptualized in terms of the expressive model, politics is viewed as an agonal encounter between actors who strive for recognition and glory; on the other hand, when action is conceptualized in terms of the communicative model, politics is viewed as the collective process of deliberation and decision-making that rests on the arts of persuasion and mutual accommodation.

I argue that Arendt was never able to resolve the tension between these two conceptions of action. However, I also stress the fact that in her later writings she progressively broadened her conception of action to include collective processes of deliberation and decision-making, and in this respect provided the basis for a politics based on mutuality, solidarity, and persuasion.

## CHAPTER 3: HANNAH ARENDT'S THEORY OF JUDGMENT

In this chapter I reconstruct Arendt's theory of judgment and relate it to some of the issues explored in the previous two chapters. As I argue in Chapter 1, Arendt's conception of modernity is characterized by a deep concern about the losses incurred as a result of world alienation, earth alienation, the rise of the social, and the victory of *animal laborans*. In her view the processes of world alienation and earth alienation have undermined the possibility of forming stable identities, of establishing an adequate sense of reality, and of endowing our existence with meaning. The rise of the social and the victory of *animal laborans* have, in turn, eroded the opportunities for engaging in spontaneous action with others and for creating free public spaces of interaction and discourse. Against this predicament Arendt sets out to revindicate the importance of memory, that is, of a selective reappropriation of the past that can critically illuminate the present, and the value of action, understood as the free and public intercourse among a plurality of agents mediated by speech and persuasion. In this chapter I examine a third proposed remedy to the losses incurred by modernity, namely, the exercise of our capacity for judgment, and attempt to provide a reconstruction of Arendt's unfinished work on judgment.

The chapter is divided into four parts. In the first part I explore the reasons that led Arendt to concentrate on the faculty of judgment and to characterize it as the most political of our cognitive faculties. I argue that Arendt's interest in judgment stemmed from her need to come to terms with the phenomenon of totalitarianism. Totalitarianism had in fact exploded our categories of political thought and our standards of moral judgment. Faced with the horror and the unprecedentedness of the Holocaust, Arendt had to reconceive our categories and standards of moral and political judgment. Her participation at the trial of Eichmann in the 1960s made her acutely aware of the need to come to terms with and to judge a reality that defied human comprehension. In her encounter with the person of Eichmann, Arendt had first to show the intelligibility of his actions, the fact that they stemmed from a lack of thought and an absence of judgment, so that ultimately we could come to terms with their enormity, with their absolutely unprecedented nature. Once Eichmann's deeds were rendered intelligible they could then be judged, and judged to be not only monstrous but "banal." Thus, to be in a position to pass judgment, Arendt had first to account for the unprecedented, and devise new standards to judge actions that would otherwise have escaped human comprehension.

In the second part of the chapter I examine the attempt made by Arendt to connect the activity of thinking to that of judging. She maintained that thinking – the silent dialogue of me and myself – dissolves our fixed habits of thought and the accepted rules of conduct, and thus prepares the way for the activity of judging particulars without the aid of pre-established universals. Thinking loosens the grip of the universal over the particular, thereby releasing judgment from ossified categories of thought and from conventional standards of behavior. She also maintained that thinking, by actualizing the dialogue between me and myself, produces conscience as a by-product. The rules of conscience concern the integrity of the self; they give no positive prescriptions, but only tell us what we should not do and what we should repent of.

Conscience as a side-effect of thinking has its counterpart in judgment as the by-product of the liberating activity of thought. Thus, if conscience represents the inner check by which we evaluate our actions, judgment represents the outer manifestation of our capacity to think critically. Both relate to the question of right and wrong, but while conscience directs attention to the self, judgment directs attention to the world – it makes possible what Arendt called "the manifestation of the wind of thought" in the sphere of appearance.

In the third part of the chapter I provide an account of Arendt's appropriation of Kant's theory of aesthetic judgment. Following Kant, Arendt identifies judgment with the capacity to think "representatively," that is, from the standpoint of everyone else. Arendt called this capacity to think representatively an "enlarged mentality," adopting the same term used by Kant in his Third Critique to characterize aesthetic judgment. She credits Kant with having dislodged the prejudice that judgments of taste lie altogether outside the political realm, since they supposedly concern only aesthetic matters. She believes, in fact, that by linking taste to that wider manner of thinking which Kant called an "enlarged mentality," the way was opened to a revaluation of judgment as a specific political ability, namely, as the ability to think from the standpoint of everyone else.

For Arendt the acquisition of an "enlarged mentality" is the *sine qua non* of both political and aesthetic judgment. She maintained that this enlarged way of thinking could only be acquired in public, in the actual or anticipated dialogue with the standpoints and perspectives of others. Political opinions, she claimed, can never be formed in private; rather, they are formed, tested, and enlarged within a public context of argumentation and debate. Public debate and discussion is indeed crucial to the formation of opinions that can claim more than subjective validity; individuals may hold personal opinions on many subject matters, but they can form representative opinions only by testing and purifying their views through a process of democratic debate and enlightenment. The same holds true for the formation of valid judgments: as "the most political of man's mental abilities," judgment can be exercised and tested only in a context of public deliberation and debate, a context where everyone is encouraged to enlarge his or her perspective and to acknowledge the standpoint of others.

In the fourth part of the chapter I address three important critiques of Arendt's theory of judgment. The first concerns the question of whether Arendt placed judgment exclusively in the sphere of the *vita contemplativa*, or whether it also played a role in the *vita activa*. The second concerns the appropriateness of Kant's aesthetics for a theory of political judgment. Was Arendt right to appeal to Kant's model of aesthetic judgment rather than to Aristotle's notion of *phronesis*? The third concerns the question of whether Arendt's theory of judgment rests on an adequate theory of knowledge and a plausible conception of rationality.

With respect to the first issue I argue that Arendt did indeed develop two distinct conceptions of judgment, one from the standpoint of the *vita activa* (judging in order to act), the other from the standpoint of the *vita contemplativa* (judging in order to cull meaning from the past), but she did not, as R. Beiner and others have claimed, opt entirely in her last writings for the latter conception, or abandon her earlier insights into the nature of judgment as a political faculty. I argue, in fact, that even in the latter, more "contemplative" conception, Arendt retained the link between judgment and the world of human affairs, stressed the public and intersubjective dimensions of judgment, and continued to emphasize its political character. In this respect, Arendt did not abandon her earlier insights about judgment, nor did she end up with a conception of judgment that excluded the concerns of the *vita activa*.

The second issue raised by Arendt's theory of judgment is whether she was right to appeal to Kant's aesthetics rather than to Aristotle's notion of practical reason. Both C. Lasch and R. Beiner have argued that Kant's theory of aesthetic judgment is too formal and abstract to serve as a basis for a theory of *political* judgment. In their view, Arendt should have drawn on Aristotle's notion of *phronesis*, in particular, its stress on the substantive ends and purposes of the political community. I argue that there are two main problems with this suggestion. The first has to do with the question of validity. Aristotle restricts the capacity for sound judgment or *phronesis* to a few individuals; as such, the validity of judgment does not depend on the potential agreement with other judging subjects, but on the experience and insight of a few privileged individuals. From a democratic standpoint, a judgment of this kind lacks the criteria of equality, impartiality, and universality. The second and related problem has to do with the appeal to community. I argue that community, in its Aristotelian sense of a congruence of *ethos* and *polis*, can neither provide an adequate standard for judgment, nor can it be taken as a valid model for modern politics. To accept the substantive ends and purposes of the community as the sole criteria for guiding our moral and political judgments means, in my view, to relapse either into a narrow and particularistic conception of judgment, or into a pre-modern and undemocratic conception of politics.

The third issue I address is whether Arendt's theory of judgment rests on an adequate theory of knowledge and a plausible conception of rationality. J. Habermas and R. Bernstein have claimed that Arendt subscribed to a Platonic conception of knowledge which prevented her from appreciating the role of rational argumentation in practical affairs. A. Wellmer, on the other hand, has argued that Arendt subscribed to an overly formalistic conception of rationality which she derived, in part, from Kant. I argue that these claims are both pertinent and valid, and that Arendt's theory of judgment was partially constrained by an antiquated conception of knowledge in which questions of truth were separated too sharply from questions of opinion, and that her theory retained some of the formalistic assumptions of Kant's conception of rationality.

## CHAPTER 4: HANNAH ARENDT'S CONCEPTION OF CITIZENSHIP

In the last chapter I reconstruct and critically evaluate Arendt's conception of citizenship with respect to three major themes: the public sphere, political agency and collective identity, and political culture. Each of these themes has been addressed in the context of larger discussions about modernity, action, and judgment. In Chapter 1 I argued that the loss or decline of the public sphere was one of the consequences of world alienation, of that "loss of the world" which for Arendt characterizes the rise of modernity. In Chapter 2 I argued that the issues of political agency and collective identity were central to Arendt's theory of action. In Chapter 3 I argued that the possibility of reactivating the capacity for political judgment depended upon the creation of public spaces for collective deliberation and on the constitution of an active political culture. The aim of this chapter is, thus, to reconstruct Arendt's conception of citizenship around the three issues of the public sphere, political agency and collective identity, and political culture, and to highlight the contribution of Arendt's conception to a theory of democratic citizenship.

The chapter is divided into three parts. In the first part I examine the connection between Arendt's conception of citizenship and the notion of the public sphere. For Arendt the public sphere comprises two distinct but interrelated dimensions. The first is the *space of appearance*, a space of political freedom and equality which comes into being whenever citizens act in concert through the medium of speech and persuasion. The second is the *common world*, a shared and public world of human artifacts, institutions, and settings that separates us from nature and that provides a relatively permanent and durable context for our activities. Both dimensions are essential to the practice of citizenship, the former providing the spaces where it can flourish, the latter providing the stable background from which public spaces of action and deliberation can arise. For Arendt the reactivation of citizenship in the modern world depends upon *both* the recovery of a common, shared world (i.e., the overcoming of world alienation), and the creation of numerous spaces of appearance in which individuals can disclose their identities and establish relations of reciprocity and solidarity.

Drawing on an article by M. Canovan, I then examine three features of the public sphere and of the sphere of politics in general that are closely connected to Arendt's conception of citizenship. These are: first, its artificial or constructed quality; second, its spatial quality; and third, the distinction between public and private interests.

As regards the first feature, Arendt always stressed the artificiality of public life and of political activities in general, the fact that they are man-made and constructed rather than natural or given. She regarded this artificiality as something to be celebrated rather than deplored. Politics for her was not the result of some natural predisposition, or the realization of the inherent traits of human nature. Rather, it was a cultural achievement of the first order, enabling individuals to transcend the necessities of life and to fashion a world within which free political action and discourse could flourish.

This stress on the artificiality of politics has a number of important consequences. For example, Arendt emphasized that the principle of political equality does not rest on a theory of natural rights or on some natural condition that precedes the constitution of the political realm. Rather, it is an attribute of citizenship which individuals acquire upon entering the public realm and which can be secured only by democratic political institutions.

A further consequence of Arendt's stress on the artificiality of political life is evident in her rejection of all neo-romantic appeals to the *volk* and to ethnic identity as the basis for political community. She maintained that one's ethnic, religious, or racial identity was irrelevant to one's identity as a *citizen*, and that it should never be made the basis of membership in a *political* community.

Finally, Arendt's emphasis on the formal qualities of citizenship made her position rather distant from those advocates of participation in the 1960s who saw it in terms of recapturing a sense of intimacy, of community, of warmth, of authenticity. For Arendt political participation was important because it permitted the establishment of relations of civility and solidarity among citizens. She claimed that the ties of intimacy and warmth can never become political, since they represent psychological substitutes for the loss of the common world. The only truly political ties are those of civic friendship and solidarity, since they make political demands and preserve reference to the world. For Arendt, therefore, the danger of trying to recapture the sense of intimacy and warmth, of authenticity and communal feelings is that one loses the public values of impartiality, civic friendship, and solidarity.

The second feature stressed by Arendt has to do with the spatial quality of public life, with the fact that political activities are located in a public space where citizens are able to meet one another, exchange their opinions, and debate their differences, and search for some collective solution to their problems. Politics, for Arendt, is a matter of people sharing a common world and a common space of appearance so that public concerns can emerge and be articulated from different perspectives. In her view, it is not enough to have a collection of private individuals voting separately and anonymously according to their private opinions. Rather, these individuals must be able to see and talk to one another in public, to meet in a public-political space, so that their differences as well as their commonalities can emerge and become the subject of democratic debate.

This notion of a common public space helps us to understand how political opinions can be formed which are neither reducible to private, idiosyncratic preferences, on the one hand, nor to a unanimous collective opinion, on the other. Arendt herself distrusted the term "public opinion," since it suggested the mindless unanimity of mass society. In her view representative opinions could arise only when citizens actually confronted one another in a public space, so that they could examine an issue from a number of different perspectives, modify their views, and enlarge their standpoint to incorporate that of others. Political opinions, she claimed, can never be formed in private; rather, they are formed, tested, and enlarged only within a public context of argumentation and debate.

Another implication of Arendt's stress on the spatial quality of politics has to do with the question of how a collection of distinct individuals can be united to form a political community. For Arendt the unity that may be achieved in a political community is neither the result of religious or ethnic affinity, nor the expression of some common value system. Rather, the unity in question can be attained by sharing a public space and a set of political institutions, and engaging in the practices and activities which are characteristic of that space and those institutions.

A further implication of Arendt's conception of the spatial quality of politics is that since politics is a public activity, one cannot be part of it without in some sense being present in a public space. To be engaged in politics means actively participating in the various public forums where the decisions affecting one's community are taken. Arendt's insistence on the importance of direct participation in politics is thus based on the idea that, since politics is something that needs a worldly location and can only happen in a public space, then if one is not present in such a space one is simply not engaged in politics.

This public or world-centered conception of politics lies also at the basis of the third feature stressed by Arendt, the distinction between public and private interests. According to Arendt, political activity is not a means to an end, but an end in itself; one does not engage in political action to promote one's welfare, but to realize the principles intrinsic to political life, such as freedom, equality, justice, solidarity. In a late essay entitled "Public Rights and Private Interests," Arendt discusses the difference between one's life as an individual and one's life as a citizen, between the life spent on one's own and the life spent in common with others. She argues that our public interest as citizens is quite distinct from our private interest as individuals. The public interest is not the sum of private interests, nor their highest common denominator, nor even the total of enlightened self-interests. In fact, it has little to do with our private interests, since it concerns the world that lies beyond the self, that was there before our birth and that will be there after our death, a world that finds embodiment in activities and institutions with their own intrinsic purposes which might often be at odds with our short-term and private interests. The public interest refers, therefore, to the interests of a public world which we share as citizens and which we can pursue and enjoy only by going beyond our private self-interest.

After having examined these three features of the public-political realm and their implications for Arendt's conception of citizenship, I then focus on an unresolved tension at the heart of Arendt's political theory, between a dramaturgical and a discursive conception of the public sphere. According to the first conception, the public sphere is a dramatic setting for the performance of noble deeds and the utterance of memorable words, that is to say, for the display of the excellence of political actors. According to the second conception, the public sphere is a discursive space that arises whenever people act together in concert, establish relations of equality and solidarity, and engage in collective deliberation through the medium of speech and persuasion. Arendt was not able to resolve the tension between these two conceptions of the public sphere, and I argue that the reason for this lies in the fundamental duality of her theory of action. When action is conceptualized in terms of an expressive model, the public sphere is viewed as a dramatic setting where actors compete for recognition and glory; conversely, when action is conceptualized in terms of a communicative model, the public sphere is viewed as a discursive space of action and unconstrained deliberation for the establishment of relations of mutuality and solidarity. I argue that insofar as Arendt was unable to integrate the expressive and the communicative models of action, she was bound to present two distinct and opposed conceptions of the public sphere. I also argue that the tension between the two models of action was responsible for Arendt's vacillation between an agonal and a participatory conception of citizenship.

In the second part of the chapter I examine the connection between Arendt's conception of citizenship and the questions of political agency and collective identity. I argue that Arendt's participatory conception of citizenship provides the best starting point for addressing both the question of the constitution of collective identity and that concerning the conditions for the exercise of effective political agency.

With respect to the first claim, I argue that one of the crucial questions at stake in political discourse is the creation of a collective identity, a "we" to which we can appeal when faced with the problem of deciding among alternative courses of action. Indeed, since in political discourse there is always disagreement about the possible courses of action, the identity of the "we" that is going to be created through a specific form of action becomes a central question. By engaging in this or that course of action we are, in fact, entering a claim on behalf of a "we," that is, we are creating a specific form of collective identity. Political action and discourse are, in this respect, essential to the constitution of collective identities.

This process of identity-construction, however, is never given once and for all and is never unproblematic. Rather, it is a process of constant renegotiation and struggle, a process in which actors articulate and defend competing conceptions of cultural and political identity and competing conceptions of political legitimacy. I argue that Arendt's participatory conception of citizenship is particularly relevant in this context, since it articulates the conditions for the establishment of collective identities. I argue, in fact, that once citizenship is viewed as the process of active deliberation about competing identity projections, its value would reside in the possibility of establishing forms of collective identity that can be acknowledged, tested, and transformed in a discursive and democratic fashion.

With respect to the second claim, concerning the question of political agency, I examine the connection between political action, understood as the active engagement of citizens in the public realm, and the exercise of effective political agency. I argue that this connection between action and agency is one of the central contributions of Arendt's participatory conception of citizenship. According to Arendt, the active engagement of citizens in the determination of the affairs of their community provides them not only with the experience of public freedom and public happiness, but also with a sense of political agency and efficacy, the sense, in Jefferson's words, of being "participators in government." In her view, only the sharing of power that comes from civic engagement and common deliberation can provide each citizen with a sense of effective political agency. Arendt's strictures against representation must be understood in this light. She saw representation as a substitute for the direct involvement of the citizens, and as a means whereby the distinction between rulers and ruled could reassert itself. As an alternative to a system of representation based on bureaucratic parties and state structures, Arendt proposed a federated system of councils through which citizens could effectively determine their own political affairs. After having examined the limits of this proposal, I show that its relevance lies in the connection it establishes between active citizenship and effective political agency. For Arendt, in fact, it is only by means of direct political participation, that is, by engaging in common action and collective deliberation, that citizenship can be reaffirmed and political agency effectively exercised.

In the third part of the chapter I explore the connection between Arendt's participatory conception of citizenship and the constitution of an active and democratic political culture. Drawing on some of the arguments presented in Chapter 3, I show that for Arendt the possibility of reactivating the political capacity for impartial and responsible judgment depends upon the creation of public spaces for collective deliberation in which citizens can test and enlarge their opinions. Where an appropriate public space exists, these opinions can be shaped, enlarged, and transformed through a process of democratic debate and enlightenment. Instead of remaining the expression of arbitrary preferences or being molded into a unanimous "public opinion," these opinions can thereby be transformed into a sophisticated political discourse.

The capacity to form valid opinions and to shape them into a sophisticated political discourse requires, therefore, a public space where individuals can test and purify their views through a process of public argumentation and debate. The same holds true for the formation of valid judgments: as the most political of our cognitive faculties, judgment can be exercised and tested only in a context of public deliberation and debate, a context where everyone is encouraged to enlarge his or her perspective and to acknowledge the standpoint of others. The cultivation of an "enlarged mentality" requires, therefore, the creation of institutions and practices where the voice and perspective of everyone can be articulated, tested, and transformed. In this respect, the creation and cultivation of a public culture of democratic participation that guarantees to everyone the right to action and opinion is essential to the flourishing of our capacity for judgment and to the formation of valid opinions.

My conclusion is that Arendt's conception of citizenship articulates the historical experience and the normative presuppositions of participatory democracy, and that such a conception is essential for the reactivation of public life in the modern world.

# Chapter 1

# Hannah Arendt's conception of modernity

I would like to consider at the outset some of the most important approaches to the study of modernity. I shall briefly sketch the outlines of two influential approaches, one stemming from Hegel, the other from Weber, so as to locate Arendt's own conception of modernity and to explore the extent of her indebtedness to previous traditions of thought. I shall then look at a major contemporary figure, Jürgen Habermas, in order to highlight the distinctiveness of Arendt's understanding of modernity.

In an article published in 1974, Manfred Riedel has shown that there is a tradition of analyzing modernity quite distinct from the Weberian one, a tradition that can be traced back to the Aristotelian distinction between *oikos* and *polis* and that found its embodiment in the writings of Scottish political economists (Smith, Ferguson, Steuart) and in Hegel's early as well as mature political philosophy.[1] For this tradition the crucial aspect of modernity is that of *institutional differentiation*, that is to say, the separation of household and economy, morality and legality, politics and economics, individual and community. Hegel described this process of differentiation as *Entzweiung*, as the division or sundering apart of previously unified spheres, and in his early writings he characterized it as the "tragedy and comedy of ethical life." In his later writings, however, he considered the breaking apart of the unity of ethical life as something positive, or rather, as the price to be paid for the gains that modernity offered in terms of increased freedom and autonomy. Nevertheless, the problem of *Entzweiung*, of the diremption of a previous unity, remained to haunt him and those who followed in his footsteps.[2]

"Hegel," Habermas writes, "is not the first philosopher who belongs to modern times, but he is the first for whom modernity has become a problem."[3] The problem that Hegel confronted was that of reconciling the achievements of modernity – the expansion of individual freedom and autonomy *vis-à-vis* traditional customs and authorities – with the need for institutional and normative integration. His solution was to identify the rational with the actual, to mediate the universal with the particular, at the cost of rationalizing a deficient actuality and universalizing what was merely contingent. The failure of Hegel's attempt at reconciliation thus set the stage for later attempts, all of which had to contend with the problem of finding an adequate institutional and normative embodiment for the new principle of subjectivity. As Habermas puts it:

A modernity that is freed of images of authority, that is open to the future, and addicted to continuous self-renewal can only create itself the criteria to judge itself by. Thus, the principle of subjectivity emerges as the only origin of normativity which grows out of the time consciousness of modernity itself.[4]

But can this principle of subjectivity alone and the structure of self-consciousness intrinsic to it "be adequate sources of normative orientation"?[5] This is the dilemma that post-Hegelian thinkers had to contend with, and none of them seemed able to provide a satisfactory answer. In Marx, for example, we find the proletariat raised to the level of universal subject of history, in Kierkegaard the overcoming of subjectivity in the sphere of faith, in Nietzsche the equation of subjectivity with the will to power, in Heidegger the displacement of subjectivity by the calling of Being. All of these thinkers were unable, in Habermas' view, to provide an adequate normative embodiment for the principle of subjectivity.

In what sense is Arendt's conception of modernity connected to, or influenced by, this tradition and its attempts to resolve the dilemmas of modernity? As we shall see in more detail later, Arendt identifies a crucial feature of modernity in the emergence of Cartesian doubt, with its distrust of the senses and its turn to introspection. She also highlights the loss in modern times of the distinction between *oikos* and *polis*, between economy and polity, which characterized the early phase of capitalism but has been blurred with the expansion of the economy in our century. In her view the rise of Cartesian doubt has led to a condition that she calls "world alienation," the loss of a commonly experienced and shared world of action and speech in favor of the private world of introspection. By giving primacy to the experiences of an isolated subject, the modern age has endowed subjectivity with the power to determine reality, at the cost, however, of making this reality a purely private affair. Furthermore, by rejecting the assumption that reality can be apprehended veridically through the senses, the modern age has lost all trust in appearances, and since for Arendt, as for Hegel, reality is manifested in appearances, this means that the modern age has lost trust in reality.

With her emphasis on the deleterious effects of subjectivity Arendt remains close to the concerns of those thinkers after Hegel (especially Nietzsche and Heidegger) who saw subjectivity as a problem to be overcome rather than as a solution to the dilemmas of modernity. Moreover, in focusing on the issue of institutional de-differentiation (the eclipse of the distinction between economy and polity, between private and public), she is addressing an issue similar to that which preoccupied Hegel and the thinkers of the Scottish Enlightenment, who were the first to address the problems of institutional differentiation and reintegration.

The second influential tradition of analyzing modernity is that associated with Weber and his studies on rationalization. For this tradition the crucial aspect of modernity is that of *cultural differentiation*, the increasing separation of value spheres (science, morality, legality, religion, art, and erotics) from one another and their embodiment in institutions characterized by distinct dynamics of rationalization. For Weber this process of increasing rationalization and cultural differentiation led to a value pluralism that undermined any attempt at reconciliation between different value spheres, a situation that Weber himself characterized in terms of an unceasing struggle between the gods of ancient pagan mythology. A polytheism of values was thus increasingly replacing the unity of value of the Judeo-Christian tradition. Weber also argued that the extension of instrumental rationality (*Zweckrationalität*) to all spheres of life and the progressive restriction of value rationality (*Wertrationalität*) to the sphere of private choice and faith resulted in what he called the "disenchantment of the world" (*Entzauberung*). As he declared in his essay "Science as a Vocation": "The fate of our times is characterized by rationalization and intellectualization and, above all, by the 'disenchantment of the world.' "[6] Faced with a world devoid of meaning and with the loss of transcendent sources of value, the individual was confronted with the task of creating meaning by an act of choice which could not be rationally grounded. Neither God, nor Nature, nor Science could possibly reunify the separate and conflicting value spheres or endow the world with meaning. The individual had thus to choose among competing values that allowed no rational adjudication, and to endow existence with a meaning no longer backed by transcendent sources of validity. As Weber wrote:

> The fate of an epoch which has eaten of the tree of knowledge is that it must know that we cannot learn the *meaning* of the world from the results of its analysis, be it ever so perfect; it must rather be in a position to create this meaning itself. It must recognize that general views of life and the universe can never be the products of increasing empirical knowledge, and that the highest ideals, which move us most forcefully, are always formed only in the struggle with other ideals which are just as sacred to others as ours are to us.[7]

Weber's diagnosis of modernity was highly ambivalent: although acknowledging the achievements of science and formal-legal rationality, he was deeply concerned with the pathologies of rationalization, especially the loss of freedom (*Freiheitsverlust*) resulting from processes of societal rationalization and the loss of meaning (*Sinnverlust*) resulting from cultural rationalization. In the concluding pages of *The Protestant Ethic and the Spirit of Capitalism* he warned that modernity threatened to become an "iron cage" and that rationalization might end in "mechanized petrification."[8] Weber's pessimistic outlook was matched by a stoical acceptance of the ambiguous fate of modernity, an acceptance that found normative expression in what he called an "ethic of responsibility."[9]

Arendt's indebtness to this tradition of analyzing modernity, which includes thinkers such as Horkheimer, Adorno, and Marcuse,[10] is evident in her concern with the loss of freedom brought about by the rise of the "social" and the loss of meaning that results from "world alienation." By the "social" Arendt means the expansion of economic activities to the point where they become the central political concern of a society, a phenomenon she traces to the progressive extension of the market since the seventeenth century. In her view the rise of the social has enabled activities connected to the necessities of life to predominate to the point where the central task of government has become that of steering the economy for the purpose of greater productivity and expanded consumption. Moreover, the exclusive preoccupation with economic matters has resulted in the destruction of the public sphere, where freedom and action could appear, and in the enforcement of predictable patterns of behavior, for every individual is now expected to conform to the dictates of economic necessity. By "world alienation" Arendt means the loss of an intersubjectively constituted world of experience and action by means of which we establish our self-identity and an adequate sense of reality. Once this world of shared experience and action is lost, our identity becomes precarious and reality more doubtful, that is, we can no longer provide a coherent narrative about ourselves, find confirmation of our identity with others, or validate the existence of a common, objective reality. In this respect world alienation represents a *Sinnverlust*, since we are no longer in a position to endow our existence or the world with any common or shared meaning.

I would like to complete this brief sketch by looking at a contemporary thinker whose conception of modernity might be usefully compared to Arendt's. Jürgen Habermas has presented what is arguably the most systematic analysis of modernity by bringing together the two traditions we have just examined – the Hegelian one with its stress on institutional differentiation and the Weberian one with its stress on cultural differentiation – and integrating them with the results of modern social systems theory (Parsons, Luhmann), with their emphasis on functional adaptation, system integration, and reduction of complexity via steering media. In *The Theory of Communicative Action* Habermas has presented the framework of his analysis of modernity, such analysis being based on a reconstructive theory of social evolution.[11] By means of the latter he can claim that human evolution occurs in two distinct but interrelated dimensions, namely, the evolution of the *forces of production* and the evolution of *normative structures*. In each of these dimensions there is a logic of development which has its own dynamic and which cannot be reduced to the other. Habermas therefore maintains that socialization processes organized in terms of normative structures are as important as production processes for the evolution of the human species. He also maintains that the transition from one stage of development to another (e.g., from archaic to traditional to modern societies) is effected by means of *learning processes* that allow an expansion of rationality in the cognitive-instrumental and moral-practical spheres. This means that at the level of the productive forces there is an increase in the steering capacity of the system, while at the level of normative structures there is an increase in reflexivity, universality, and discursive redemption of validity claims.

With respect to the processes of modernization characteristic of Western societies, Habermas operates a distinction between *social modernization* and *cultural modernization*. Social modernization is characterized by the rationalization of the life-world, the differentiation of institutional spheres, and the expansion of instrumental rationality. Cultural modernization, by contrast, is characterized by the decentration of worldviews, the differentiation of value spheres and their respective claims to validity, and the extension of universalistic norms.[12]

Habermas is fully aware of the pathological consequences of one-sided rationalization processes that threaten the communicative infrastructure of the life-world. The over-extension of instrumental rationality leads to the *erosion of traditions* that nourish the processes of reaching understanding in everyday life, and to what Habermas calls the "colonization of the life-world," whose pathological manifestations he identifies in *loss of meaning* in the domain of cultural reproduction, *anomie* in the domain of social integration, and *personality disorders* in the domain of socialization. He is not willing, however, to take a tragic stance toward modernity in the manner of Weber, or to reject the project of the Enlightenment in the manner of Nietzsche, Foucault, Derrida, and Horkheimer and Adorno in their *Dialectic of Enlightenment*.[13] His aim, rather, is to complete the project of the Enlightenment, in the sense of reconciling the decayed parts of modernity and preserving the experiences of undistorted intersubjectivity.[14]

With respect to the concerns that have characterized Arendt's writings, especially the loss of meaning, the erosion of the public sphere, and the reduction of politics to administration, Habermas is in fundamental agreement. He has devoted his first book to the origin, development, and eventual demise of the public sphere (*The Structural Transformation of the Public Sphere*), subjected to critical examination the claims of those who defended a scientistic and technocratic conception of politics (*Toward a Rational Society; Theory and Practice*), analyzed the tendencies toward political apathy and familial-vocational privatism (*Legitimation Crisis*), addressed the issue of whether complex societies could form a rational identity ("Können komplexe Gesellschaften eine vernünftige Identität ausbilden?" in *Zur Rekonstruktion des Historischen Materialismus*), and written a series of recent essays on the crisis of the welfare state and the exhaustion of utopian energies (*The New Conservatism*). But there is no doubt that, aside from sharing these fundamental concerns, Habermas' attitude toward modernity departs in several respects from Arendt's. To put it very schematically, while Arendt expresses a tragic pathos with respect to the losses incurred in the modern age as a result of secularization, rationalization and socio-cultural modernization, Habermas is more inclined to assume an affirmative stance *vis-à-vis* the same processes, in the sense of emphasizing their progressive aspects and highlighting the potential for communicative rationality that they have opened up. Second, with respect to the problem of value pluralism, Arendt's response is much closer to Weber's stoic embrace of an ethic of responsibility in the face of the modern polytheism of values than to Habermas' defense of discursive proceduralism for the consensual resolution of conflicting norms and interests. As we shall see when treating Arendt's theory of judgment, Arendt questions the possibility of assessing value judgments in terms of cognitive criteria; in her view they can only be evaluated in terms of the criteria of disinterestedness and generality that she derives from Kant's theory of aesthetic judgment.[15] Finally, as regards the underlying assumptions guiding their work, Arendt emphasizes the importance of a selective reappropriation of the past, of a remembrance of past actions and events (what she calls the "forgotten treasures") for the purpose of redeeming and illuminating the present, while Habermas stresses the critical function of a future-oriented analysis of the present which highlights its pathologies and indicates the communicative potentials that still await realization.[16]

If this characterization of their respective assumptions is correct, then it is possible to say that from the standpoint of Habermas' future-oriented thinking modernity is an incomplete project that needs to be fulfilled, while from the standpoint of Arendt's past-oriented thinking modernity appears as a deficient project that stands in need of redemption.[17] To this fundamental motive of Arendt's thought we may now turn.

## METHODOLOGICAL OBSERVATIONS

Arendt's writings on modernity display a continuing concern with the losses incurred as a result of the eclipse of tradition, religion and authority, and offer a number of illuminating suggestions with respect to the resources still left in the modern age to cope with the problems of meaning, identity, action, and value. For Arendt modernity is characterized by the *loss of the world*, by which she means the restriction or elimination of the public sphere, of the sphere of appearance, in favor of the private world of introspection. Modernity is the age of mass society, of the rise of the "social" out of a previous distinction between the public and the private, and of the victory of *animal laborans* over *homo faber* and the conception of man as *zoon politikon.* It is the age of bureaucratic administration and anonymous labor, rather than politics and action, and of the emergence of totalitarian forms of government based on the institutionalization of terror and violence. It is the age where history as a natural process has replaced history as a fabric of actions and events, where homogeneity and conformity have replaced plurality and freedom, and organized loneliness has replaced all spontaneous forms of human living-together. Modernity is the age where the past no longer carries any certainty of evaluation, where individuals, no longer being the measure of things, must search for new grounds of human community as such.

This is Arendt's vision of modernity, a vision so stark and unredeeming as to offer at first sight little room for alternative accounts or different characterizations. But as we shall see, this is not the whole of Arendt's understanding of modernity; moreover, she provides us with a number of fruitful insights that may help us to confront the dilemmas of the modern age. Let us then listen to her words from the closing statements of *The Life of the Mind*:

> I have clearly joined the ranks of those who for some time now have been attempting to dismantle metaphysics, and philosophy with all its categories, as we have known them from their beginning in Greece until today. Such dismantling is possible only on the assumption that the thread of tradition is broken and that we shall not be able to renew it. Historically speaking, what actually has broken down is the Roman trinity that for thousands of years united religion, authority, and tradition . . . What has been lost is the continuity of the past as it seemed to be handed down from generation to generation, developing in the process its own consistency . . . What you then are left with is still the past, but a *fragmented* past, which has lost its certainty of evaluation.[18]

The fragmentation of the past and the loss of its relevance for the present have created a *gap* between past and future. For a very long time this gap was bridged by tradition, which "selects and names, which hands down and preserves, which indicates where the treasures are and what their worth is."[19] But with the breakdown of tradition we must move within this gap without any secure sense of direction, without the help of any established principle. Each new generation "must discover and ploddingly pave it anew,"[20] since no precedent, no testament, no authoritative instructions have been bequeathed to us from tradition. In this situation, where, as Arendt says, "notre héritage n'est précédé d'aucun testament,"[21] her thinking seeks to preserve the meaning of the past outside the framework of any tradition. The break in our tradition has, in fact, become complete after the terrible events of this century and the triumph of totalitarian movements in East and West. In the form of Stalinism and Nazism, totalitarianism has exploded the established categories of political thought and the accepted standards of moral judgment, and has thereby broken the continuity of our history. These events have brought us to the point where, in the words of Arendt:

> We can no longer afford to take that which was good in the past and simply call it our heritage, to discard the bad and simply think of it as a dead load which by itself time will bury in oblivion. The subterranean stream of Western history has finally come to the surface and usurped the dignity of our tradition. This is the reality in which we live. And this is why all efforts to escape from the grimness of the present into nostalgia for a still intact past, or into the anticipated oblivion of a better future, are vain.[22]

Faced with the reality of the Holocaust we cannot go back to traditional concepts and values, so as to explain the unprecedented by means of precedents or understand the monstrous by means of the familiar. "Comprehension," says Arendt,

> does not mean denying the outrageous . . . It means, rather, examining and bearing consciously the burden which our century has placed on us − neither denying its existence nor submitting meekly to its weight. Comprehension, in short, means the unpremeditated, attentive facing up to, and resisting of, reality − whatever it may be."[23]

The burden of our time must, therefore, be faced without the aid of tradition, or, as Arendt once declared, "without a bannister."[24] Our inheritance has been dissolved under the impact of modern political events, and the task now is to re-establish the meaning of the past outside the framework of any tradition, since none has retained its original validity. It is the *past*, then, and not tradition, as Stan Spyros Draenos rightly observes, that Arendt attempts to redeem from the rupture in modern time-consciousness. Only through such a re-demption of the past can we hope to restore meaning to our lives and throw some light on the contemporary situation. In Draenos' words:

> If we have forgotten or are rapidly in the process of forgetting our past, this means nothing less than that we have forgotten what we

are. And if this is our situation, then to remember the past involves no exercise in utopian idealism or philosophical abstraction. On the contrary, only by so doing might we restore the sense of ourselves and thereby gain some practical bearings by which to orient ourselves toward the future.[25]

This exercise in *remembrance*, without the aid of tradition, embodying a continuity between past and present now irrevocably lost, is compared by Arendt to the activity of the pearl diver who brings to the surface the pearls and corals hidden in the depths of the sea. Just as the pearl diver recovers these treasures by extracting them forcibly from their surroundings, so anamnestic thinking delves into the depths of the past, not to resuscitate it the way it was or to glorify past ages, but to recover and save from forgetfulness those fragments that are still able to illuminate our situation. Arendt's indebtness to Benjamin's notion of "profane illumination" is made clear in the following passage:

> Like a pearl diver who descends to the bottom of the sea, not to excavate the bottom and bring it to light but to pry loose the rich and the strange, the pearls and the coral in the depths and to carry them to the surface, this thinking [of Benjamin] delves into the depths of the past – but not in order to resuscitate it the way it was and to contribute to the renewal of extinct ages. What guides this thinking is the conviction that although the living is subject to the ruin of time, the process of decay is at the same time a process of crystallization, that in the depth of the sea, into which it sinks and is dissolved what once was alive, some things "suffer a sea-change" and survive in new crystallized forms and shapes that remain immune to the elements, as though they waited only for the pearl diver who one day will come down to them and bring them up into the world of the living – as "thought fragments," as something "rich and strange," and perhaps even as everlasting *Urphaenomene*.[26]

For Arendt these thought fragments have to be preserved against the collapse of tradition and against the obliteration of memory. In her view it is no longer possible, after the breakdown of tradition, to save the past as a whole; we are faced, rather, with the task of redeeming from oblivion those elements of the past that are relevant to our present. To re-establish a linkage with the past is not, for Arendt, an antiquarian exercise; on the contrary, without the critical reappropriation of the past our temporal horizon becomes disrupted, our experience precarious, and our identity less and less secure.[27] In Arendt's view, therefore, it is necessary to redeem from the past those moments worth preserving, to save those fragments from past treasures that are significant for us. Only by means of this *selective reappropriation* can we discover the past anew, endow it with relevance and meaning for the present, and make it the source of inspiration for a future yet to come.[28]

Arendt's hermeneutic strategy is also indebted to Heidegger's deconstruction of Western metaphysics, the uncovering and subsequent displacement of our philosophical categories by a mode of thinking that identifies and recovers their ontological, as opposed to their ontic, determinations.[29] Heidegger called this mode of thinking a "destructive hermeneutics," since in order to recover the original meaning of our categories we had to do violence to the philosophical tradition in which they were embedded; the Western metaphysical tradition was, in his view, no longer to be trusted as a valid source of insight.[30] In an essay written on the occasion of Heidegger's eightieth birthday, Arendt claimed that Heidegger's thinking has a peculiar "digging quality," since

> he penetrates to the depths, but not to discover, let alone bring to light, some ultimate, secure foundations which one could say had been undiscovered earlier in this manner. Rather, he persistently remains there, underground, in order to lay down pathways and fix "trail marks" [*Wegmarken*] . . . On this deep plane, dug up and cleared, as it were, by his own thinking, Heidegger has laid down a vast network of thought-paths; and the single immediate result . . . is that he has caused the edifice of traditional metaphysics . . . to collapse, just as underground tunnels and subversing burrowings cause the collapse of structures whose foundations are not deeply enough secured.[31]

The undermining of the categories of the Western metaphysical tradition is not, however, a purely destructive enterprise; as Heidegger himself remarked, the aim is to "stake out the positive possibilities of that tradition" by recovering those "primordial experiences" out of which it originated.[32] Once liberated from the artificial and distorting incrustations of the tradition, the original meaning of our metaphysical categories could be discovered anew. It is in this *redemptive* sense that we must do violence to the tradition, so as to recover for the present the forgotten and occluded *Urphaenomene*. Arendt herself made an interesting comparison between Heidegger and Benjamin on this point:

Without realizing it, Benjamin actually had more in common with Heidegger's remarkable sense for living eyes and living bones that had sea-changed into pearls and coral, and as such could be saved and lifted into the present only by doing violence to their context in interpreting them with "the deadly impact" of new thoughts, than he did with the dialectical subtleties of his Marxist friends.[33]

The "deadly impact" of new thoughts can thus re-establish our links with the past in fresh and novel ways, endowing it with an authority that issues from a critical reappropriation of its meaning. Arendt maintained that in this way

the cultural treasures of the past, believed to be dead, are being made to speak, in the course of which it turns out that they propose things altogether different from the familiar, worn-out trivialities they had been presumed to say.[34]

As we shall see shortly, Arendt's writings on modernity have a disturbing capacity to unsettle our fixed categories, to shake our inherited conceptual habits, and to let us see phenomena in a new light. And what enables her to do this, I would argue, is the loss of tradition, the loss of the thread which safely guided us through the vast realms of the past, but which also constrained our understanding of it. Arendt herself maintains that only after the rupture introduced by modernity can the past "open up to us with unexpected freshness and tell us things no one has yet had ears to hear."[35] Indeed, the loss of authority in the modern age may signal "the great chance to look upon the past with eyes undistorted by any tradition, with a directness which has disappeared from Occidental reading and hearing ever since Roman civilization submitted to the authority of Greek thought."[36]

It could be argued at this point that Arendt's claims are, to some extent, hermeneutically naive. To look upon the past with eyes undistorted by any tradition or, for that matter, to read past authors as though nobody had ever read them before, goes against the hermeneutic principle that we are *always already* situated in a tradition (in a horizon of meaning, to use Gadamer's terms), so that our appreciation of the past is always mediated by our present standpoint, with its forestructure of understanding and prejudgments. The understanding and reappropriation of the past can, in this view, be achieved only by an effective historical consciousness (*Wirkungs-geschichtliches Bewusstsein*) that links past and present (or text and interpreter) in what Gadamer calls a "fusion of horizons" (*Horizontver-*

*schmelzung*). Any direct, unmediated return to the past would thus be excluded on methodological (and, for Gadamer, ontological) grounds. Arendt's intent, however, is not to do away with the notion of tradition *per se*, but to make us aware that the extant traditions of thought and interpretation have been dissolved under the impact of the tragic events of the twentieth century, so that we are left in the unprecedented situation of having to reconstitute our hermeneutic standpoint.[37]

I would therefore claim that Arendt's return to the original experience of the Greek *polis* represents an attempt to break the fetters of a worn-out tradition and to rediscover a past over which tradition has no longer a claim. Against tradition Arendt sets the criterion of genuineness, against the authoritative that which is forgotten, concealed, or displaced at the margins of history.[38] Only in this way can the past be made meaningful again, provide sources of illumination for the present, and yield its treasures to those who search for them with "new thoughts" and saving acts of remembrance.[39]

## MODERNITY AND *THE HUMAN CONDITION*

With these reflections in mind, we might be in a better position to understand Arendt's treatment of the modern age contained in *The Human Condition*. In this work she provides the framework of a phenomenological anthropology which addresses those aspects of the human condition that pertain to the *vita activa*. She makes clear that her attempt to describe phenomenologically the internal articulations of the *vita activa* and to determine the proper ranking of activities does not amount to a theory of human nature, since nothing in her view can determine our existence in an absolute sense. As she puts it: "The conditions of human existence . . . can never 'explain' what we are or answer the question of who we are for the simple reason that they never condition us absolutely."[40] No account of the human condition can, in her view, identify essential traits or fundamental characteristics in the absence of which we should cease to be human. Even the most radical change in the human condition, such as the emigration to another planet, would be unable to affect us to the point of making us different creatures. Such an event, she writes:

> would imply that man would have to live under man-made conditions, radically different from those the earth offers him. Neither labor nor work nor action nor, indeed, thought as we know it would then make sense any longer. Yet even these hypothetical

wanderers from the earth would still be human; but the only statement we could make regarding their "nature" is that they still are conditioned beings, even though their condition is now self-made to a considerable extent.[41]

The human condition, then, is not the same as human nature, and the description of all the human activities and capacities which correspond to the human condition does not amount to a theory of human nature, but only to what may be called a phenomenological anthropology.[42] Let us then turn to a brief account of the latter.

In the opening section of *The Human Condition* Arendt lays out the *conditions*, the *activities*, and the *spaces* of the *vita activa*. The conditions she identifies are life, natality, mortality, plurality, worldliness, and the earth. The activities are labor, work, and action. The spaces in which the activities take place are the private and the public.[43] Conditions, activities, and spaces are interrelated: thus life itself is the condition that corresponds to the activity of labor, worldliness the condition that corresponds to the activity of work, plurality the condition that corresponds to action. All three activities are in turn related to the most general conditions of human existence: birth and death, or natality and mortality.[44] As for spaces, labor and work take place in the private sphere, that is, they can be carried out in isolation from others, while action, since it requires the presence of others, can only take place in a public sphere. Arendt employs the Greek distinction between *oikos* and *polis* to emphasize the separation of the private from the public. The household is the sphere of satisfaction of material needs by means of labor and work carried out in private and under the rule of necessity; the *polis* is the sphere of freedom where equality reigns and where citizens act with a view to excellence and distinction, with the aim of achieving a measure of immortality by glorious deeds and memorable words.

Arendt's purpose is to recover the categories of the *vita activa* from the distortions they have suffered at the hands of the tradition of political thought since Plato. As she writes:

> My contention is simply that the enormous weight of contemplation in the traditional hierarchy [in which the *vita contemplativa* stood on a higher and nobler plane than the *vita activa*] has blurred the distinctions and articulations within the *vita activa* itself and that, appearances notwithstanding, this condition has not been changed essentially by the modern break with the tradition and the eventual reversal of its hierarchical order in Marx and Nietzsche.[45]

For present purposes I shall leave aside her criticism of the tradition of political thought, responsible in her view for the imposition of alien schemes, drawn primarily from the realm of fabrication or making (*poiesis*), upon political life, with the consequence that the model of *ruling*, rather than action and participation, became paradigmatic for the understanding, as well as the conduct, of political affairs. I would like rather to focus on her characterization of modernity, on such themes as world alienation, earth alienation, the rise of the social, and the victory of *animal laborans*.

A few methodological remarks are in order. Arendt's account of the emergence of the modern age is a combination of historical and conceptual analysis in which each concept is traced back to its origins in Greek and Roman experience, followed by a close account of its modifications during Christianity and the Middle Ages and its eventual displacement with the emergence of modernity.[46] The historical background of these conceptual changes is normally made up of entire epochs, so that what is often lost is a sense of the complexity, differentiation, and internal tensions of each epoch, as well as the underlying continuity from one historical period to another. Moreover, such conceptual changes are not integrated with a sociological or economic analysis of the emergence and development of capitalism from the sixteenth century onwards. What Arendt offers, instead, are broad cultural periodizations that serve as a background for the examination of some crucial categories of our experience and of the transformation undergone by each.[47]

Arendt identifies a number of key features of the modern age: world alienation, earth alienation, the blurring of the distinction between the private and the public brought about by the rise of the social, the reversal of the priority of contemplation over action and subsequently of the hierarchy within the *vita activa*, the loss of public freedom and public happiness, the loss of the Roman trinity of tradition, religion, and authority, the reduction of politics to administration, and the disappearance of the public realm.

She identifies a number of causes: the discovery of America and the corresponding shrinking of the earth, the waves of expropriation started by the Reformation, the invention of the telescope challenging the adequacy of the senses, the rise of modern science and philosophy and subsequently of a conception of man as part of a process of Nature and History, and the expansion of the realm of the economy, of the production and accumulation of social wealth.

She also identifies two main stages: the first, from the sixteenth to the nineteenth century, corresponds to world alienation and the rise of the social, the second, from the beginning of our century, corresponds to earth alienation and the victory of *animal laborans*.[48]

These then are the key features, the main causes, and the principal stages. What are we to make of them? Or, to put it differently, how are we to assess them? Perhaps the best way is to explore each in turn and to see if a coherent picture can emerge. Let us then begin with world alienation.

## WORLD ALIENATION: FIRST STAGE OF MODERNITY

The world and its correlative condition, worldliness, are part of what Arendt considers to be the human condition; in contradistinction to nature, the world is the artificial environment of humanly created objects, institutions, and settings that provide us with an abode upon this earth, with a shelter from the natural elements, and, insofar as it is relatively stable and permanent, with a sense of belonging, of being at home with our surroundings. Without such a stable human world our lives would lack points of reference by which to orient ourselves, our identities would be difficult to sustain, and our actions would not form coherent stories. We would instead be part of the endless cycles of nature, part of its endless flux. The world also provides us with a touchstone of reality: since it is lived in common with others, our experiences can become objective by being shared, our senses can be confirmed by the testimony of others, and our self-identity can be sustained by intersubjective acknowledgment. The reality of the world and of the self can thus be secured only by sharing our existence with others, that is, by living in a world which is public and common.

What happens then when this world is lost, when we find ourselves in that condition that Arendt calls "world alienation"? The first and most important consequence is that we lose our sense of being at home in the world and, with that, our identity, our sense of reality, and the possibility of endowing our existence with meaning.[49] Some writers have claimed that Arendt displays here a religious commitment to the notion that we exist to be at home in the world and that our identity depends on it.[50] However valid, this claim must be complemented by another, namely, that in order to live meaningful lives our human environment must present certain features (e.g., relative familiarity, stability, permanence) that enable our expectations to be satisfied in a non-random manner. The fact that our sense of belonging, of rootedness, and of self may have religious underpinnings does not therefore invalidate certain of our existential predicaments.

Another consequence of the condition of world alienation is that, lacking a world in common, the individual is thrown back upon herself, into the private sphere of introspection, which, being devoid of agreed-upon standards, can never provide secure principles of conduct. Moreover, being thrown back upon ourselves means also losing ourselves, losing the faith in our senses and, ultimately, in our reason, a condition that Arendt insists on calling world alienation, though it might well be defined as self-alienation. The result is that, alienated from ourselves and from others, we become doubtful of our experiences and of the reality of the world.[51] Such a situation is conducive, in Arendt's eyes, to mass manipulation and totalitarian indoctrination, if only as a way of relieving individuals of their anxiety and their sense of isolation.

These extreme developments are also encouraged by another phenomenon arising from world alienation: the restriction or elimination of the public sphere, of the sphere of appearances, where the words and deeds of individuals can be preserved for posterity and the identity of each disclosed and sustained. Being at home in the world is, in fact, one of the preconditions for the constitution of a public realm; with the loss of the world the framework for public activities can never come into being, nor can those capacities that flourish within it, such as judgment, common sense, impartiality, and memory. What remains in common is then only the bare fact of life, the natural life-cycle of the human species governed by sheer animal needs. Having lost the world, we are left with only nature in common.

Arendt identifies two main causes of world alienation: expropriation and wealth accumulation. Expropriation is a process that started with the Reformation and the concomitant separation of church and state. All stable forms of landed property, beginning with church property, were eliminated and replaced with an ever-increasing accumulation of social wealth. This, in turn, brought into existence a laboring class directly compelled by life's necessities, stimulated an enormous increase of productivity, and generated more expropriation and further wealth accumulation. As she describes it:

> Expropriation, the deprivation for certain groups of their place in the world and their naked exposure to the exigencies of life, created both the original accumulation of wealth and the possibility of transforming this wealth into capital through labor. These together constituted the conditions for the rise of a capitalist economy . . .

What distinguishes this development at the beginning of the modern age from similar occurrences in the past is that expropriation and wealth accumulation did not simply result in new property or lead to a new redistribution of wealth, but were fed back into the process to generate further expropriations, greater productivity, and more appropriation.[52]

This remorseless dynamic of economic growth, which Arendt compares to a natural process in its compulsion and inexhaustibility, destroys all worldly stability and durability; everything becomes an object of production and consumption, of acquisition and exchange, and individuals are forced to concentrate on their purely biological needs, that is, on *laboring* to reproduce their condition of existence on an ever-expanding scale. All values attached to the world – permanence, stability, durability – are sacrificed in favor of the values of labor – life, productivity, and abundance. The introduction of automation would only make matters worse, since "the rhythm of machines would magnify and intensify the natural rhythm of life enormously, but it would not change, only make more deadly, life's chief character with respect to the world, which is to wear down durability."[53]

Arendt then sketches the later phases of this process of expropriation and wealth accumulation: having started with the uprooting of people from their land and their transformation into a class of wage-laborers, it then substituted membership in a social class and identity with the nation-state for their previous allegiances. But with the decline of the nation-state and the integration of the world economy we have reached a stage where *mankind* as a whole replaces nationally bound societies, and the *earth* the limited state territories. Far from representing a progressive development, this elimination of cultural specificities in favor of a global and undifferentiated society is viewed with apprehension by Arendt, since in her view "men cannot become citizens of the world as they are citizens of their country, and social men cannot own collectively as family and household men own their private property."[54]

## EARTH ALIENATION: SECOND STAGE OF MODERNITY

"Earth alienation," to which we may now turn, represents an intensification of the trends identified with world alienation. It was partly induced by the discovery of America and the subsequent exploration of the whole earth, culminating in the invention of the airplane and in the conquest of space. This had the unintended effect of making the earth seem much smaller, to the point where modern man could see it as a mere ball from which, first in imagination and then in reality, he could detach himself and view it from a point in space. The more proximate cause, however, was the invention of the telescope which, beside destroying man's faith in the evidence of the senses, established an Archimedean standpoint from which the earth could be viewed as part of an infinite universe.[55] This cosmic standpoint not only displaced the geocentric worldview but enabled man to view the universe, including the earth, as subject to the same universal laws, so that nothing occurring in earthly nature was viewed any longer as a mere earthly happening. It also enabled a tremendous expansion in knowledge and mastery over nature, culminating in the ability of contemporary science to introduce cosmic processes into the earth – such as the splitting of the atom – and, in so doing, to endanger the survival not only of the human species but of the earth itself. In Arendt's view, then, while world alienation determined the course of modern society, earth alienation has been the hallmark of modern science.[56] But as she notes:

> Compared with the earth alienation underlying the whole development of natural science in the modern age, the withdrawal from terrestrial proximity contained in the discovery of the globe as a whole and the world alienation produced in the twofold process of expropriation and wealth accumulation are of minor significance.[57]

Earth alienation epitomizes the desire to escape from the confines of the earth: spurred by modern science and technology, we have searched for ways to overcome our earth-bound, and thus limited, condition by setting out on the exploration of space, by attempting to recreate life under laboratory conditions, and by trying to extend our given life-span. In doing this we seem to be driven by "a rebellion against human existence"[58] which we wish to exchange for something we have made entirely by ourselves. Earth alienation represents thus, in the helpful formulation of George Kateb, a resentment against the human condition.[59] The paradox of this resentment, however, is that it will not lead to a liberation, a freedom from earthly constraints. Rather, it will only lead us back to the prison of our own minds, since we will be able to know only those patterns that we ourselves have created. Modern science and technology thus make it more and more unlikely "that man will encounter anything in the world around him that is not man-made and hence is not, in the last analysis, he himself in a different disguise."[60] Moreover, the conquest of space can only lead to an infinite regress, because once we have reached the Archimedean point with respect to the earth, we would need "a new Archimedean point, and so on *ad infinitum*. In other words, man can only get lost in the immensity of the universe, for the only true Archimedean point would be the absolute void behind the universe."[61]

Arendt's reflections are here shaped by the further preoccupation that in wilfully departing from our earthly and worldly condition we might reach a point where we shall no longer be able to recognize ourselves in our creations, and that, as a result, the modern epistemological precept of knowing only that which we have made ourselves might be rendered obsolete. The new universe that has emerged from our most advanced theoretical constructions seems, paradoxically, to escape all possible representation, since − in the words of Erwin Schrödinger − it is not only "practically inaccessible but not even thinkable," for "however we think it, it is wrong; not perhaps quite as meaningless as a triangular circle, but much more so than a winged lion."[62] By abandoning our faith in the senses to reveal reality and in the capacity of reason to discover truth we have reached the point where the world and our theories have lost all intelligibility. Arendt thus sees a continuity from the rise of Cartesian doubt to the most recent developments in quantum mechanics and relativity theory, insofar as they all rejected the identity of Being and Appearance, that is, the idea that reality could be disclosed to our senses veridically and that our reason could apprehend the truth. Cartesian doubt doubted the existence of truth itself, and thereby discovered that

> the traditional concept of truth, whether based on sense perception or on reason or on belief in divine revelation, had rested on the twofold assumption that what truly is will appear of its own accord and that human capabilities are adequate to receive it.[63]

Thus, what started as universal doubt has been deepened and extended by the most recent discoveries of science. The unsettling philosophical implications of the discoveries of Einstein, of Max Planck, of Bohr, of Schrödinger and Heisenberg are taken by Arendt as the confirmation of her views about the losses incurred in world and earth alienation. For her the possibility of truly understanding what we are doing has disappeared in the modern world, and she fears that with the escape from our earthly condition we might face a radically novel situation:

The most radical change in the human condition we can imagine would be an emigration of men from the earth to some other planet. Such an event, no longer totally impossible, would imply that man would have to live under man-made conditions, radically different from those the earth offers him. Neither labor nor work nor action nor, indeed, thought as we know it would then make sense any longer.[64]

## THE HIERARCHY OF HUMAN ACTIVITIES AND THE VICTORY OF *ANIMAL LABORANS*

It is to the activities of labor, work, and action that I would like now to turn, since in the reversal of their priority, as well as in the reversal of the hierarchy between the *vita activa* and the *vita contemplativa*, Arendt sees a key manifestation of the modern age. As regards the second reversal, Arendt claims that in the tradition of Western philosophy, starting with Plato, there occurred a shift away from the activities connected with political life, with action and the striving for earthly immortality, in favor of the silent contemplation of eternal truths which a privileged few could enjoy by willfully detaching themselves from all worldly concerns and activities. For Arendt, in fact, our tradition of political philosophy was founded in explicit opposition to the *polis* and its activities, with the philosopher turning away from politics and then returning to it in order to impose his alien standards upon human affairs.[65] This debasement of the values of the *vita activa*, and especially of political action, was continued by the Christian tradition, insofar as it gave a religious sanction to the activity of contemplation and stressed the sinfulness of our worldly activities. The "glad tidings" announced by Christianity, the belief in the immortality of the soul and in a world beyond this one where the faithful will be gathered, had fateful consequences for the esteem and dignity of politics. Politics was now no longer seen as the sphere where individuals could perform noble deeds, reach agreement on matters of mutual concern, and achieve a measure of justice; it became, instead, the instrument for checking and controlling men's sinful nature, for punishing their evil conduct, and for looking after their earthly necessities. As Arendt puts it:

Political activity, which up to then had derived its greatest inspiration from the aspiration toward worldly immortality, now sank to the low level of an activity subject to necessity, destined to remedy the consequences of human sinfulness, on one hand, and to cater to the legitimate wants and interests of earthly life, on the other.[66]

What Platonism and Christianity achieved, then, was an elevation of the values and concerns associated with the *vita contemplativa* and a corresponding denigration of those associated with the *vita activa*. Henceforth all the values of the *vita activa* had to serve and be justified in terms of the values of the *vita contemplativa*.

With the emergence of modernity we witness a reversal of this hierarchy, although such reversal was not straightforward. What it affected, in fact, was not the relation of contemplation and action, but that of *thinking* and *making*, of *thought* and *fabrication*. Contemplation, in the original sense of silently beholding the truth, was altogether eliminated, since it was associated with a passive state of the mind, with the stillness required for the revelation or apprehension of truth. Thinking, on the other hand, was associated with a highly active state, with the engagement of the mind with itself, the inner dialogue of me and myself. Thus, when in Bacon's well-known formulation science became the acquisition of power over nature (*scientia propter potentiam*), it was thinking, and not contemplation, that became the servant of making. And it became the servant of making because with the scientific revolution it became evident that our claim to knowledge was restricted to what we ourselves could produce with our tools and instruments (e.g., through the setting up of artificial experiments, through the invention of the telescope).

According to Arendt, the principle that we could only know what we ourselves had produced was summed up in Vico's statement that truth was a product of making (*verum factum*). Vico's claim, to be sure, was restricted to history, since only history could be "made" by man. She argues, however, that the principle itself was already established at the time of the discoveries of Galileo. Galileo's telescope had demonstrated that merely contemplating the heavens in the belief that truth would disclose itself was no longer an adequate way to knowledge. Knowledge was arrived at not through contemplation or passive observation, but through *making* and *fabricating*.[67] Thus the reversal in the modern age elevated *homo faber* to the position previously enjoyed by contemplation, and channeled all human activities into the pursuit of knowledge through making, that is, to intervening in nature in order to extract from her universal laws that applied to the whole cosmos.

Furthermore, the knowledge thus obtained was no longer concerned with the *why* or the *what* of phenomena, with the cause or the substance of things, but only with the *how*, that is, with the processes of generation and development. To know something meant to know how it came into being and to be able to reproduce its processes artificially. One of the reasons for this shift, in Arendt's view, was that "the scientist made only in order to know, not in order to produce things, and the product was a mere by-product, a side effect."[68] The result was that in the place of the concept of *Being* we now find the concept of *Process*: nature itself became a process governed by immutable laws, and it was not long before history too was viewed in the same light.[69] One of the key concepts of physical science, that of development, was in fact taken up by the historical sciences.[70]

For Arendt, then, the break with contemplation was finally consummated "not with the elevation of man the maker to the position formerly held by man the contemplator, but with the introduction of the concept of *process* into making."[71] This break had fateful consequences, insofar as it led to the final reversal, namely, the elevation of *labor* to the highest position in the hierarchical order of the *vita activa*, at the expense of both fabrication (*poiesis*) and action (*praxis*). Man as *animal laborans* now became the standard against which *homo faber* and man as *zoon politikon* were assessed and found wanting. And what permitted this to happen was precisely the central position that the concept of process assumed with the emergence of modernity. As Arendt points out:

> It deprived man as maker and builder of those fixed and permanent standards and measurements which, prior to the modern age, have always served him as guides for his doing and criteria for his judgment ... For the mentality of modern man, as it was determined by the development of modern science and the concomitant unfolding of modern philosophy, it was at least as decisive that man began to consider himself part and parcel of the two superhuman, all-encompassing processes of nature and history, both of which seemed doomed to an infinite progress without ever reaching any inherent *telos* or approaching any preordained idea.[72]

Submerged in the overall process of nature and later, with the rise of the historical sciences, of history, man lost all contact with the permanent and durable features of the world, and with the objects and standards that previously governed his activities. Arendt finds an example of this loss in the transformation of the principle of utility, characteristic of the worldview of *homo faber*, into Bentham's principle of the greatest happiness of the greatest number.[73] In the principle of greatest happiness all worldly values are replaced by the subjective sensations of pleasure and pain, which are geared exclusively to the promotion of life and the survival of the species. *Life*, then, and not the world, became the highest good of man, and all activities previously directed at the construction of a human world and at the establishment of public spaces where speech and action could flourish were reduced to the single and monotonous activity of labor.

Arendt mantains that the Christian emphasis on the sacredness of life was partly responsible for the obliteration of the ancient distinctions within the *vita activa*, since it viewed labor, work, and action as equally subject to the necessities of life.[74] In this respect Christianity helped to free labor from the contempt in which it was held in antiquity, paving the way for its revaluation and eventual triumph in the modern age. But as we saw, the impact of modern science and the loss of trust in the senses were also contributing factors in the emergence of the worldview of *animal laborans*, insofar as both forced man to concentrate on processes as found in nature or in the internal workings of the mind. The overall result was to make *labor*, the endless repetitive cycle of man's metabolism with nature, the highest of man's capacities, and to elevate *life*, or the preservation of our biological species, into the highest value. In Arendt's words:

> What was left was a "natural force," the force of the life process itself, to which all men and all human activities were equally submitted and whose only aim, if it had an aim at all, was survival of the animal species man. None of the higher capacities of man was any longer necessary to connect individual life with the life of the species; individual life became part of the life process, and to labor, to assure the continuity of one's own life and the life of his family, was all that was needed.[75]

A world whose chief values are dictated by labor is a world were private activities, previously enclosed in the sphere of the household (*oikos*), have taken over the public realm and turned it into that oxymoron going under the name of the "public household."[76] In this respect the victory of *animal laborans* has carried forward the obliteration of the distinction between the public and the private that started in the eighteenth century with the rise of the social. It has enabled the activities connected to the necessities of life to appear in public and predominate to the point where the public itself (the polity) has become a function of the private (the economy).[77] This is indeed one of the major objections of Arendt against the modern age, since the latter's exclusive preoccupation with economic matters has resulted in the disappearance of the public sphere, the creation of a society of job-holders, the imposition of conformity and isolation, the enforcement of predictable behavior, and the establishment of bureaucratic forms of government. All these phenomena are connected, in Arendt's view, to the rise of society, or, more precisely, to its most extreme development, mass society. Let us then examine in more detail this constellation of factors.

## THE RISE OF THE SOCIAL AND THE RULE BY NOBODY

In Chapter 2 of *The Human Condition* Arendt presents the distinction between the private and the public realm and offers a series of reflections on the events that have made that distinction obsolete. As we saw previously, she maintains that the private is the sphere governed by *necessity*, by the need to labor to satisfy our biological needs, while the public is the sphere of *freedom*, of the disclosure of the "who" in speech and action among a community of equals. The distinction private–public also coincides with the opposition of, respectively, futility and permanence, shame and honor, hidden and disclosed.[78] Each human activity has thus a proper location in the world, an appropriate space of operation. When one such activity systematically transgresses the space of another and establishes its values upon it, as labor has done in respect of the public sphere, it deprives it of its autonomy and transforms it into something altogether different (the public has now become the sphere of "national housekeeping," of the bureaucratic steering of the economy). It may also, in conjunction with the rise of mass society, displace it entirely and put into its place a hybrid called "the social," which will endanger the private realm as well. Arendt:

> We know that the contradiction between private and public, typical of the initial stages of the modern age, has been a temporary phenomenon which introduced the utter extinction of the very difference between the private and public realms, the submersion of both in the sphere of the social.[79]

Both the private and the public realm suffer from the threat of extinction: in the case of the former it would mean the destruction of a private space in which to hide and in which to find comfort and rest from the activities of work, labor, and action; it would also mean the loss of initiative that springs from necessity and the blurring of the distinction between freedom and necessity.[80] In the case of the latter it would mean the elimination of a public space of appearance where our identities are revealed, our deeds remembered, our traditions renewed and our history preserved; it would also mean the loss of objectivity, the disappearance of stability and permanence, and the destruction of freedom and plurality.[81]

All these baneful consequences are seen to follow the emergence of mass society in the modern age. Such a society, for Arendt, constitutes a novel form of living together characterized by the fact that individuals are united only by their common membership in the human species, that is, by their common biological needs of life and survival, and not by a public world of action and speech. In such society people are expected to conform, to share the same private interests (economic by definition), and to behave in a predictable manner, rather than to act in original and distinctive fashion. Arendt claims that this form of living together allows for forms of despotic rule which have varied from the more benign one-man rule of monarchical absolutism to the more terrifying forms of totalitarianism;[82] in Western democracies it has encouraged the rule by nobody, namely, by a bureaucracy. But this rule by nobody is not, she writes, "no rule; it may indeed, under certain circumstances, even turn out to be one of its cruelest and most tyrannical versions,"[83] since no one appears to be responsible, and no one in particular can be blamed for certain policies or programs. As she remarks:

A complete victory of society will always produce some sort of "communistic fiction," whose outstanding political characteristic is that it is indeed ruled by an "invisible hand," namely, by nobody. What we traditionally call state and government gives place here to pure administration.[84]

Such form of rule is moreover perfectly suited to a society that, in Arendt's view, has done away with all distinctions of rank, status, or title and replaced them with mere function. This process started with the absorption of the family and its economic activities by larger social groups; these groups, in turn, expanded and became consolidated as social classes; but with the emergence of mass society these classes have themselves been absorbed by society, and we are left with a situation where every individual is identified only by his or her function. Thus with the establishment of mass society the realm of the social "has finally, after several centuries of development, reached the point where it embraces and controls all members of a given community equally and with equal strength";[85] and the reason for this is that no boundaries between public and private, no distinctions among individuals, and no world common to them all, are allowed to exist. In their place we now have the relentless dynamic of wealth accumulation characteristic of a society in which, as Arendt puts it, "the fact of mutual dependence for the sake of life and nothing else assumes public significance, and where the activities connected with sheer survival are permitted to appear in public."[86]

## THE FUTILITY OF THE MODERN WORLD

Arendt's indictment of modern mass society and of the values of *animal laborans* appears to be exceedingly harsh in light of the fact that vast numbers of people have gained, thanks to the expansion of productivity and the struggles to redistribute its fruits equally, a measure of economic security and of self-respect unmatched in previous ages. But the point of her accusation actually lies elsewhere. It is not just that, in her opinion, economic emancipation does not lead by itself to political freedom, but rather, if pursued exclusively, to an expansion of the sphere of necessity. The real issue for her is that in a world where the values of *animal laborans* have triumphed, all human activities have been reduced to the lowest common denominator, that is, to the task of securing life's necessities and providing for their abundance. She is not against the activity of labor *per se*, but rather against its undisputed predominance over all the other activities of the *vita activa*, that is, over work and especially over action. What worries her most is that since the products of labor are perishable, their increasing availability only makes our existence more futile. A society entirely devoted to labor and consumption might reach a stage where "dazzled by the abundance of its growing fertility and caught in the smooth functioning of a never-ending process, [it] would no longer be able to recognize its own futility."[87]

Against the futility of the labor process, of the life-process of the species, Arendt sets the values of permanence and earthly immortality that are to be found, respectively, in a common artificially constructed world and in a public sphere of speech and action. Her act of recovery of the central political categories of the Greek and Roman experience must therefore be seen as an attempt to save the modern world from its growing futility, from its absorption in endless labor and consumption, by reminding us of the values that make our existence meaningful, of those activities that enable us to share a world in common, and of the joys of public freedom and happiness that come from acting in concert. For Arendt, in this respect, the Greek *polis* stands as an exemplar, since like the Roman *res publica*, it stood for a "guarantee against the futility of individual life, the space protected against this futility and reserved for the relative permanence, if not immortality, of mortals."[88] Within this space the words and deeds of individuals were turned into stories that could be recorded and saved for posterity. Those who acted were thus able to establish "the everlasting remembrance of their good and bad deeds, to inspire admiration in the present and in future ages,"[89] and thereby "prove themselves to be of a 'divine' nature."[90] The public space of the *polis* represented, therefore, a form of "organized remembrance"[91] that assured everlastingness to the words and deeds of political actors and, in so doing, endowed human existence with a measure of immortality.

The redeeming qualities of political action and remembrance are not, however, restricted to the experience of the Greek *polis*; on the contrary, they are to be found throughout history whenever organs of self-government have been established and individuals have tasted the joys of public freedom and public happiness. They have also been reactivated whenever public spaces for action and deliberation have been set up, from town hall meetings to workers' councils, from demonstrations and sit-ins to struggles for justice and equal rights. Arendt's vision is thus not a nostalgic return to the greatness of a past now irremediably lost,[92] but represents the attempt to articulate for the present those experiences of political action and collective self-determination that have occurred again and again in history, providing human life with greater meaning and purpose, and human affairs with some dignity and hope.

Arendt's critique of modernity must be understood against the background of these experiences of public action and their redeeming qualities. If her criticism is harsh, it is because of her concern that the trends she has identified in the modern age might become permanent, thereby impoverishing our existence. Her most worrisome conviction is that the modern age, by restricting the opportunities for political action and allowing the unlimited expansion of the social, has undermined the redeeming and immortalizing possibilities of politics. Furthermore, by eroding the stability and permanence of the public world and concentrating human energies on the unlimited accumulation of wealth, it has left individuals isolated and vulnerable to political manipulation. As she argued in her essay "The Concept of History," modern mass society stands for a society of men who, without a common world which would at once relate and separate them, either live in desperate lonely separation or are pressed together into a mass. For a mass-society is nothing more than that kind of organized living which automatically establishes itself among human beings who are still related to one another [in virtue of being members of the human species] but have lost the world once common to all of them.[93]

And as we know from her writings on totalitarianism, these characteristics of mass society carry grave political dangers, since "loneliness, the common ground for terror, the essence of totalitarian government . . . is closely connected with uprootedness and superfluousness which have been the curse of modern masses since the beginning of the industrial revolution."[94] It is important to stress this connection, because in Arendt's indictment of modernity the novel and catastrophic event of totalitarianism plays a crucial role. Without a deep appreciation of this event and the impact it had on Arendt's life and work, it is difficult to understand the harshness of her judgment. In her view the terrible originality of totalitarianism consisted in the fact that through its terror and violence, and through the brutality of its ideology, it constituted a radical break with all the standards and categories of our moral and political tradition. As she put it in the essay "Tradition and the Modern Age":

> Totalitarian domination as an established fact, which in its unprecedentedness cannot be comprehended through the usual categories of political thought, and whose "crimes" cannot be judged by traditional moral standards or punished within the legal framework of our civilization, has broken the continuity of Occidental history. The break in our tradition is now an accomplished fact.[95]

This tragic rupture in our history forced Arendt to rethink the whole tradition of political thought in the West and to refashion, in the form of a phenomenological anthropology, those categories of the human condition that could serve to orient us again in the modern world. I will shortly present some objections to her understanding and evaluation of modernity, but I hope to have shown the provocative and original character of her thinking. If her work still admits, indeed, requires criticism, such criticism is nourished by the originality of her insights as much as by one's disagreement with them.

## CRITICAL QUESTIONS

I would like now to devote my concluding section to a critique of a number of categories employed by Arendt in her evaluation of modernity. The categories I want to focus on are those of *nature*, of *process*, and what Arendt calls the *social*.

## 1

As we saw previously, one of the categories that defines our human condition is that of worldliness (the others being life, natality, mortality, plurality, and the earth). Worldliness is created and reproduced by the activity of work, being the result of those activities of fabrication that provide us with an artificial environment of objects, institutions, and settings that separates us from nature. Without such a humanly created environment we would be subject to the endless cycles of nature, to the recurring patterns of growth and decay through which nature "forever invades the human artifice, threatening the durability of the world and its fitness for human use."[96]

Now, one of the distinctive features of the modern age is to have allowed these natural processes an unrestricted sway, thereby undermining the stability and permanence of the world and producing that condition which Arendt calls worldlessness. By elevating labor, the most natural of human activities, to the highest position within the *vita activa*, the modern age has in this respect brought us *too close* to nature. Deprived of a common artificial world in which our actions and projects could find an embodiment that preserved them in time, we are reduced now to the activity of sheer survival and to the production of things that are by definition perishable. The growing sense of futility that characterizes the modern age is thus connected, in Arendt's view, to the loss of a humanly created, artificial world, and the corresponding exposure and subordination to the natural life-cycle of the species.

There is, however, another account of the distinctive features of modernity where Arendt stresses not the increasing naturalness but the increasing *artificiality* of our condition. This account can be found in her essay "The Concept of History," where Arendt claims that:

> The modern age, with its growing world-alienation, has led to a situation where man, wherever he goes, encounters only himself. All the processes of the earth and the universe have revealed themselves either as man-made or as potentially man-made. These processes, after having devoured, as it were, the solid objectivity of

the given, ended by rendering meaningless the one over-all process which originally was conceived in order to give meaning to them ... This is what happened to our concept of history, as it happened to our concept of nature. In the situation of radical world-alienation, neither history nor nature is at all conceivable.[97]

It is thus the loss of any *given* world, of anything that is not man-made and artificial, that characterizes the modern age. As an instance of this we can cite the following elements of Arendt's analysis of modernity. First, natural processes have been recreated artificially by means of scientific experiment, so that what was previously a natural occurrence has become a matter of human intervention. Second, our natural environment has been extensively transformed by technology and in some instances replaced by an entirely artificial habitat. Third, even life itself, the most natural condition of human beings, has become an object of artificial manipulation in our attempts to extend it or to recreate it by means of genetic engineering. Fourth, we have searched for ways to overcome our natural condition as earth-bound creatures by setting out on the exploration of space and envisaging the possibility of inhabiting other planets. All this leads to a situation where, thanks to our efforts, nothing around us will be a naturally given event, object, or process, "a free gift from nowhere," as Arendt puts it,[98] but rather will be the product of our instruments and of the will to refashion the world in our image. The progress in science and the advances in technology will, therefore, make it "more unlikely every day that man will encounter anything in the world around him that is not man-made and hence is not, in the last analysis, he himself in a different disguise."[99]

It is difficult to reconcile this account of modernity, where art replaces nature, with the previous one, where nature intrudes upon the human artifice. One reason for this difficulty is that in the former account Arendt views nature from the standpoint of labor, while in the latter it is viewed from the standpoint of fabrication. The result is to make nature an ambiguous category, since in one case the victory of *animal laborans* indicates our subjection to natural processes (to the life-process of the species), while in the other case the expansion of scientific knowledge and of technological mastery indicates the overcoming of all natural limits (including that of life itself). The modern world is thus both too natural and too artificial, too much under the dominance of *labor* as well as too much under the dominance of *techne*.

This ambiguity in Arendt is never properly resolved: in some writings she seems more concerned to stress the importance of the human artifice, with its qualities of permanence, stability, and durability; in others she emphasizes our connection to nature and our dependence on the given conditions of existence, especially life, mortality, and the earth. One way to resolve this ambiguity would be to argue that for Arendt the proper relation between art and nature is one where art *completes* nature instead of either creating it or being totally subject to it. It is worth noting that this conception was held by the ancients (since they maintained that art could only perfect nature), and was later reformulated in religious terms by Aquinas, with his notion that grace does not eliminate nature but completes it. Against this conception the moderns asserted that art could reconstruct nature, that is, could create it and thereby master it.[100] Now, if Arendt's understanding of the relation between art and nature is indeed the one being suggested here, she would be siding with the ancients and criticizing modernity for its technological hubris as well as for its enslavement to nature.

I cannot pursue this suggestion further, since it cannot be found explicitly in Arendt's writings, and would in any case be open to the charge of setting up an unhistorical contrast between ancients and moderns. The point was merely to see if a specific conception of art's relation to nature could resolve the ambiguity of Arendt's understanding of modernity, or at least reconcile the two contrasting accounts we have examined. My contention is that it could, and that Arendt's category of nature would have gained in clarity if she had pursued a more explicit articulation of the relation of art to nature.

## 2

I would like now to examine another category whose status is problematic, that of *process*. We have seen that for Arendt the modern worldview is characterized by its emphasis on the idea of Process, on the "how" of phenomena, be they natural or historical, and by the corresponding loss of the idea of Being. The shift from the "what" and the "why" to the "how" that occurred with the rise of modern science meant that it was no longer important to inquire into the nature of things and to discover their causes; rather, the purpose of science was to gain knowledge of processes, of the way things came into being and of their mode of development. Beginning with modern physics, this shift of emphasis became consolidated with the rise of the historical sciences, to the point where nature and history were seen as two all-encompassing processes governed by universal laws but devoid of any inherent purpose or *telos*.[101]

The subsumption of nature and history under the category of process is explored in more detail in the essay "The Concept of History."[102] In that essay Arendt argues that there is a close connection between the modern conception of history as a process unfolding by its own laws, and the understanding of nature in terms of processes which is characteristic of the worldview of modern science. History is no longer conceived as a record of human actions and events but as a process transcending all these earthly happenings and endowing them from time to time with significance. The problem with this conception is that just as the particular occurrences in the physical world become meaningful by being located within the overall processes of nature, so the actions and sufferings of particular individuals only gain significance if they happen to be part of the unfolding pattern of history. In both instances, Arendt writes, "the particular incident, the observable fact or single occurrence of nature, or the reported deed and event of history, have ceased to make sense without a universal process in which they are supposedly embedded."[103] Yet, by locating meaning at the level of process we are confronted by the dangerous paradox that any meaning we may choose to impose upon either nature or history may turn out to be valid. As Arendt puts it:

> The trouble is that almost every axiom seems to lend itself to consistent deductions and this to such an extent that it is as though men were in a position to prove almost any hypothesis they might choose to adopt, not only in the field of purely mental constructions like the various over-all interpretations of history which are all equally well supported by facts, but in the natural sciences as well ... This means quite literally that everything is possible not only in the realm of ideas, but in the field of reality itself.[104]

One might argue that the possibility of proving any hypothesis is only to acknowledge the possibility of what Nietzsche called perspectivism, namely, that the world is open to any number of interpretations, none of which is epistemically privileged. If we were to accept this doctrine, what appears as a dangerous paradox to Arendt might no longer be so. Arendt's concern, however, is that once we start acting on the assumption that any hypothesis can be made true (i.e., that any interpretation is possible and legitimate), the consequences for the world, especially for the world of politics, can be disastrous. As she points out, the totalitarian phenomenon was based on the conviction that everything is possible and that any hypothesis, if acted upon consistently, will become true. In this respect, it does not matter that the hypothesis is, as she writes

> as mad as it pleases; it will always end in producing facts which are then "objectively" true. What was originally nothing but a hypothesis, to be proved or disproved by actual facts, will in the course of consistent action always turn into a fact, never to be disproved.[105]

The point, therefore, is that the moment we try to escape the contingent character of events or the factuality of the world in order to find meaning in an overall process, we find ourselves confronted by the possibility that any meaning we wish to impose will be found acceptable; moreover, once this possibility is made the basis of consistent action it can transform the world in ways that we may come to regret profoundly.

I shall now turn to another set of considerations made by Arendt in the concluding section of *The Human Condition*. In that work, as we saw, Arendt mantained that the modern age brought about two reversals, first in the priority of contemplation over action, and second in the hierarchical order within the *vita activa*. In both instances it appears that the category of process was involved. As regards the first, Arendt claims that the break with contemplation was finally con-summated with the introduction of the concept of process into making. Previous to that the making and fabricating activities of *homo faber* had been guided by certain fixed standards and models provided by contemplation; but once in the understanding of fabrication the emphasis shifted from these standards and models to the fabrication process, the relevance of contemplation was altogether lost.[106] This, in turn, prepared the way for the second reversal, since, according to Arendt, having lost the connection with contemplation, the privileged position of *homo faber* within the *vita activa* was no longer secure. Deprived of those permanent standards that precede and outlast the process of fabrication, man the maker was soon eclipsed by *animal laborans*. The shift in emphasis from the "what" to the "how," from the models and standards which guide fabrication to the processes by which an object can be produced, was thus partly responsible for the second reversal, that is, for the elevation of labor to the highest position in the hierarchical order of the *vita activa*.[107] The victory of *animal laborans* is, in turn, associated with a whole number of disturbing features of modernity: the valuing of life over freedom and worldliness, the loss of the capacity to act, the erosion of the public sphere, the imposition of conformity and isolation, the distrust of permanence and durability, and the absorption in endless production and consumption.

From the foregoing account we might conclude that everything associated with the category of process is judged in very negative terms by Arendt. This, however, would be a rash conclusion. If we examine her writings more carefully we discover, in fact, a deep ambivalence in her attitude toward processes. For example, in the same essay where she criticizes the modern understanding of history and nature ("The Concept of History") she also claims that processes are started by human action, and in *The Human Condition* she devotes a section to the process character of action. Let us look a bit more closely at the first claim. In a surprising passage contained in "The Concept of History" we read:

> The notion of process does not denote an objective quality of either history or nature; it is the inevitable result of human action. The first result of men's acting into history is that history becomes a process, and the most cogent argument for men's acting into nature in the guise of scientific inquiry is that today, in Whitehead's formulation, "nature is a process."[108]

Just before the epilogue she reiterates that:

> The very notion of process, which is so highly characteristic of modern science, both natural and historical, probably had its origin in this fundamental experience of action ... [which] in contrast to all other human activities consists first of all of starting processes.[109]

It is surprising to find such claims, because one of the principal features of action, according to Arendt, is to introduce the unexpected, to break the continuum of time, to interrupt the automatism of processes. Action seems therefore to carry the burden both of initiating processes and of constantly disrupting them. The truth, as Arendt says, is that "automatism is inherent in all processes, no matter what their origin may be," that is, whether they originate in nature or as a result of human action, which is why "no single act, and no single event, can ever, once and for all, deliver and save a man, or a nation, or mankind."[110] This means that we must constantly interrupt by action those processes that were started by the same miracle, the miracle of beginning which every act contains. Historical processes, for example, are "created and constantly interrupted by human initiative, by the *initium* man is insofar as he is an acting being."[111] Similarly, natural processes are nowadays initiated by our greatly increased capacity to "act into nature," to the point where some of them become irreversible and need to be countered by further action.[112] Our struggle against the automatism of processes resembles in this respect the never-ending labors of Sisyphus.

Let us now look at the second claim made by Arendt, that pertaining to the process quality of action. In the chapter on action contained in *The Human Condition* there is a section entitled "The Process Character of Action" where Arendt repeats the claim that:

> The central concept of the two entirely new sciences of the modern age, natural science no less than historical, is the concept of process, and the actual human experience underlying it is action. Only because we are capable of acting, of starting processes of our own, can we conceive of both nature and history as systems of processes.[113]

But we also find the further claim that the reason why action is able to start processes is because action itself is process-like, since it sets in motion a chain of events which is irreversible and whose outcome is unpredictable. No one, Arendt claims, is able to undo or even to control reliably any of the processes started by action, since irreversibility and unpredictability are built into the very core of it. As she put it:

> Not even oblivion and confusion, which can cover up so efficiently the origin and the responsibility for every single deed, are able to undo a deed or prevent its consequences. And this incapacity to undo what has been done is matched by an almost equally complete incapacity to foretell the consequences of any deed or even to have reliable knowledge of its motives ... The reason why we are never able to foretell with certainty the outcome and end of any action is simply that action has no end.[114]

It could be easily objected that Arendt confuses the nature of the consequences with the nature of that which causes them; in other words, that action does not have to be process-like simply because it sets in motion processes which are irreversible and unpredictable. However, even if we accept this criticism, it remains the case that Arendt identifies some of the worst features of modernity (e.g., the understanding of history and nature as all-encompassing processes and the endangering of life on this planet) with the consequences of that capacity for action which is otherwise held to be the highest and most rare of all human capacities. How are we to account for this contradiction? In my view part of the explanation is to be found in the type of action involved, since Arendt makes clear that "acting into nature" (the predominant form of action in the modern age) is not the same as acting in the world, since it lacks the revelatory and historical qualities of the latter.[115] But even if we grant this distinction, the problem of the relation between action and process would remain, for we would still have to explain how the miracle of beginning something new can be reconciled with the irreversibility of its consequences, with the automatism of what follows. It is not sufficient to argue, as Arendt does, that the power to forgive is what saves the doer from the consequences of his/her actions.[116] We are still confronted by the puzzle of relating freedom (i.e., action) to necessity (i.e., process), and of reconciling the negative assessment of all those features of modernity associated with the automatism of processes with the acknowledgment that action is responsible for initiating many of those processes. What Arendt said of Marx — that his attitude toward labor never ceased to be equivocal[117] — can be said of Arendt too: her attitude towards process is characterized by a deep ambivalence, an ambivalence which affected her assessment of modernity as well as her understanding of the relation between freedom and necessity.[118]

3

I would like to conclude with a critique of Arendt's category of the *social*. We have seen previously that for Arendt the distinction between the public and the private realm has been blurred and finally dissolved by what she calls "society" or "the social," a sphere whose origin coincides with the emergence of the modern age. Arendt identifies the social with all those activities formerly restricted to the private sphere of the household and having to do with the necessities of life, labor, and reproduction. Her claim is that with the tremendous expansion of the economy from the end of the eighteenth century, all such activities have taken over the public realm and transformed it into a sphere for the satisfaction of our material needs. Society has thus "invaded" and "conquered" the public realm, turning it into a function of what previously were private needs and concerns. As she puts it: "With the rise of society, that is, the rise of the 'household' (*oikia*) or of economic activities to the public realm, housekeeping and all matters pertaining formerly to the private sphere of the family have become a 'collective' concern."[119] Having become a matter of collective concern, economic activities now shape the purpose and content of politics, to the point where the whole of political life is understood on the model of a family, "whose everyday affairs have to be taken care of by a gigantic, nation-wide administration of housekeeping."[120] The destruction of the boundary separating the private from the public has thus reduced politics to a matter of national housekeeping, that is, to an activity no longer characterized by action, freedom, participation, and deliberation, but by labor, necessity, rule, and bureaucratic administration.

Arendt maintains that one of the causes of the breakdown of the distinction between public and private has to do with the nature of the social realm. What characterizes the latter are in fact all those activities connected to life and survival; once these are displaced onto the public realm, they acquire, as Arendt says, "an irresistible tendency to grow, to devour the older realms of the political and the private as well as the more recently established sphere of intimacy."[121] Confronted by this unnatural growth, no institutional boundaries are able to remain in place or to secure that which lies within them. As Arendt writes:

> The social realm, where the life process has established its own public domain, has let loose an unnatural growth, so to speak, of the natural; and it is against this growth, not merely against society but against a constantly growing social realm, that the private and intimate, on the one hand, and the political . . . on the other, have proved incapable of defending themselves.[122]

Arendt's concern, however, is not restricted to such phenomena as the erosion of the public and the private spheres and the reduction of politics to administration. She also wants to emphasize the fact that with the expansion of the social realm the tripartite division of human activities has been undermined to the point of becoming meaningless. In her view, once the social realm has established its monopoly, the distinction between labor, work, and action has no longer a rationale, since every effort is now expended on reproducing on an ever-expanding scale the material conditions of existence. Obsessed with life, productivity, and abundance, we can no longer appreciate the values associated with work, nor those associated with action. Our society has become one of laborers and job-holders, where "the fact of mutual dependence for the sake of life and nothing else assumes public significance,"[123] and where the very possibility of action is excluded, since everyone is expected to perform his/her assigned role in the productive process, and to conform to the prevailing standard of behavior.[124]

It is clear from the foregoing account that the category of the social plays a crucial role in Arendt's assessment of modernity. It enables her to highlight a number of important trends in contemporary societies toward conformism, anonymity, apathy, and consumerism. It also enables her to mount a critique of modern politics, of its growing bureaucratization as well as its exclusive concentration on economic matters. By means of this category she is also able to challenge the liberal model of politics, which is based on the assumption that the public is subordinate to the private, and the Marxist one, which is based on the idea that politics is only a reflection of economic interests.[125] But when examined more closely, we see that it blinds her to many important issues and leads her to a series of questionable judgments.

To begin with, Arendt's characterization of the social seems overly restricted. She claims that the social is the realm of labor, of biological and material necessity, of the reproduction of our conditions of existence. She also claims that the rise of the social coincides with the expansion of the economy from the end of the eighteenth century. Now it seems to me that, having identified the social with the growth of the economy in the past two centuries, Arendt cannot characterize it in terms of a subsistence model of simple reproduction. Such characterization may be adequate for the activities that are carried out in the household, in the sphere that Arendt defines as private, but is totally inappropriate as a description of modern industrial forms of production, with their high rates of capital accumulation and high levels of economic growth. By identifying the social with the economic activities of simple reproduction Arendt remains blind to the fact that modern capitalist economies generate a surplus far beyond the needs of reproduction. Moreover, the activities connected with the generation of this surplus are much better characterized in terms of the model of fabrication, rather than that of labor, since they create the entire material infrastructure upon which our society depends, as well as the technology by means of which we are able to create an entirely artificial environment.

Arendt's identification of the social with the activities of the household was responsible for another major shortcoming in her analysis of the economy. She was, in fact, unable to acknowledge that a modern capitalist economy constitutes a structure of power, determining the allocation of resources and the distribution of burdens and rewards. By relying on the misleading analogy of the household, Arendt maintained that all questions pertaining to the economy were pre-political, and therefore ignored the crucial question of economic power and exploitation. A number of writers, otherwise sympathetic to her, have noted this central deficiency. Sheldon Wolin, for example, writes that Arendt

> never succeeded in grasping the basic lesson taught not only by Marx but by the classical economists as well, that an economy is not merely work, property, productivity, and consumption: it is a structure of power, a system of ongoing relationships in which power and dependence tend to become cumulative, and inequalities are reproduced in forms that are ever grosser and ever more sophisticated.[126]

Similarly, Hanna Pitkin has noted that the question of justice is conspicuously absent in the writings of Arendt.[127] This is not because she was opposed to it or thought it unimportant, but because she was determined to insulate the public realm from all questions pertaining to the social, which in her view could only destroy it.[128] By insisting on a strict separation between the social and the political Arendt was therefore unable to give justice the central place it ought to occupy in any political theory.[129] Moreover, in claiming that social and economic questions were bound to destroy politics, she lent support to the view that they should be treated as technical questions, amenable to administrative solutions.[130] But as Richard Bernstein has perceptively pointed out: "Issues or problems do not simply come labeled 'social,' 'political,' or even 'private.' Indeed, the question whether a problem is itself properly social (and therefore not worthy of public debate) or political is itself frequently the central *political* issue."[131] Once we give up the distinction between the political and the social, we are able to acknowledge that any particular issue may be transformed into a political one, and that what were previously "private" concerns may turn out to be public problems.[132] One of the achievements of the feminist movement has been, precisely, to redefine the personal in political terms, to show the political nature of many issues classified as private.[133] To be sure, this redefinition of the personal *as* political does not aim at the complete dissolution of the distinction between the private and the public. Rather, the feminist critiques of the separation between the private and the public have emphasized the fact that these categories refer to two *interrelated* dimensions of the structure of liberal-patriarchal societies. As Carol Pateman has noted:

> Feminists are trying to develop a theory of a social practice that, for the first time in the western world, would be a truly general theory – including women and men equally – grounded in the inter-relationship of the individual to collective life, or personal to political life, instead of their separation and opposition.[134]

The boundary between the public and the private is thus not as fixed as Arendt thought; nor is the one between the social and the political. Indeed, many of the struggles for social equality which for Arendt were non-political in nature were decisive in enlarging our conception of citizenship.[135] Jean Bethke Elshtain, one of the feminist political thinkers who has attempted to reformulate the public–private distinction on more adequate grounds,[136] has noted how Arendt's insulation of the political sphere from the concerns of the "social" prevented her from appreciating the many instances of citizenship that have emerged in the modern age. As she writes:

> To lament the absence of a "public space" – even the notion of a "space" conveys an aura of pristine exclusion, apart from, floating above the concerns of everyday life – becomes a self-fulfilling prophecy as well as a self-indulgent nostalgia. It means one is blinded to authentic instances of citizenship within one's own society. It means one nurtures the concept of the "citizen" in a hothouse of purity so as to keep it untainted by the struggles of the present.[137]

In sum, by insulating the political sphere from the concerns of the social, and by rigidly distinguishing the private from the public, Arendt was unable to account for some of the most important achievements of modernity – the struggles for the extension of citizenship and the redrawing of the boundaries between the public and the private.

I would like to conclude with a brief account of the possible lines of inquiry which have opened up as a result of the changes in the relation between the political, the economic, and the private dimensions of late capitalist societies. Nancy Fraser, in two important articles,[138] has looked at the kind of changes that the political-public sphere must undergo in order to accomodate the transformations of the economy and of our conception of the private (i.e., the family and the so-called "domestic" sphere). With respect to the relation between the political and the economic, she poses the following questions:

> When, in the late modern period, even capitalist economic production is socialized to the point of defying the label "private enterprise"; when, therefore, justice requires that the domain of the political be *quantitatively* enlarged so as to include the previously excluded "social question"; and when, *pace* Arendt, politics must, as a result, become political economy; what *qualitative* transformations of the political are needed to prevent its being overrun by instrumental reason and reduced to administration? . . . What new, still uninvented, postliberal and postmarxian models of democratic, decentralized, socialist or mixed political-economies can do justice both to the specificity of the political and to its connectedness with the socio-economic?[139]

Second, concerning the relationship between the political and the private (familial-domestic) spheres of contemporary societies, she asks:

> If, as Arendt contended, the institution of the political in the West depended upon, indeed was the flip side of, the institution of the familial; and if the familial, as a sphere of inequality and exploitation, can no longer be immune from critique and transformation; then how must and ought the political sphere change as well? . . . How might an equitable reorganization of childrearing, one which put it at the center of public concern, help to revitalize and transform the political? . . . How might the political be transformed in case women's cultures were liberated from domesticity and permitted to infuse public life?[140]

These are the questions that, in my view, need to be addressed, at both the normative and empirical level, in order to confront the transformations that the private and the public, the political and the social, the political and the familial, have undergone in contemporary Western societies. Only on the basis of an adequate diagnosis of these transformations, a diagnosis that transcends Arendt's categorial distinctions and incorporates the insights of contemporary feminist theory, can we hope to highlight the emancipatory possibilities of the present and anticipate the conditions of a non-repressive, egalitarian, post-capitalist, and post-patriarchal society of the future.

# Chapter 2

# Hannah Arendt's theory of action

In the previous chapter we examined Arendt's conception of modernity and found that for Arendt the losses incurred in the modern age as a result of secularization, rationalization, and socio-cultural modernization could be partially redeemed by a selective reappropriation of the past, by an anamnestic thinking in which the remembrance of past actions and events could serve to illuminate and orient us in the present.

In this chapter I want to examine Arendt's theory of action and defend the claim that Arendt's revival of the ancient notion of *praxis* represents her most original attempt to respond to the aporias of the modern age. By distinguishing action (*praxis*) from fabrication (*poiesis*), by linking it to freedom and plurality, and by showing its connection to speech and remembrance, Arendt is able to articulate a conception of politics in which questions of meaning, identity, and value can be addressed in a pertinent manner. Moreover, by viewing action as a mode of human togetherness, Arendt is able to develop a conception of participatory democracy which stands in direct contrast to the bureaucratized and elitist forms of politics so characteristic of the modern epoch.

In the first part I will provide an exposition of Arendt's theory of action, focusing on its principal components such as freedom, plurality, and disclosure. I will also examine the links between action and narrative, the importance of remembrance, and of what I call "communities of memory." I will then show the connection between action, power, and the space of appearance. Lastly, I will look at the remedies for the unpredictability and irreversibility of action, namely, the power of promise and the power to forgive.

In the second part I will examine and respond to a number of criticisms that have been made of her theory. These criticisms, I will suggest, stem from an inadequate appreciation of the complexity, as well as the tensions, of Arendt's theory of action. My response will be to show that her theory incorporates two models of action, an expressive and a communicative one, and that her critics have concentrated almost exclusively on the expressive model at the expense of the communicative one.

I will also address the criticism that Arendt oscillates between a heroic and a participatory conception of politics, and will show that these two conceptions of politics are connected to the two models of action. Although Arendt was not able to resolve the tension between these two conceptions – and their respective models of action – in a satisfactory manner, I will try to show that in her later writings she did progressively broaden her theory of action to include collective processes of deliberation and decision-making based on mutuality, solidarity, and persuasion. I will thus defend the claim that Arendt's theory of action articulates the historical experience and normative presuppositions of participatory democracy, and that such a theory remains essential for the reactivation of public life in the modern world.

## ACTION, FREEDOM, AND PLURALITY

Action, the only activity that goes on directly between men without the intermediary of things or matter, corresponds to the human condition of plurality . . . this plurality is specifically *the* condition – not only the *conditio sine qua non*, but the *conditio per quam* – of all political life.[1]

To address Arendt's theory of action means to enter into the very center of her thought about politics, since action represents for her the category around which political life is centered, and constitutes the highest realization of the *vita activa*. As we saw in the preceding chapter, Arendt analyzes the *vita activa* via three categories which correspond to the three fundamental activities of our being-in-the-world: labor, work, and action. Labor is the activity which is tied to the human condition of life, work the activity which is tied to the condition of worldliness, and action the activity tied to the condition of plurality. For Arendt each activity is autonomous, in the sense of having its own distinctive principles and of being judged by different criteria. Labor is judged by its ability to sustain human life, to cater to our biological needs of consumption and reproduction, work is judged by its ability to build and maintain a world fit for human use and for human enjoyment, and action is judged by its ability to disclose the identity of the agent, to affirm the reality of the world, to actualize our capacity for freedom and to endow our existence with meaning.[2]

Although Arendt considers the three activities of labor, work, and action equally necessary to a complete human life, in the sense that each contributes in its distinctive way to the realization of our human capacities, it is clear from her writings that she takes action to be the *differentia specifica* of human beings, that which distinguishes them from both the life of animals (who are similar to us insofar as they need to labor to sustain and reproduce themselves) and the life of the gods (with whom we share, intermittently and with great effort, the activity of contemplation). In this respect the categories of labor and work, while significant in themselves, must be seen as counterpoints to the category of action, helping to differentiate and highlight the place of action within the order of the *vita activa*. It is therefore important to stress that Arendt, almost alone among contemporary political philosophers,[3] accords action the central place in the hierarchy of human activities and endows it with the potential to realize our highest human capacities, such as freedom and individuality. Moreover, in giving primacy to the category of action, Arendt is attempting to recover those features of human experience – such as innovation, plurality, membership, and remembrance – which have been denigrated by the tradition of political philosophy that originated with Plato,[4] but whose importance for political life was recognized by thinkers such as Aristotle, Machiavelli, and Tocqueville, and which found expression in the Greek *polis*, the Renaissance republics and in the formative stages of modern revolutions.

Let us then turn to an examination of Arendt's theory of action. The two central features of action are *freedom* and *plurality*. By freedom Arendt does not mean simply the ability to choose among a set of possible alternatives (the freedom of choice so dear to the liberal tradition) or the faculty of *liberum arbitrium* which, according to Christian doctrine, was given to us by God (who also gave us the capacity to receive grace, so that our freedom could at the same time be the freedom to do the good). Rather, by freedom Arendt means the capacity to begin, to start something new, to do the unexpected, with which all human beings are endowed by virtue of being born. Action as the realization of freedom is therefore rooted in natality, in the fact that each birth represents a new beginning and the introduction of novelty in the world. As Arendt says:

> Because they are *initium*, newcomers and beginners by virtue of birth, men take initiative, are prompted into action. *Initium ergo ut*

*esset, creatus est homo, ante quem nullus fuit* ("that there be a beginning, man was created before whom there was nobody"), said Augustine in his political philosophy . . . With the creation of man, the principle of beginning came into the world itself, which, of course, is only another way of saying that the principle of freedom was created when man was created but not before.[5]

To be sure, Arendt recognizes that all activities are in some way related to the phenomenon of natality, since both labor and work are necessary to create and preserve a world into which new human beings are constantly born. However, of the three activities, action is the one most closely connected with natality, because by acting individuals re-enact the miracle of beginning inherent in their birth. For Arendt, therefore, the beginning that each of us represents by virtue of being born is actualized every time we act, that is, every time we begin something new. As she says: "the new beginning inherent in birth can make itself felt in the world only because the newcomer possesses the capacity of beginning something anew, that is, of acting."[6]

Arendt also stresses the fact that since action as beginning is rooted in natality, since it is the actualization of freedom, it carries with it the capacity to, as it were, perform miracles, that is, to introduce what is totally unexpected. "It is in the nature of beginning" – she claims –

that something new is started which cannot be expected from whatever may have happened before. This character of startling unexpectedness is inherent in all beginnings . . . The fact that man is capable of action means that the unexpected can be expected from him, that he is able to perform what is infinitely improbable. And this again is possible only because each man is unique, so that with each birth something uniquely new comes into the world.[7]

To act means therefore to be able to take the initiative and to do the unanticipated, to exercise that capacity for freedom which was given to us the moment we came into the world. To act and to be free are, in this respect, synonymous: to be free means to engage in action, while through action our capacity for freedom is actualized. As Arendt puts it: "Men *are* free – as distinguished from their possessing the gift for freedom – as long as they act, neither before nor after; for to *be* free and to act are the same."[8]

Arendt also highlights the fact that by acting we preserve the world of human affairs from the corruption and decay it would be subject to were it left to the automatism of natural processes. Although labor and work do play a part in preserving such world, they are not sufficient to save it, because neither of them embodies the principle of beginning from which action springs, and, consequently, neither of them can interrupt processes and introduce the unexpected. As she says:

> If left to themselves, human affairs can only follow the law of mortality . . . The life span of man running toward death would inevitably carry everything human to ruin and destruction if it were not for the faculty of interrupting it and beginning something new, a faculty which is inherent in action like an ever-present reminder that men, though they must die, are not born in order to die but in order to begin.[9]

For Arendt, therefore:

> the miracle that saves the world, the realm of human affairs, from its normal, "natural" ruin is ultimately the fact of natality, in which the faculty of action is ontologically rooted. It is, in other words, the birth of new men and the new beginning, the action they are capable of by virtue of being born.[10]

The birth of every individual is thus the promise of a new beginning: to act means to be able to disclose one's self and to do the unanticipated, and it is entirely in keeping with this conception that most of the concrete examples of action in the modern age that Arendt discusses are cases of revolutions and popular uprisings. Her claim is that "revolutions are the only political events which confront us directly and inevitably with the problem of beginning,"[11] since they represent the attempt to found a new political space, a space where freedom can appear as a worldly reality. The favorite example for Arendt is the American Revolution, because there the act of foundation took the form of a constitution of liberty. Her other examples are the revolutionary clubs of the French Revolution, the Paris Commune of 1871, the creation of Soviets during the Russian Revolution, the French Resistance to Hitler in the Second World War, and the Hungarian revolt of 1956. In all these cases individual men and women had the courage to interrupt their routine activities, to step forward from their private lives in order to create a public space where freedom could appear, and to act in such a way that the memory of their deeds could become a source of inspiration for future generations. In doing so, according to Arendt, they rediscovered the truth known to the ancient Greeks that action is the supreme blessing of human life, that which bestows significance to the lives of individuals.

In the book *On Revolution* Arendt devotes much attention to the rediscovery of this truth by those who participated in the American

Revolution. In her view the Founding Fathers, although they might have pretended that they longed for private life and engaged in politics only out of a sense of duty, made clear in their letters and recollections that they had discovered unexpected delights in action and had acquired a taste for public freedom and for earning distinction among their peers. In Arendt's words:

> The point is that the Americans knew that public freedom consisted in having a share in public business, and that the activities connected with this business by no means constituted a burden but gave those who discharged them in public a feeling of happiness they could acquire nowhere else. They knew very well, and John Adams was bold enough to formulate this knowledge time and again, that the people went to the town assemblies . . . neither exclusively because of duty nor, and even less, to serve their own interests but most of all because they enjoyed the discussions, the deliberations, and the making of decisions. What brought them together was "the world and the public interest of liberty" (Harrington), and what moved them was "the passion for distinction" which John Adams held to be more essential and remarkable than any other human faculty.[12]

Similarly, Arendt quotes a passage in which John Adams makes clear that the evils of poverty derive not so much from material hardship but from being excluded from the public realm; such a view, she notes, could only have come from someone who had tasted the joys of public life, of appearing in public and acting together with others:

> The poor man's conscience is clear; yet he is ashamed . . . He feels himself out of the sight of others, groping in the dark. Mankind takes no notice of him. He rambles and wanders unheeded. In the midst of a crowd, at church, in the market . . . he is in as much obscurity as he would be in a garret or a cellar. He is not disapproved, censured, or reproached; *he is only not seen.*[13]

And with reference to the new understanding of freedom articulated by the French *philosophes*, she notes that:

> they used the term freedom with a new, hitherto almost unknown emphasis on *public* freedom . . . Their public freedom was not an inner realm into which men might escape at will from the pressures of the world, nor was it the *liberum arbitrium* which makes the will choose between alternatives. Freedom for them could exist only in public; it was a tangible, worldly reality, something created by men

to be enjoyed by men rather than a gift or a capacity, it was the man-made public space . . . which antiquity had known as the area where freedom appears and becomes visible to all.[14]

*Plurality*, to which we may now turn, is the other central feature of action. For if to act means to take the initiative, to introduce the *novum* and the unexpected into the world, it also means that it is not something that can be done in isolation from others, that is, independently of the presence of a plurality of actors who from their different perspectives can judge the quality of what is being enacted. In this respect action needs plurality in the same way that performance artists need an audience; without the presence and acknowledgment of others, that is, without the presence of a community of like-minded actors who can see and judge the performance, action would cease to be a meaningful activity. Action, therefore, to the extent that it requires appearing in public, making oneself known through words and deeds, and eliciting the consent of others, can only exist in a context defined by plurality.

Arendt also maintains that by virtue of its public acknowledgment action acquires a tangible, worldly reality, and is endowed with a measure of permanence by being turned into stories which can be preserved for posterity.[15] Plurality is therefore one of the essential conditions of action – it confirms the reality of the actor and his or her deeds – and creates the condition for remembrance – since through the telling of (plural) narratives deeds can be made to outlast the life of the doer.

Arendt establishes the connection between action and plurality by means of an anthropological argument. In her view just as *life* is the condition that corresponds to the activity of labor and *worldliness* the condition that corresponds to the activity of work, so *plurality* is the condition that corresponds to action.[16] She defines plurality as "the fact that men, not Man, live on the earth and inhabit the world," and says that it is the condition of human action "because we are all the same, that is, human, in such a way that nobody is ever the same as anyone else who ever lived, lives, or will live."[17] Plurality thus refers both to *equality* and *distinction*, to the fact that all human beings belong to the same species and are sufficiently alike to understand one another, but yet no two of them are ever interchangeable, since each of them is an individual endowed with a unique biography and perspective on the world. In Arendt's words:

Human plurality, the basic condition of both action and speech, has the twofold character of equality and distinction. If men were not equal, they could neither understand each other and those who came before them nor plan for the future and foresee the needs of those who will come after them. If men were not distinct, each human being distinguished from any other who is, was, or will ever be, they would need neither speech nor action to make themselves understood. Signs and sounds to communicate immediate, identical needs and wants would be enough.[18]

It is by virtue of plurality, then, that each of us is capable of acting and relating to others in ways that are unique and distinctive, and in so doing of contributing to a network of actions and relationships that is infinitely complex and unpredictable. This network of actions is what makes up the realm of human affairs, that space where individuals relate directly without the intermediary of things or matter — that is, through *language*. Let us examine briefly this connection between action and language.

In *The Human Condition* Arendt stresses repeatedly that action is primarily symbolic in character and that the web of human relationships is sustained by communicative interaction.[19] We may formulate it as follows. *Action entails speech*; by means of language we are in fact able to articulate the meaning of our actions and to coordinate the actions of a plurality of agents. Conversely, *speech entails action*, not only in the sense that speech itself is a form of action, or that most acts are performed in the manner of speech (as in performative speech-acts), but in the sense that action is often the means whereby we check the sincerity of the speaker (since by acting he or she will reveal whether his or her intentions were sincere). Thus, just as action without speech runs the risk of being meaningless and would be impossible to coordinate with the actions of others, so speech without action would lack one of the means by which we may confirm the veracity of the speaker. As we shall see later, this link between action and speech is central to Arendt's characterization of power, that potential which springs up between people when they act "in concert," and which is actualized

only where word and deed have not parted company, where words are not empty and deeds not brutal, where words are not used to veil intentions but to disclose realities, and deeds are not used to violate and destroy but to establish relations and create new realities.[20]

## ACTION AND SPEECH AS DISCLOSURE

Let us now turn to an examination of the disclosing power of action and speech. In the opening section of the chapter on action in *The Human Condition* Arendt discusses one of its central functions, namely, the disclosure of the identity of the agent. In action and speech, she maintains, individuals reveal themselves as the unique individuals they are, disclose to the world their distinct personalities. In terms of Arendt's distinction, they reveal "who" they are as distinct to "what" they are — the latter referring to individual abilities and talents, as well as deficiencies and shortcomings, which are traits all human beings share. As she puts it:

> In acting and speaking, men show who they are, reveal actively their unique personal identities and thus make their appearance in the human world . . . This disclosure of "who" in contradistinction to "what" somebody is . . . is implicit in everything somebody says and does.[21]

Neither labor nor work enable individuals to disclose their identities, to reveal "who" they are as distinct from "what" they are. In labor the individuality of each person is submerged by being bound to a chain of natural necessities, to the constraints imposed by biological survival. When we engage in labor we can only show our sameness, the fact that we all belong to the human species and must attend to the needs of our bodies. In this sphere we do indeed "behave," "perform roles," and "fulfill functions," since we all obey to the same imperatives. In work there is more scope for individuality, in that each work of art or production (of *techne* or *poiesis*) bears the mark of its maker; but the maker is still subordinate to the end product, both in the sense of being guided by a model before the production and during the execution, and in the sense that the product will generally outlast the maker. Moreover, the end product reveals little about the maker except the fact that he or she was able to make it. It does not tell us who the creator was, only that he or she had certain abilities and talents. Mere productive activity, says Arendt,

> from the humble making of use objects to the inspired creation of art works, has no more meaning than is revealed in the finished product and does not intend to show more than is plainly visible at the end of the production process. Action without a name, a "who" attached to it, is meaningless, whereas an art work retains its relevance whether or not we know the master's name.[22]

It is thus only in action and speech, in interacting with others through words and deeds and initiating common projects, that individuals reveal who they personally are and can affirm their unique identities. Action and speech are in this sense very closely related because both contain the answer to the question asked of every newcomer: "Who are you?" This disclosure of the who is made possible by both deeds and words, but of the two, Arendt notes, it is speech that has the closest affinity to revelation. Without the accompaniment of speech, action would lose its revelatory quality and could no longer be identified with an agent. It would lack, in other words, the conditions of ascription of agency. As Arendt puts it:

> Speechless action would no longer be action because there would no longer be an actor, and the actor, the doer of deeds, is possible only if he is at the same time the speaker of words. The action he begins is humanly disclosed by the word, and though his deed can be perceived in its brute physical appearance without verbal accompaniment, it becomes relevant only through the spoken word in which he identifies himself as the actor, announcing what he does, has done, and intends to do.[23]

Actions, therefore, do not speak louder than words: they require speech, that is, words which will disclose the aims and intentions of the actor while articulating the meaning of the act. But speech, in turn, requires action, the intersubjective confirmation of intentions and the willingness to share one's motives. The disclosure of the who in speech and action is therefore contingent on the willingness of the participants to reach a mutual understanding and to reciprocally share one's motives and intentions. In this respect, the revelatory quality of speech and action is contingent on *plurality* and *solidarity*, and is only fully realized, in Arendt's memorable expression, "where people are *with* others and neither for nor against them – that is, in sheer human togetherness."[24]

## ACTION, NARRATIVE, AND REMEMBRANCE

We have seen, then, how through action and speech individuals are able to disclose their identities, to reveal their specific uniqueness – their *who* – as distinct from their personal abilities and talents – their *what*. However, while engaging in speech and action individuals can never be sure or be able to know in advance what kind of self they will reveal. Only retrospectively, that is, only through the stories that will arise from their deeds and performances, will their identity become fully manifest. As Arendt puts it:

> *Who* somebody is or was we can know only by knowing the story of which he is himself the hero – his biography, in other words . . . Thus, although we know much less of Socrates, who did not write a single line and left no work behind, than of Plato and Aristotle, we know much better and more intimately who he was, because we know his story."[25]

The function of the storyteller is thus crucial not only for the preservation of the doings and sayings of actors, but also for the full manifestation of the identity of the actor. The narratives of a storyteller, Arendt claims, "tell us more about their subjects, the 'hero' in the center of each story, than any product of human hands ever tells us about the master who produced it."[26] Without a Plato to tell us who Socrates was, what his conversations with fellow Athenian citizens were like, without a Thucydides to set down Pericles' Funeral Speech and refashion it in his powerful and dramatic style, we would not have known what made Socrates and Pericles such outstanding personalities, nor would the reason for their uniqueness have been made fully manifest. Indeed, it is one of Arendt's most important claims that the meaning of action itself, that is, its significance and import, is dependent upon the articulation retrospectively given to it by historians and narrators. As she writes:

> Action reveals itself fully only to the storyteller, that is, to the backward glance of the historian, who indeed always knows better what it was all about than the participants . . . What the storyteller narrates must necessarily be hidden from the actor himself, at least as long as he is in the act or caught in its consequences, because to him the meaningfulness of his act is not in the story that follows. Even though stories are the inevitable results of action, it is not the actor but the storyteller who perceives and "makes" the story.[27]

Storytelling, or the weaving of a narrative out of the actions and pronouncements of individuals, is therefore partly constitutive of their meaning, because it enables the retrospective articulation of their significance and import, both for the actors themselves and for the participants. Being absorbed by their immediate aims and concerns, not aware of the full implications of their actions, actors are often not in a position to assess the true significance of their doings, or to be fully aware of their own motives and intentions. Only when action has run a certain course, and its relationship to other actions has unfolded, can its significance be made fully manifest and be embodied in a narrative, whether of poets or historians. The fact that this narrative is temporally deferred, that it is at some distance from the events it describes, is moreover one of the reasons why it can provide further insight into the motives and aims of the actors. As Arendt puts it:

> All accounts told by the actors themselves, though they may in rare cases give an entirely trustworthy statement of intentions, aims, and motives, become mere useful source material in the historian's hands and can never match his story in significance and truthfulness.[28]

Narratives thus provide a measure of truthfulness and a higher degree of significance to the actions of individuals. But they also preserve the memory of deeds through time, and in so doing, they enable these deeds to become sources of inspiration and encouragement for the future, that is, models to be imitated, and, if possible, surpassed. One of the principal drawbacks of action is, in fact, to be extremely fragile, to be subject to the erosion of time and forgetfulness; unlike the products of the activity of work, which acquire a measure of permanence by virtue of their sheer facticity, deeds and words do not survive their completion unless they are remembered. *Remembrance* alone, the retelling of deeds *as* stories, can save the lives and deeds of actors from oblivion and futility. And it is precisely for this reason, Arendt points out, that the Greeks valued poetry and history so highly, because they rescued the glorious deeds of the past (as well as the less glorious and the shameful) for the benefit of future generations.[29] It was the poet's and the historian's political function to preserve the memory of past actions and to make them a source of instruction for the present as well as for the future. Homer was known as the "educator of Hellas," since he immortalized for all those who came after him the events of the Trojan War; Thucydides, in his *History of the Peloponnesian War*, told a story of human ambition and folly, of courage and unchecked greed, of ruthless struggle and inevitable defeat. In their work the past became a repository of instruction, of actions to be emulated as well as deeds to be shunned. Through their narratives the fragility and perishability of human action was overcome and made to outlast the lives of their doers and the limited life-span of their contemporaries.

However, to be preserved, such narratives needed in turn an *audience*, that is, a community of hearers who became the transmitters of the deeds that had been immortalized. As Sheldon Wolin has aptly put it, "audience is a metaphor for the political community whose nature is to be a community of remembrance."[30] In other words, *behind the actor stands the storyteller, but behind the storyteller stands a community of memory*.

It was one of the primary functions of the *polis* to be precisely such a community, to preserve the words and deeds of its citizens from oblivion and the ravages of time, and thereby to leave a testament for future generations. The Greek *polis*, beyond making possible the sharing of words and deeds and multiplying the occasions to win immortal fame, was meant to remedy the frailty of human affairs. It did this by establishing a framework where action and speech could be recorded and transformed into stories, where every citizen could be a witness and thereby a potential narrator. What the *polis* established, then, was a space where *organized remembrance* could take place, and where, as a result, the mortality of actors and the fragility of human deeds could be partially overcome. In Arendt's words:

> men's life together in the form of the *polis* seemed to assure that the most futile of human activities, action and speech, and the least tangible and most ephemeral of man-made "products," the deeds and stories which are their outcome, would become imperishable. The organization of the *polis* . . . is a kind of organized remembrance. It assures the mortal actor that his passing existence and fleeting greatness will never lack the reality that comes from being seen, being heard, and, generally, appearing before an audience of fellow men, who outside the *polis* could attend only the short duration of the performance and therefore needed Homer and "others of his craft" in order to be presented to those who were not there.[31]

## ACTION, POWER, AND THE SPACE OF APPEARANCE

The metaphor of the *polis* recurs constantly in the writings of Arendt, and I say metaphor because in employing this term Arendt is not simply referring to the political institutions of the Greek city-states, bounded as they were to their time and circumstance, but to all those instances in history where a public realm of action and speech was set up among a community of free and equal citizens.

> The *polis*, properly speaking, is not the city-state in its physical location; it is the organization of the people as it arises out of acting and speaking together, and its true space lies between people living together for this purpose, no matter where they happen to be.[32]

Thus the famous motto: "Wherever you go, you will be a *polis*" expressed the conviction among Greek colonists that the kind of political association they had set up originally could be reproduced in their new settlements, that the space created by the "sharing of words and deeds" could find its proper location almost anywhere.

For Arendt, in this respect, the *polis* stands for the *space of appearance*, for that space "where I appear to others as others appear to me, where men exist not merely like other living or inanimate things, but to make their appearance explicitly."[33] Such public space of appearance can be always recreated anew wherever individuals gather together politically, that is, "wherever men are together in the manner of speech and action."[34] However, since it is a creation of action, this space of appearance is highly fragile and exists only when actualized through the performance of deeds or the utterance of words. Its peculiarity, as Arendt says, is that:

> unlike the spaces which are the work of our hands, it does not survive the actuality of the movement which brought it into being, but disappears not only with the dispersal of men – as in the case of great catastrophes when the body politic of a people is destroyed – but with the disappearance or arrest of the activities themselves. Wherever people gather together, it is potentially there, but only potentially, not necessarily and not forever.[35]

The space of appearance must therefore be continually recreated by action; its existence is secured whenever actors gather together for the purpose of discussing and deliberating about matters of public concern, and it disappears the moment these activities cease. It is therefore always a *potential space* that finds its actualization in the actions and speeches of individuals who have come together to undertake some common project. It may arise suddenly, as in the case of revolutions, or it may develop slowly out of the efforts to change some specific piece of legislation or policy, for example, saving an historic building or a natural landscape, extending the public provision of housing and health care, protecting groups from discrimination and oppression, fighting for nuclear disarmament, and so on. Historically, it has been recreated whenever public spaces of action and deliberation have been set up, from town hall meetings to workers' councils, from demonstrations and sit-ins to struggles for justice and equal rights.

This capacity to act in concert for a public-political purpose is what Arendt calls *power*. Power needs to be distinguished from strength, force, and violence.[36] Unlike strength, it is not the property of an individual, but of a plurality of actors joining together for some common political purpose. Unlike force, it is not a natural phenomenon but a human creation, indeed, a collective achievement. And unlike violence, it is based not on coercion but on consent and rational deliberation.

For Arendt, therefore, power is a *sui generis* phenomenon, since it is a product of *action* and rests entirely on *persuasion*. It is a product of action because it arises out of the concerted activities of a plurality of agents, and it rests on persuasion because it consists in the ability to secure the consent of others through rational means, that is, through unconstrained discussion and debate. Its only limitation is the existence of other people, but this limitation, she notes, "is not accidental, because human power corresponds to the condition of plurality to begin with."[37] It is actualized in all those cases where action is undertaken for communicative (rather than strategic or instrumental) purposes, and where speech is employed to disclose our intentions and to articulate our motives to others. As Arendt says:

> Power is actualized only where word and deed have not parted company, where words are not empty and deeds not brutal, where words are not used to veil intentions but to disclose realities, and deeds are not used to violate and destroy but to establish relations and create new realities.[38]

Arendt also maintains that the legitimacy of power is derived from the initial getting together of people, that is, from the original pact of association that establishes a political community, and is reaffirmed whenever individuals act in concert through the medium of speech and persuasion. For her

> Power needs no justification, being inherent in the very existence of political communities; what it does need is legitimacy . . . Power springs up whenever people get together and act in concert, but it derives its legitimacy from the initial getting together rather than from any action that then may follow.[39]

This distinction between legitimation and justification is based on the fact that, for Arendt, "legitimacy, when challenged, bases itself on an appeal to the past, while justification relates to an end that lies in the future."[40] Power may thus be legitimized by tracing it back to the original act of foundation, when mutual promises and commitments were made by those who came together to form a political community;

violence, on the other hand, since it aims to achieve some end in the future, may at most be justifiable, but can never be legitimate.

Beyond appealing to the past, power also relies for its continued legitimacy on the rationally binding commitments that arise out of a process of free and undistorted communication. Because of this, power is highly independent of material factors: it is sustained not by economic, bureaucratic, or military means, but by the power of common convictions that result from a process of fair and unconstrained deliberation.[41]

Power is also not something that can be relied upon at all times or accumulated and stored for future use. Rather, it exists only as a *potential* which is actualized when actors gather together for political action and public deliberation. It is thus closely connected to the space of appearance, that public space that arises out of the actions and speeches of individuals. Indeed, for Arendt, "power is what keeps the public realm, the potential space of appearance between acting and speaking men, in existence."[42] Like the space of appearance, power is always "a power potential and not an unchangeable, measurable and reliable entity like force or strength . . . [it] springs up between men when they act together and vanishes the moment they disperse."[43] This means that, in order to remain effective, power needs to be constantly exercised and recreated through action.

Power, then, lies at the basis of every political community and is the expression of a potential that is always available to actors. It is also the source of vitality and legitimacy of political and governmental institutions, the means whereby they are transformed and adapted to new circumstances and made to respond to the opinions and needs of the citizens.

> It is the people's support that lends power to the institutions of a country, and this support is but the continuation of the consent that brought the laws into existence to begin with . . . All political institutions are manifestations and materializations of power; they petrify and decay as soon as the living power of the people ceases to uphold them. This is what Madison meant when he said "All governments rest on opinion."[44]

The legitimacy of political institutions is therefore dependent on the power, that is, the active consent of the people; and insofar as governments may be viewed as attempts to preserve power for future generations by institutionalizing it, they require for their vitality the continuing support and active involvement of all citizens.[45]

## ACTION, UNPREDICTABILITY, AND IRREVERSIBILITY

Our discussion so far of Arendt's theory of action has stressed a number of features, chief among which is action's capacity to disclose the identity of the agent, to enable freedom to appear and be actualized as a worldly reality, to create and sustain a public space of appearance, and to make possible the generation of power. We have also emphasized the importance of narrative and remembrance, of the retrospective articulation of the meaning of action by means of storytelling and its preservation through a community of memory. It is now time to examine two other features of action, namely, unpredictability and irreversibility, and their respective remedies, the power of promise and the power to forgive.

Action is *unpredictable* because it is a manifestation of freedom, of the capacity to innovate and to alter situations by engaging in them; but also, and primarily, because it takes place within the web of human relationships, within a context defined by plurality, so that no actor can control its final outcome.[46] Each actor sets off processes and enters into the inextricable web of actions and events to which all other actors also contribute, with the result that the outcome can never be predicted from the intentions of any particular actor. The open and unpredictable nature of action is therefore a consequence of human *freedom* and *plurality*: by acting we are free to start processes and bring about new events, but no actor has the power to control the consequences of his or her deeds.

This entanglement of action in what Arendt calls the "web of human relationships" is one of the reasons for her claim that nobody is the author or producer of his or her own life-story; these stories, the result of action and speech, reveal an agent, but this agent is neither an author nor a producer, but rather an actor and a sufferer. As Arendt says:

> It is because of this already existing web of human relationships, with its innumerable, conflicting wills and intentions, that action almost never achieves its purpose; but it is also because of this medium, in which action alone is real, that it "produces" stories with or without intention as naturally as fabrication produces tangible things.[47]

Thus

> Although everybody started his life by inserting himself into the human world through action and speech, nobody is the author or producer of his own life story . . . Somebody began it and is its

subject in the twofold sense of the word, namely, its actor and sufferer, but nobody is its author.[48]

Unpredictability, in this respect, is closely linked to the unfinished narrative that each actor has to live with until the moment of death. Only retrospectively, that is, through the eyes of the historian, can we identify the author of certain deeds, but even then we cannot point unequivocally to him or her as the author of their eventual outcome. This helps to explain Aristotle's dictum that no one can be truly called happy until after his death; the consequences of his actions may, in fact, still affect his happiness on earth by affecting the memory of his person among those who survive him.

Another and related reason for the unpredictability of action is that its consequences are *boundless*: every act sets in motion an unlimited number of actions and reactions which have literally no end. As Arendt puts it:

> While the strength of the production process is entirely absorbed in and exhausted by the end product, the strength of the action process is never exhausted in a single deed but, on the contrary, can grow while its consequences multiply . . . The reason why we are never able to foretell with certainty the outcome and end of any action is simply that action has no end.[49]

And the reason for this, in turn, is that action,

> though it may proceed from nowhere, so to speak, acts into a medium where every action becomes a chain reaction and where every process is the cause of new processes . . . This boundlessness is characteristic not of political action alone . . . the smallest act in the most limited circumstances bears the seed of the same boundlessness, because one deed, and sometimes one word, suffices to change every constellation.[50]

Closely connected to the boundlessness and unpredictability of action is its *irreversibility*. Every action sets off processes which cannot be undone or retrieved in the way, say, we are able to undo a faulty product of our hands. If one builds an artifact and is not satisfied with it, it can always be destroyed and recreated again. This is impossible where action is concerned, because action always takes place within an already existing web of human relationships where every action becomes a reaction, every deed a source of future deeds, and none of these can be stopped or subsequently undone. The consequences of each act are thus not only unpredictable but also irreversible; the processes started by action can neither be controlled nor be reversed. As Arendt says:

> Whereas men have always been capable of destroying whatever was the product of human hands . . . men never have been and never will be able to undo or even control reliably any of the processes they start through action. Not even oblivion and confusion, which can cover up so efficiently the origin and the responsibility for every single deed, are able to undo a deed or prevent its consequences.[51]

The remedy which the tradition of Western thought has proposed for the unpredictability and irreversibility of action has consisted in abstaining from action altogether, in the withdrawal from the sphere of interaction with others, in the hope that one's freedom and integrity could thereby be preserved. Platonism, Stoicism and Christianity elevated the sphere of contemplation above the sphere of action precisely because in the former one could be free from the entanglements and frustrations of action.[52] Arendt's proposal, by contrast, is not to turn one's back on the realm of human affairs, but to rely on two faculties inherent in action itself, the faculty of *forgiving* and the faculty of *promising*. These two faculties are closely connected, the former mitigating the irreversibility of action by absolving the actor from the unintended consequences of his or her deeds, the latter moderating the uncertainty of its outcome by binding actors to certain courses of action and thereby setting some limit to the unpredictability of the future. Both faculties are, in this respect, connected to *temporality*. From the standpoint of the present forgiving looks backward to what has happened and absolves the actor from what was unintentionally done, while promising looks forward as it seeks to establish islands of security in an otherwise uncertain and unpredictable future. As Arendt writes:

> The two faculties belong together in so far as one of them, forgiving, serves to undo the deeds of the past, whose "sins" hang like Damocles' sword over every new generation; and the other, binding oneself through promises, serves to set up in the ocean of uncertainty, which the future is by definition, islands of security without which not even continuity, let alone durability of any kind, would be possible in the relationships between men.[53]

Forgiving enables us to come to terms with the past and liberates us to some extent from the burden of irreversibility; promising allows us to face the future and to set some bounds to its unpredictability.

Without being forgiven, released from the consequences of what we have done, our capacity to act would, as it were, be confined to one single deed from which we could never recover; we would remain the victims of its consequences forever.[54]

On the other hand, "without being bound to the fulfilment of promises, we would never be able to keep our identities,"[55] since we could no longer have trust in each other or have our expectations reciprocally acknowledged. Both faculties, in this sense, depend on *plurality*, on the presence and acting of others, for no one can forgive himself and no one can feel bound by a promise made only to him or herself.[56] At the same time, both faculties are an expression of human *freedom*, since without the faculty to undo what we have done in the past, and without the ability to control at least partially the processes we have started, we would be the victims, in Arendt's words, "of an automatic necessity bearing all the marks of inexorable laws."[57] For Arendt, therefore:

Only through this constant mutual release from what they do can men remain free agents, only by constant willingness to change their minds and start again can they be trusted with so great a power as that to begin something new.[58]

On the other hand, only through the force of mutual promises can freedom be sustained in a world where no one is able to master the consequences of his or her actions. For Arendt the faculty of promising corresponds to the existence of a freedom which was given to us under conditions of *non-sovereignty*. The faculty of promising represents, in this respect, the only alternative to a mastery which relies on domination of one's self and rule over others, rather than on plurality, reciprocity, and solidarity.[59]

## CRITICAL OBSERVATIONS

Having examined thus far the principal components of Arendt's theory of action, I would like now to turn to a discussion of the most significant critiques that have been made of it by figures such as Jay, Kateb, Canovan, Parekh, and Habermas. It is worth noting at the outset that these critiques differ considerably both in substance and in terms of the implications that are drawn with respect to the validity of Arendt's theory. Jay and Kateb are concerned with the apparent lack of a normative or moral dimension in Arendt's theory of action and maintain that this seriously impairs its validity. Canovan and Parekh, on the other hand, are more concerned with the political feasibility of her theory and argue that it contains a tension between two different visions of politics, an elitist and a democratic one in the case of Canovan, a heroic and participatory one in the case of Parekh. Habermas, finally, thinks that Arendt remains bound to the constellation of classical Greek philosophy and is unable for this reason to conceptualize adequately the phenomenon of power in modern capitalist societies. I want to argue, however, that these different assessments of Arendt's theory of action can be explained in terms of a fundamental tension in her theory between an *expressive* and a *communicative* model of action.

As we saw in the preceding discussion, Arendt conceives action as that mode of human activity in which individuals are able to disclose their identity, their distinctive "who" as against their shared "what." But we have also seen that the disclosure of identity is subject to a twofold process of interpretation and retrospective articulation, that is, that the identity of actors can only become manifest within a community of interpreters and is preserved, confirmed, or modified through the retrospective narrative of historians.[60] Both an expressive and a communicative component are therefore present in the articulation of one's identity. Arendt provides a further communicative dimension to action in her claim that action enables individuals to establish relations of reciprocity and solidarity, since it is based on speech, on equality, and on the acknowledgment of plurality. In short, action enables individuals both to express their unique identities and to establish communicative relations with others. There is little doubt, however, that these two components of action coexist in an uneasy tension, and that Arendt is prone at times to emphasize too strongly the expressive dimension at the expense of the communicative one.[61]

This tension, moreover, does not affect only Arendt's conceptualization of action but also her vision of politics. As Peter Fuss and Bhikhu Parekh have pointed out, Arendt provides us with two models of politics, the first being an agonal or heroic model, the second an accommodational or participatory one, and argue that that she never manages to integrate the two in a satisfactory manner.[62] I shall examine this charge later in the chapter. What I want to stress in this context is that these two models of politics correspond rather closely to the two models of action we have just examined. Thus, to the expressive model of action there corresponds the agonal or heroic model of politics, while to the communicative model of action there corresponds the accommodational or participatory model of politics.

This mapping of action types to distinct models of politics may be elaborated with the help of Seyla Benhabib's reformulation of Habermas' categories. She distinguishes between four types of human action: instrumental, communicative, expressive, and strategic. For our purposes the two relevant ones are the communicative and the expressive, since they are the ones with which Arendt operates. Communicative action is oriented to reaching understanding and is characterized by the norms of symmetry and reciprocity between subjects who are recognized as equal. Expressive action, on the other hand, allows for the self-actualization or self-realization of the person, and its norms are the recognition and confirmation of the uniqueness of the self and its capacities by others.[63] Insofar as Arendt's theory of action rests upon an unstable combination of both expressive and communicative models (or action types), it is clear that her account of politics will vary in accordance with the emphasis given to one or the other. When the emphasis falls on the expressive model of action, politics is viewed as the performance of noble deeds by outstanding individuals; conversely, when her stress is on the communicative model of action, politics is seen as the collective process of deliberation and decision-making that rests on equality and solidarity.

Having identified this fundamental tension at the center of Arendt's conceptualization of politics and action, I would like to examine the arguments of a number of important critics. My purpose will not be so much to defend Arendt, but to show that these arguments can be made plausible and, in turn, criticized, only if we acknowledge the duality to be found throughout Arendt's writings between the expressive and the communicative models of action.

## ARENDT: POLITICAL EXISTENTIALIST?

Martin Jay's critique covers a broad range of topics and addresses some of the most disputed issues of Arendt's political philosophy, such as the distinction between the social and the political, the separation of truth from opinion, and the insulation of action from normative and instrumental standards of assessment. For our purposes his most important charge is that Arendt, in her efforts to give politics the utmost possible autonomy, fell into the danger of aestheticizing politics and came close to a position known as "decisionism." In making this charge Jay relies on an essay published in 1946 called "What is Existenz Philosophy?"[64] which he claims contained all the themes that were subsequently developed in *The Human Condition*.

Indeed, by restricting his attention to this essay Jay wants to show the connection between Arendt's thought and the political existentialists of the 1920s in Germany which included, in addition to her teacher Heidegger, Carl Schmitt, Ernst Jünger, and Alfred Bäumler. He recognizes that Arendt found much of their thought intolerable, that she wrote against the celebration of violence in Jünger, the emphasis on sovereignty and the "exception" in Schmitt, the "mythologizing confusions" of Heidegger, and yet he maintains that

> despite these criticisms, Hannah Arendt's political philosophy can justly be situated in the political existentialist tradition of the 1920's, albeit as one of its "tender" rather than "tough" variants. To stress this link is useful not because it establishes some sort of guilt by association, but rather because it provides the historical context in which her apparently uncategorizable position begins to make sense. On the most general level, it allows us to see the broad movement of which she was a part, a movement which asserted the primacy of the political realm over society, culture, economics, or religion as the arena in which man's most quintessentially human quality, his capacity for freedom, could be realized.[65]

Thus, he continues

> In attempting to liberate political action from its subordination to other modes of the *vita activa*, Hannah Arendt, like the political existentialists of the twenties, was anxious to assure its utmost possible autonomy. Thus, she saw politics not merely as irreducible to socioeconomic forces, but also as unhampered by all normative or instrumental constraints as well, a position often known as "decisionism." As its own end, politics should not be conceived as a means to anything else whether it be domination, wealth, public welfare, or social justice: in short, *politique pour la politique*.[66]

This reading of Arendt can be criticized on several grounds: first, for its dubious identification of her thought with the tradition of political existentialism, a tradition which laid great stress on the *will* as the motor of political action and on *decision* as an act of existential choice unconstrained by principles or norms. Arendt was in fact highly critical of the will as a faculty of political action,[67] and never maintained that decisions, or the political initiative exercised by actors in the public sphere, could be justified for their own sake. Rather, these decisions had to be justified in the light of public principles which were recognized to be binding for every member of the political community.[68] Second, Jay restricts his attention to the early essay "What is Existenz Philosophy?" and claims that it contains the philosophical principles whose political implications were developed later in *The Human Condition* and in the essays collected in *Between Past and Future.* This, however, betrays a cursory reading of Arendt's texts, for in that early essay Arendt was not so much presenting or articulating her own theory, but rather giving an account of a tradition of thought which originated with Kierkegaard and ended, in her view, with the writings of Jaspers and Heidegger. As Leon Botstein has correctly noted, the real purpose of this essay was

> to explicate a movement to an American and English audience, an audience quite unfamiliar with a body of work written in often impenetrable German. She clearly had more sympathy with Jaspers, her teacher. But her own writing does not support Jay's view that, like the existentialists, she admired the self-centered and melodramatic reasons behind political action, mere heroism and glory. Her use of the notion of glory is ancient, not modern. Arendt uses it in the Roman and biblical sense, which endows glory with ethical rather than narrow self-serving qualities.[69]

Moreover, some of the philosophical figures examined in that essay were subsequently criticized in her essay "Tradition and the Modern Age,"[70] and a careful reading of *The Human Condition* hardly supports the claim that Arendt had any sympathy for an existentialist ethics or for a politics based on existentialist principles. Finally, to impute to Arendt any affinity with the thought of Schmitt or Bäumler is a travesty of her political philosophy, which stressed the principles of freedom, equality, plurality, and solidarity.

It is true, nevertheless, that Arendt asserted the primacy of the political realm and sought to give politics the "utmost possible autonomy" from socio-economic factors. But here again we must be careful in our interpretation of her political standpoint. Arendt, in fact, did not view politics as *unhampered* by normative or instrumental constraints, but as not *determined* by them. She believed that action should be inspired by *public principles* – such as freedom, dignity, honor, solidarity, and love of equality – and that the Christian virtues of goodness and love could not be applied to the public realm, since they were essentially private and bound to be destroyed or distorted when made public.[71] But she did not think that action was thereby freed from normative considerations; rather, these considerations were embodied in public principles which inspired, but could never totally determine, the actions of individuals.

The same can be said of Arendt's view of the relation of politics and instrumentality: she did not assert that political action was for its own sake or that it shunned all instrumental considerations. She maintained, rather, that action is engaged for the sake of freedom and that it is free to the extent that it transcends mere instrumental concerns. Most action, she wrote, is

> concerned with the matters of the world of things in which men move, which physically lies between them and out of which arise their specific, objective, worldly interests. These interests constitute, in the word's most literal significance, something which *interest*, which lies between people and therefore can relate and bind them together.[72]

Action is therefore always *about*, and to this extent, *constrained by*, our instrumental concerns; the point, for Arendt, is that it can never be entirely determined by them, that we are able to transcend our worldly interests for the sake of a political principle, be it the principle of freedom, or equality, or communal solidarity.

Jay's criticism seems therefore to miss the nuance and the complexity of Arendt's thought. In a subsequent passage he even suggests that Arendt's conception of politics has totalitarian implications because of the absolute separation she imposes between political and instrumental action. In her book *The Origins of Totalitarianism*, Jay argues, Arendt had stressed that

> one of the most sinister characteristics of totalitarian systems, best shown in the Nazi attitude toward the Jews, is their indifference to utilitarian considerations. A politics that is *oblivious* to the means–ends continuum and the consequences of its actions risks descending into the realm of fantasy in which the inexorable logic of an ideology can justify even self-destructive behavior. The "expresssive" moment of politics need not be seen as the *absolute negation* of the instrumental.[73]

Of course Arendt's notion of politics is neither "oblivious" to consequences nor is it the "absolute negation" of the instrumental. What Jay produces here is a caricature of Arendt's actual position. She believed that action did indeed have consequences, and that these consequences had to be controlled by means of laws, constitutions, and mutual promises.[74] Laws and constitutions protect the community from the undesirable or unintended consequences of action, and mutual promises establish some limit to its unpredictability. Action is moreover guided by principles which include, beyond freedom and love of equality, prudence or moderation. As Arendt writes: "The boundlessness of action is only the other side of its tremendous capacity for establishing relationships . . . this is why the old virtue of moderation, of keeping within bounds, is indeed one of the political virtues par excellence."[75] And finally, in those cases that allow for it, there is the faculty of forgiving which releases the actor from the consequences of his or her deeds. This faculty, together with that of making and keeping promises, enables us to control, if not to eliminate, the risks associated with action. The readiness to forgive and to be forgiven, to make promises and to keep them are like moral precepts which, as Arendt puts it, "arise directly out of the will to live together with others in the mode of acting and speaking, and thus they are like control mechanisms built into the very faculty to start new and unending processes."[76]

It is misleading therefore to claim that Arendt is oblivious to consequences, nor is it correct to say that her notion of politics is the "absolute negation of the instrumental." As I have argued, Arendt maintains that action has to transcend mere instrumental concerns for the sake of a political principle, but is fully aware that we can never eliminate them entirely. Her point is that politics should not be seen as just another kind of instrumental action or as a means to the pursuit of private advantage; it is the active engagement of citizens in all matters of public concern, the public discussion, deliberation, and decision-making with respect to issues affecting the political community (which may be local, national, or international). It follows that politics has to take into account many matters, including those of a more instrumental character; it should not, however, be determined exclusively by them.

Jay is nonetheless correct in noting that Arendt often conceives of politics as an expressive activity, as the performance of noble deeds or the uttering of memorable words which are judged by their beauty or greatness. He notices the analogy that Arendt makes between politics and the performing arts. As he writes: "If politics has any analogy outside itself, it is to the performing arts where virtuosity is its own ephemeral end."[77] There are many passages in Arendt to support this claim. In "What is Freedom?" she writes that

> performing artists — dancers, play-actors, musicians, and the like — need an audience to show their virtuosity, just as acting men need the presence of others before whom they can appear; both need a

publicly organized space for their "work," and both depend upon others for the performance itself.[78]

And in *The Human Condition* she says that "the theater is the political art par excellence; only there is the political sphere of human life transposed into art. By the same token, it is the only art whose sole subject is man in his relationship to others."[79] Although she never championed the "aestheticization of politics,"[80] it is true that her theory of action often stresses the expressive component at the expense of the communicative one. The urge to self-disclosure is not always compatible with the establishment of intersubjective relations, nor is self-realization the same as communicative understanding. Furthermore, action as "beginning" may stand in tension with action as participation or with action as collective deliberation. Finally, the "virtuosity" of action is not by itself sufficient to validate it; the greatness of a political performance should be judged also by the standards of rightness, that is, whether it allows for reciprocal recognition and the establishment of fair or just relations among actors. By giving emphasis to the expressive dimension of action Arendt often obscures the other side of her theory, and leaves herself open to the – in my view misleading – charge that she aestheticized politics.

## ARENDT: POLITICAL IMMORALIST?

The charge that Arendt aestheticized politics is repeated, in a modified and more sophisticated form, by George Kateb. In his highly illuminating and thorough study of Arendt he accuses her of disallowing moral judgment in her theory of action and, consequently, of falling into a dangerous form of amoralism. He claims that: "If amorality is one kind of immorality, then in a few moments of recklessness Arendt celebrates immorality."[81] He maintains that in some passages "Arendt talks about particular acts in a way that seems to strengthen one's alarmed sense that her general theory of action can too easily accommodate great substantial evils, even the system of evil known as totalitarianism."[82]

How can we make sense of this accusation in a study that in many respects shows a deep and nuanced understanding of Arendt's thought? My answer is that, as in the case of Jay, Kateb does not account sufficiently for the communicative dimension of Arendt's theory of action.

Kateb opens his discussion with a characterization of Arendt's theory in terms of the "existential supremacy of political action"[83] and goes on to describe it in the following terms:

> Action is its own end: its greatness as revelation needs no further validation, only philosophical elaboration. For Arendt, to press beyond the revelatory qualities of action is absurd because it is to demand an answer to the question, Why be human?[84]

Arendt is seen as displaying "a single-minded adherence to the unique and supreme existential achievement of political action as revelatory speech."[85] It follows, therefore, that "insofar as Arendt confines her thought to the action of the *polis*, she severs the whole point of political action – its revelatory existential achievement, its creation of human identity – from moral motivation or intention."[86] In Kateb's view, an acceptance of moral limits to action must be accompanied by a full acknowledgment of its moral motives. In the absence of moral criteria Arendt's theory is open to the charge of being arbitrary:

> That action may often be revelatory and therefore existentially supreme for those who engage in it, and that it may be beautiful for the outsider to witness, read about, or contemplate, is not sufficient. The phenomenon of totalitarianism, which she did so much to conceptualize, must haunt us as we attend to her thought on the ideal. It is not really possible to overlook the conceptual resemblance.[87]

In this and many other passages Kateb clearly identifies Arendt's theory with an expressive model of action – what he calls her "Greek conception" of political action – and faults it for lacking moral criteria. Not surprisingly, he advocates a substantial revision which would reduce the "existential achievement" of action and subordinate it to moral considerations.[88]

My disagreement with Kateb is twofold: first, as I have tried to show, he focuses almost exclusively on the expressive dimension at the expense of the communicative one. This leads him to accuse Arendt of immoralism, an accusation which could not bear scrutiny had Kateb given the same emphasis to all those passages where Arendt acknowledges that action grows out of moral concerns and is guided by criteria of justice and human dignity. In her essay "On Violence" Arendt declares that the student movement of the 1960s was "almost exclusively inspired by moral considerations,"[89] and in her "Thoughts on Politics and Revolution" she says that it "acted almost exclusively from moral motives."[90] Moreover, when asked whether she agreed with Ernst Bloch, who had argued that the student protest movement acted on principles derived from the natural law tradition and, in so doing, had made an important contribution "to the history of revolutions and very likely to the structure of the coming revolutions," she replied that:

> What Ernst Bloch calls "natural law" is what I was referring to when I spoke of the conspicuous moral coloration of the movement. However, I would add – and on this point I am not in agreement with Bloch – that something similar was the case with all revolutionaries. If you look at the history of revolutions, you will see that it was never the oppressed and degraded themselves who led the way, but those who were not oppressed and not degraded but could not bear it that others were. Only, they were embarassed to admit their moral motives – and this shame is very old. I don't want to go into the history of it here, though it has a very interesting aspect. But the moral factor has always been present, although it finds clearer expression today because people are not ashamed to own up to it.[91]

Arendt was therefore not insensitive to moral considerations. If in *The Human Condition* she was more inclined to stress the glory and the beauty of action, to take the Greek model as her exemplar, and to emphasize the expressive component of action, in her other writings (from *On Revolution* to *Crises of the Republic*) she made explicit her commitment to moral principles and articulated more clearly the communicative dimension of action.

My second disagreement has to do with Kateb's notion of morality and with the nature of the moral principles to which politics should be subordinated. Although he acknowledges that politics should be guided by ordinary moral considerations (he says that "the lesser evil must be, in fact, the dominant ethic of any public realm"[92]), he subscribes to an absolute conception of morality and maintains that the potential evils of politics should be resisted in the name of such an absolute conception. He identifies absolute morality with the Socratic morality of *conscience* and with the Christian morality of *goodness*, and claims that Arendt's main emphasis "is to ease acceptance of political action in the face of that resistance to it which comes from some deep or even merely residual attachment to the spirit of absolute morality."[93] My reservations as to Kateb's argument are twofold: first, he claims that there are absolute standards of morality upon which everyone agrees, or ought to agree, but never explains what makes these standards absolute or by what processes we are supposed to come to recognize their absolute validity. He seems unconcerned with the whole debate about the universality of moral standards, the degree of their bindingness, the problem of skepticism, and the question of moral conflict.[94] He believes that these standards are just there, awaiting to be discovered by all those with a minimum of good will and integrity, and that they should be binding regardless of circumstances. The Socratic morality of conscience, in its universality and abstractness, seems to be his favorite model. The problem of mediating its abstract principles with the concrete circumstances and conflicts of daily life seems therefore to elude him. His position is well captured by Bernard Williams' opening statement in *Ethics and the Limits of Philosophy*:

> It is not a trivial question, Socrates said: what we are talking about is how one should live. Or so Plato reports him, in one of the first books written about this subject. Plato thought that philosophy could answer the question. Like Socrates, he hoped that one could direct one's life, if necessary redirect it, through an understanding that was distinctively philosophical – that is to say, general and abstract, rationally reflective, and concerned with what can be known through different kinds of inquiry.[95]

My second reservation has to do with the validity of the application of absolute morality to politics. Kateb claims that Arendt views politics as a realm that is either

> not charged with moral purposes (politics as imagined in the light of the *polis*) or is made moral only from an indissociable connection to a political artifice, a constitution (modern politics). Her writing continually disparages the transfer of moral preoccupations to political life. She adopts a severe attitude toward *absolute* as distinguished from *ordinary* morality, especially activist absolute morality; and she finds only minimal uses for abstentionist absolute morality.[96]

Now, the reason why Arendt was opposed to the introduction of absolute morality into politics was that such morality was essentially private and bound to be distorted or to become destructive when introduced into the public realm. Goodness loses its essential quality when proclaimed to the public, for "the moment a good work becomes known and public, it loses its specific character of goodness, of being done for nothing but goodness' sake."[97] Thus, despite her deep admiration for the teachings of Jesus, she believed that the Christian tradition of hostility to the public realm was a direct result of his commitment to the activity of goodness. Similarly, she maintained that love harbors an anti-political tendency, since it is by its very nature unworldly and, by reason of its passion, "destroys the in-between which relates us to and separates us from others."[98] As for pity and compassion, she believed that they were unsuited for a realm characterized by relations of equality and were responsible for the excesses of the French Revolution. Finally, with respect to the morality of conscience, she believed that it was too subjective in character, more concerned with self-reproach than with injustice, and only effective in emergencies (for example, in resisting atrocities). To each of these moral absolutes she opposed political principles: in place of goodness she advocated *virtue*, in place of love *respect*, in place of compassion and pity *solidarity*, in place of conscience *active citizenship*. And the reason for advocating these principles was not that she disparaged the transfer of moral preoccupations to political life, but that she did not believe that politics should be guided by moral absolutes. The search for absolute goodness in politics often ended, in her view, in absolute evil.[99] Politics should be guided by ordinary moral considerations, such as respect for others, responsibility for self, reciprocity and mutuality, as well as fairness and solidarity. It does not need to appeal to absolute moral principles.

There is a final aspect of Kateb's criticism that I would like to address. Kateb claims that to purge politics of "love, goodness, conscience, compassion, and pity is to purge it of the largest part of moral inhibition."[100] This may be true, if politics is viewed as an extension of *private* morality. Arendt, however, sought the remedy to the dangers of action in *public* principles, and – as Kateb himself admits – always relied on the power of *ordinary* morality to check the excesses of political actors.[101] In particular, Arendt relied on our capacity to forgive, our power to make and keep promises, our ability to think and our capacity to judge.[102] These were, in her view, the moral resources available to actors in their public capacity, the faculties through which they could set some limit to action. But they are not faculties which we could exercise in isolation, withdrawn from others or absorbed in the privacy of our own conscience. Rather, they always require the presence of others (even thought, when it addresses public matters, becomes "representative"; and judgment is the capacity to imagine ourselves in the place of others), and can be exercised or find their realization only in a public context. It follows, therefore, that for Arendt the morality appropriate to politics must be grounded in public criteria and finds expression not in private sentiments, but in the exercise of our ordinary moral capacities for promising, forgiving, judging, and thinking.[103]

## ARENDT: DEMOCRAT OR ELITIST?

I would like now to turn to an examination of the criticisms advanced by Margaret Canovan, Bhikhu Parekh, and Peter Fuss. In her essay "The Contradictions of Hannah Arendt's Political Thought"[104] Canovan identifies two problems at the heart of Arendt's theory: first, a contradiction between her democratic and elitist attitudes, and second, an uncertainty about the relation of her political thought to practice.

With respect to the first problem Canovan maintains that Arendt

can be read as one of the most radical of democrats. Her political ideal is a vision of ancient Athens, a polity in which there were neither rulers nor ruled, but all citizens were equal within the agora, acting among their peers. She asserts that every man is a new beginning, and is capable of acting in such a way that no one, not even he himself, can know what he may achieve. She cites again and again the revolutionary situations in which the people have sprung spontaneously into action, and she shares Jefferson's desire to perpetuate that revolutionary impulse by means of direct democratic participation. However, if Arendt in some moods can seem preeminently the theorist of participatory democracy, she can also be read as an elitist of almost Nietzschean intensity. She attributes totalitarianism largely to the rise of "mass society"; she expresses contempt not only for the activity of labouring but for the characteristic tastes and dispositions of labourers; and she shows what is, for a modern political thinker, a truly astonishing lack of interest in the social and economic welfare of the many, except in so far as the struggle to achieve it poses a threat to the freedom of the few.[105]

I am not entirely in disagreement with this characterization of Arendt's political thought. Canovan is right to suggest that there is an inconsistency between her democratic and her elitist stance; what she fails to explore, however, is the reason for this inconsistency. As I have tried to show, Arendt's theory of action incorporates both an expressive and a communicative model of action which she was never able to integrate adequately. In her earlier writings, covering the period up to *The Human Condition*, she did lay great stress on the expressive model, and produced a vision of politics which was both too elitist and too individualistic. Politics is here seen as the performance of great and beautiful deeds, as the uttering of memorable words, as the disclosure of one's unique identity. The public realm is characterized as a dramatic stage for the display of one's excellence, rather than as a discursive setting in which individuals acquire a public identity and establish relations of reciprocity and solidarity. Canovan suggests that in this period Arendt was influenced by the theory of mass society "with its inbuilt elitist bias of distrust for the common people"[106] – a bias which was probably due to her experience of Fascism in the 1930s. But it would be incorrect to focus exclusively on this side of Arendt's thought. As Canovan notes Arendt progressively broadened her conception of action to include collective processes of deliberation and decision-making, and under the impact of the Hungarian revolutionary uprising of 1956, overcame her pessimistic vision of the modern masses. As Canovan puts it:

> From 1956 on, by no means simply or straightforwardly, but recognisably nevertheless, her theory shifts away from the view of modern men as mass men with only the labourer's consciousness, toward seeing them as people capable of political action, and away from a view of action itself as something lost since the Greeks, toward seeing it as an ever-present possibility.[107]

Thus, together with a renewed faith in the possibility of political action by all members of the society, Arendt began to lay greater stress on the deliberative and communicative dimensions of action, on the importance of direct or participatory democracy, and on the joys to be found in civic engagement and public deliberation (i.e., the joys of "public freedom" and "public happiness").[108] It is true, nevertheless, that Arendt was not able to integrate the two perspectives in a satisfactory manner, that her thought retained both democratic and elitist strains. But this, as I have tried to argue, was a result of her inability to integrate the two models of action in her theory.

The second problem identified by Canovan has to do with the political feasibility of Arendt's theory. In her writings of the 1960s, particularly in *On Revolution* and *Crises of the Republic*, Arendt proposed as an alternative to a bureaucratized system of representation based on parties and state structures a federated system of councils where people could be actively involved at various levels in the determination of their affairs.[109] For Canovan Arendt's ideal of the council system represents an attempt to reconcile the democratic and elitist sides of her thought; however, viewed as a political proposal, it must be judged as highly problematic. One obvious problem, she says, is what would people in those councils actually do, since they are not supposed to concern themselves with social or economic matters.[110] Another problem has to do with the interests and welfare of those who might choose not to enter the public arena, "perhaps because they are too old, too ill, overburdened with work, or too inarticulate."[111] And, finally, how could Arendt hope to prevent the corruption or internal erosion of the council system, or hope that it could overcome its history of defeat and suppression? In the light of these objections Canovan maintains that Arendt's rejection of representative democracy and her desire to replace it with a federated system of councils must be seen as "wildly utopian."[112] She remarks that Arendt had a keen sense of the fragility of human deeds, of the brief duration of every attempt to institutionalize direct democracy, but argues that

> if it was her sense of the rarity and fragility of great deeds that led her to desperately utopian schemes for institutionalising greatness, the same insight should surely have led her to make a crucial distinction that is sadly lacking in her thought. The distinction is that between what one may call *normal* politics and *extraordinary* politics, and it is unfortunate that the same concern for rare events that gave her unparalleled insight into extraordinary politics should have led her to overlook normal politics altogether.[113]

I am not in serious disagreement with this criticism: Arendt did indeed see politics as an "extra-ordinary" event and often downplayed the normal, everyday politics of interests. Nevertheless, there is a sense in which her vision can still inform us by reminding us of those experiences of participatory citizenship in which individuals were able, however briefly, to taste the joys of public happiness and to establish spaces of public freedom and solidarity. In a world where citizenship has often to be reactivated through memory, Arendt's contribution remains important and relevant.[114]

## POLITICS: AGONAL OR DISCURSIVE?

The criticisms of Parekh and Fuss are both a development and a qualification of Canovan's views, and they are worth considering together. They both show that Arendt strove to reconcile two different visions of politics, but that the attempt was not entirely successful.

Fuss argues that Arendt oscillates between an *agonal* and an *accommodational* conception of politics: when she looked back to the Greek *polis*, and particularly to the Athens portrayed by Pericles' Speech, Arendt articulated the agonal conception; on the other hand, when she turned to the American Revolution, she praised its institutionalization of the arts of persuasion and accommodation. Fuss notes that Arendt's works published after *The Human Condition* have tended to accentuate the latter conception and that

> her laudatory assessment of the roots of the American political experience in *On Revolution* is, in the final analysis, a tribute to a politics of persuasion and mutual accommodation rather than to a *polis* dedicated to the manifestation of individual excellence.[115]

Parekh makes a similar criticism and shows that Arendt in *The Human Condition* formulated a *heroic* view of politics, while in her later writings she took a far more realistic *participatory* view. In these later writings, he says,

> she justifies political participation and the political way of life not in terms of glory and historical immortality, but public freedom and happiness. Not surprisingly, she takes persuasion to be the paradigmatic form of political speech, emphasizes the "relativity" of opinion, insists on the importance of compromise and consensus, and explores new institutions upon which a participatory community could be constructed.[116]

Both Fuss and Parekh suggest ways of reconciling these two models of politics. For Fuss it is a question of reconciling the substantive and the procedural dimensions of politics: politics is *substantially* the realm of personal initiatives "individually enacted and plurally responded to," and *procedurally* the persuasion and accommodation required in the decision-making process with respect to the best way to preserve the substance of the political realm.[117] For Parekh it is a question of recognizing the connection between *ordinary* and *extraordinary* politics: the two are interdependent "in the sense that participatory politics creates and sustains the climate necessary for heroic politics, and the latter inspires and encourages men to take active interest in public life."[118] Both Fuss and Parekh recognize in the end that Arendt failed to integrate these two models of politics in a satisfactory way. This failure, however, can be traced back to the tension in Arendt's theory between a communicative and an expressive model of action.

## POWER: STRATEGIC OR COMMUNICATIVE?

I would like to conclude with a brief account of Habermas' essay on Arendt's concept of power. In contrast to both Jay and Kateb, Habermas maintains that Arendt's concept of power was developed on the basis of a communicative model of action, and that as a result it never lacked a normative content. In his view Arendt starts with a communicative model of action and derives from it a concept of power as "the formation of a *common* will in a communication directed to reaching agreement."[119] For Arendt

> power is built up in communicative action; it is a collective effect of speech in which reaching agreement is an end in itself for all those involved . . . it becomes consolidated and embodied in political institutions which secure those very forms of life that are centered in reciprocal speech.[120]

The weaknesses of Arendt's concept are therefore not to be found in a supposed lack of normative content; rather, they derive from the fact that "Arendt remains bound to the historical and conceptual constellation of classical Greek philosophy."[121] By separating *praxis* from *poiesis* and from *theoria*, and by conceiving power as a communicative phenomenon, Arendt is unable to account for the strategic, the systemic, and the structural dimensions of politics. As Habermas puts it:

> Arendt's concept of communicatively generated power can become a sharp instrument only if we extricate it from the clamps of an Aristotelian theory of action. In separating praxis from the unpolitical activities of working and laboring on the one side and of thinking on the other, Arendt traces back political power *exclusively* to praxis, to the speaking and acting together of individuals. Over against the production of material objects and theoretical knowledge, communicative action has to appear as the *only* political category. This narrowing of the political to the practical permits illuminating contrasts to the presently palpable elimination of essentially practical contents from the political process. But for this Arendt pays a certain price: (a) she screens all strategic elements, as force, out of politics; (b) she removes politics from its relation to the economic and social environment in which it is embedded through

the administrative system; and (c) she is unable to grasp structural violence.[122]

Habermas is essentially correct in highlighting these three deficits of Arendt's concept of power. My only reservation has to do with Habermas' elaboration of point (a), where he makes a distinction between the *acquisition* and *maintenance* of political power, involving power struggles and strategic considerations, and the *generation* of power understood in terms of Arendt's theory of action.[123] As Habermas himself acknowledges, Arendt formulated what was essentially a *normative* conception of power in terms of which the legitimacy of political institutions could be assessed. She was not unaware of the strategic competition for political power; her point, rather, was to show that political institutions had to rest on the consent of the people, that their legitimacy derived from the power of common conviction attained through a process of unconstrained deliberation. As Habermas himself notes:

> These phenomena of power acquisition and maintenance have misled political theorists from Hobbes to Schumpeter to identify power with a potential for successful strategic action. Against this tradition ... Arendt rightly urges that strategic contests for political power neither call forth nor maintain those institutions in which that power is anchored. Political institutions live not from force but from *recognition*.[124]

It is precisely this *normative* component that Arendt's concept of power tries to explicate; political institutions may indeed be the locus of a strategic competition for power, but they are legitimate only so long as structures of undistorted communication find their expression in them. Habermas' distinction between the acquisition and maintenance of political power and its generation through communicative action does not affect, therefore, the validity of Arendt's argument; what it shows, rather, is Arendt's determination to assess institutions in terms of the standards of a normative theory of action.

# Chapter 3

# Hannah Arendt's theory of judgment

In this chapter I would like to reconstruct Hannah Arendt's theory of judgment and relate it to some of the issues I have explored in the last two chapters. In Chapter 1 I argued that Arendt's conception of modernity is characterized by a deep concern about the loss of meaning (*Freiheitsverlust*) and loss of freedom (*Sinnverlust*) brought about by world alienation, earth alienation, the rise of the social, and the disappearance of the public sphere. In Arendt's view the processes of world alienation and earth alienation have undermined the possibility of forming stable identities, of establishing an adequate sense of reality, and of endowing our existence with meaning. The rise of the social and the disappearance of the public sphere have, in turn, eroded the opportunities for engaging in spontaneous action with others and for creating free public spaces of interaction and discourse. Against this predicament Arendt sets out to revindicate the importance of memory, that is, of a selective reappropriation of the past that can critically illuminate the present, and the value of action, understood as the free and spontaneous intercourse among a plurality of agents mediated by speech and persuasion. In this chapter I want to examine another proposed remedy to the losses incurred by modernity, namely, the exercise of our capacity for judgment, and to reconstruct Arendt's theory with respect to this most crucial faculty. As Michael Denneny has observed, "action, the central category in Arendt's political thought, is matched by judgment as the faculty that responds to and evaluates actions." Indeed, "with the wisdom of hindsight it is now fairly clear that the whole corpus of Hannah Arendt's political thought can be articulated around two foci: the concept of action and the significance of judgment in the world of opinion."[1] Let us then look more closely at the way in which Arendt developed her theory of judgment, and the reasons why it plays such a central role in her theory of politics.

## JUDGMENT: PRELIMINARY CONSIDERATIONS

Among the faculties with which human beings are endowed, judgment – which Arendt saw as "the ability to tell right from wrong, beautiful from ugly"[2] – occupies a central place while being at the same time one of the most difficult to conceptualize. The reason for this difficulty probably lies in the fact that judgment, especially moral and political judgment, is closely bound to the sphere of action and thus exhibits all the problems of mediating theory (i.e., the reflection and inner deliberation that accompanies judgment) and practice. Moreover, compared to the faculties of thinking and willing, it lacks clear criteria of operation as well as precise standards of assessment. Thinking can be assessed in terms of consistency, logic, soundness, and coherence; willing by its resoluteness or capacity to determine our actions. Judgment, on the other hand, although it may share some of these features, is never exhausted by them. In judgment we look not only for soundness or consistency, or for the ability to determine our choices in problematic situations, but also for discrimination, discernment, imagination, sympathy, detachment, impartiality, and integrity. The combination of these factors makes judgment, both in its mode of operation and in its standards of validity, one of the most difficult topics to explore and to theorize about. In turning to Arendt's theory of judgment we will thus be confronted with a number of difficulties, due not only to the way she tried to articulate her theory by appealing to two distinct models of judgment, but to the very nature of this capacity which enables us "to tell right from wrong, beautiful from ugly."

## JUDGMENT: TWO MODELS

Arendt's theory of judgment was never developed as systematically or extensively as her theory of action. She intended to complete her study of the life of the mind by devoting the third volume to the faculty of judgment, but was not able to do so because of her untimely death in 1975. What she left was a number of reflections scattered in the first two volumes on *Thinking* and *Willing*,[3] a series of lectures on Kant's political philosophy delivered at the New School for Social Research in the fall of 1970,[4] an essay entitled "Thinking and Moral

Considerations" written at the time she was composing *The Life of the Mind*,[5] and two articles included in *Between Past and Future*, where judgment and opinion are treated in relation to culture and taste ("The Crisis in Culture") and with respect to the question of truth ("Truth and Politics").[6] Thus, in our reconstruction of her theory of judgment we will have to avail ourselves of these writings in place of the systematic treatment that she was not able to complete. Moreover, these writings do not present a unified theory of judgment but, rather, two distinct models, one based on the standpoint of the actor, the other on the standpoint of the spectator, which are somewhat at odds with each other. As Ronald Beiner has noted in his interpretive essay contained in the *Lectures on Kant's Political Philosophy*, Arendt's writings on the theme of judgment can be seen to fall into two more or less distinct phases, an early one in which judgment is the faculty of political actors acting in the public sphere, and a later one in which it is the privilege of non-participating spectators.

> In her earlier writings (for example, in "Freedom and Politics," "The Crisis in Culture," and "Truth and Politics") Arendt had introduced the notion of judgment to give further grounding to her conception of political action as a plurality of actors acting in concert in a public space . . . In the later formulation, which begins to emerge in the Kant Lectures as well as in both "Thinking and Moral Considerations" and the *Thinking* volume, she approaches judging from a quite different, and much more ambitious, point of view.[7]

Here judgment is located in the sphere of the *vita contemplativa*, it is the faculty of the non-participating spectators, primarily poets and historians, who seek to understand the meaning of the past and to reconcile us to what has happened.[8] In this later formulation Arendt is no longer concerned with judging as a feature of political life as such, as the faculty which is exercised by actors in order to decide how to act in the public sphere, but with judgment as a component in the life of the mind, the faculty through which the privileged spectators can recover meaning from the past and thereby reconcile themselves to time and, retrospectively, to tragedy.[9]

Finally, beside presenting us with two models of judgment which stand in tension to each other, Arendt did not clarify the status of judgment with respect to two of its philosophical sources, Aristotle and Kant. As Seyla Benhabib has observed,

> Arendt's reflections on judgment do not only vacillate between judgment as a moral faculty, guiding action, versus judgment as a

retrospective faculty, guiding the spectator or the storyteller. There
is an even deeper philosophical perplexity about the status of
judgment in her work. This concerns her attempt to bring together
the Aristotelian conception of judgment as an aspect of *phronesis*
with the Kantian understanding of judgment as the faculty of
"enlarged thought" or "representative thinking."[10]

This attempt appears puzzling insofar as the two conceptions seem to
pull in opposite directions, the Aristotelian toward a concern with the
particular, the Kantian toward a concern with universality and
impartiality.

It would appear, therefore, that Arendt's theory of judgment not
only incorporates two models, the actor's – judging in order to act –
and the spectator's – judging in order to cull meaning from the past –
but that the philosophical sources it draws upon are somewhat at odds
with each other. I shall examine these problems in the course of the
chapter, and will attempt to show that the two models not only
articulate two distinct functions of judgment (action-guiding and
future-oriented versus meaning-endowing and past-oriented), but that
the tension between them can be interpreted as a fruitful one. With
respect to the two philosophical sources, that is, Aristotle and Kant, I
will argue that their opposition is more apparent than real, and that by
drawing upon both Arendt was able to stress the importance of
attention to the particular and concern for the universal that is the
hallmark of good judgment.[11] Let us begin by examining judgment
from the standpoint of the *vita contemplativa*.

## JUDGMENT AND THE *VITA CONTEMPLATIVA*

Arendt's concern with judgment as the faculty of retrospective
assessment that allows meaning to be redeemed from the past
originated in her attempt to come to terms with the twin political
tragedies of the twentieth century, Nazism and Stalinism. Faced with
the horrors of the extermination camps and the Gulag, Arendt strove
to understand these phenomena in their own terms, neither deducing
them from precedents nor placing them in some overarching scheme
of historical necessity. "Comprehension," she wrote in *The Origins of
Totalitarianism*,

> does not mean denying the outrageous, deducing the unprece-
> dented from precedents, or explaining phenomena by such
> analogies and generalities that the impact of reality and the shock of

experience are no longer felt. It means, rather, examining and bearing consciously the burden which our century has placed on us – neither denying its existence nor submitting meekly to its weight. Comprehension, in short, means the unpremeditated, attentive facing up to, and resisting of, reality – whatever it may be.[12]

This need to come to terms with the traumatic events of our century, and to understand them in a manner that does not explain them away but faces them in all their starkness and unprecedentedness, is something to which Arendt returned in her *Partisan Review* essay of 1953, "Understanding and Politics." Understanding, she wrote, "is an unending activity by which . . . we come to terms with, reconcile ourselves to reality, that is, try to be at home in the world."[13] However, faced with the horrors of totalitarianism, we suddenly discover the fact that "we have lost our tools of understanding. Our quest for meaning is at the same time prompted and frustrated by our inability to originate meaning."[14] Totalitarianism has in fact "exploded our categories of political thought and our standards for moral judgment."[15] We cannot make sense of this evil phenomenon by means of such categories as tyranny, despotism, or authoritarianism, or through such conventional moral standards as vice, depravity, or sinfulness.[16] Our inherited framework for judgment fails us "as soon as we try to apply it honestly to the central political experiences of our own time."[17] Even our ordinary common-sense judgment is rendered ineffective, since "we are living in a topsy-turvy world, a world where we cannot find our way by abiding by the rules of what once was common sense."[18]

The crisis in understanding is therefore coeval with a crisis in judgment, insofar as understanding for Arendt is "so closely related to and interrelated with judging that one must describe both as the subsumption of something particular under a universal rule."[19] Once these rules have lost their validity we are no longer able to understand and to judge the particulars, that is, we are no longer able to subsume them under our accepted categories of moral and political thought. Arendt, however, does not believe that the loss of these categories has brought to an end our capacity to judge; on the contrary, since human beings are distinguished by their capacity to begin anew (here Arendt invokes the principle of natality, expressed in the Augustinian saying *Initium ergo ut esset, creatus est homo, ante quem nullus fuit;* "that there be a beginning, man was created, before whom there was nobody"), they are able to fashion new categories and to formulate new standards of judgment for the events that have come to pass and for those that may emerge in the future. Thus:

> In the light of these reflections, our endeavoring to understand something which has ruined our categories of thought and our standards of judgment appears less frightening. Even though we have lost yardsticks by which to measure, and rules under which to subsume the particular, a being whose essence is beginning may have enough of origin within himself to understand without preconceived categories and to judge without the set of customary rules which is morality.[20]

For Arendt, therefore, the enormity and unprecedentedness of totalitarianism have not destroyed, strictly speaking, our ability to judge; rather, they have destroyed our accepted standards of judgment and our conventional categories of interpretation and assessment, be they moral or political. And in this situation the only recourse is to appeal to the imagination, which allows us to view things in their proper perspective and to judge them without the benefit of a pre-given rule or universal. As Arendt puts it:

> Imagination alone enables us to see things in their proper perspective, to put that which is too close at a certain distance so that we can see and understand it without bias and prejudice, to bridge abysses of remoteness until we can see and understand everything that is too far away from us as though it were our own affair. This "distancing" of some things and bridging the abysses to others is part of the dialogue of understanding.[21]

The imagination therefore enables us to create the distance which is necessary for an impartial judgment, while at the same time allowing for the closeness that makes understanding possible. In this way, Arendt notes, it makes possible our reconciliation with reality, even with the tragic reality of the twentieth century:

> Without this kind of imagination, which actually is understanding, we would never be able to take our bearings in the world. It is the only inner compass we have . . . If we want to be at home on this earth, even at the price of being at home in this century, we must try to take part in the interminable dialogue with its essence.[22]

It is worth noting that the imagination here plays a role akin to memory in making possible our reconciliation with reality. As we saw in Chapter 1, Arendt wants to revindicate the importance of memory, of a selective reappropriation of the past that could serve to illuminate and orient us in the present. The events of our century have in fact dissolved the comfortable truths of our moral and political tradition (e.g., that tyranny would not degenerate into barbarism, that despotism would not become absolute terror, that morality would not be utterly destroyed), and the task now is to re-establish some linkage to the past outside the framework of traditional standards, since none has retained its original validity. Thus, only through a process of selective remembrance of the past can we hope to restore meaning to our lives and throw some light on the contemporary situation. The imagination here plays a role akin to memory, insofar as it enables us to formulate those categories and standards of judgment through which we can come to terms with what "irrevocably happened" and be reconciled with what "unavoidably exists."[23] Imagination and memory are, in this sense, the handmaidens of judgment, since they reconcile us to a reality that has escaped traditional standards of evaluation, and provide the resources for the ever-renewed attempt to judge it. Indeed, it is by virtue of reconciling ourselves to reality that we are able, ultimately, to judge it. As Arendt puts it:

> The political function of the storyteller – historian or novelist – is to teach acceptance of things as they are. Out of this acceptance, which can also be called truthfulness, arises the faculty of judgment – that . . . in Isak Dinesen's words, "at the end we shall be privileged to view, and review, it – and that is what is named the day of judgment.[24]

Arendt's participation at the trial of Eichmann in the early 1960s made her once more aware of this need to come to terms with a reality that initially defied human comprehension. How could such an ordinary, law-abiding, and all-too-human individual have committed such atrocities? In her encounter with the person of Eichmann Arendt had first to show the intelligibility of his actions, the fact that they stemmed from a lack of thought and an absence of judgment, so that ultimately we could come to terms with their enormity, with their absolutely unprecedented nature. Once Eichmann's deeds were rendered intelligible they could be judged, and judged to be not only monstrous but "banal." In other words, in order to be in a position to pass judgment, Arendt had first to come to terms with what "irrevocably happened" and find some meaning for actions that would otherwise have escaped human comprehension.

The impact of the Eichmann trial forced Arendt to raise another problem concerning judgment, namely, whether we are entitled to presuppose "an independent human faculty, unsupported by law and public opinion, that judges anew in full spontaneity every deed and intent whenever the occasion arises."[25] The conduct of Eichmann was in fact typical of all those individuals who, during the Nazi period, had abstained from judgment, who had blindly followed the orders of their leaders, and in so doing, committed the most unspeakable atrocities. Eichmann's guilt resided in his banal thoughtlessness, in his failure to engage in responsible judgment when confronted with Hitler's orders to exterminate the Jews. Those few individuals who refused to carry out the orders of their superiors were thus left entirely to their own resources, that is, had to be capable

> of telling right from wrong even when all they [had] to guide them [was] their own judgment, which, moreover, happen[ed] to be completely at odds with what they must [have regarded] as the unanimous opinion of all those around them.[26]

In this respect, Arendt notes,

> those few who were still able to tell right from wrong went really only by their own judgments, and they did so freely; there were no rules to be abided by, under which the particular cases with which they were confronted could be subsumed. They had to decide each instance as it arose, because no rules existed for the unprecedented.[27]

## JUDGMENT AND THE WIND OF THOUGHT

Arendt returned to this issue in *The Life of the Mind*, a work which was meant to encompass the three faculties of thinking, willing, and judging. In the introduction to the first volume she declared that the immediate impulse to write it came from attending the Eichmann trial in Jerusalem,[28] while the second, equally important motive, was to provide an account of our mental activities that was missing from her previous work on the *vita activa* (this was in fact the title she had chosen for German edition of *The Human Condition*). It was Eichmann's absence of thinking, his "thoughtlessness," that struck her most, because it was responsible in her view for his inability to judge in those circumstances where judgment was most needed. "It was this absence of thinking," she wrote,

> that awakened my interest. Is evil-doing (the sins of omission, as well as the sins of commission) possible in default of not just "base

motives" . . . but of any motives whatever, of any particular prompting of interest or volition? Is wickedness . . . *not* a necessary condition for evil doing? Might the problem of good and evil, our faculty for telling right from wrong, be connected with our faculty of thought?[29]

Indeed, she continued,

could the activity of thinking as such, the habit of examining whatever happens to come to pass or to attract attention, regardless of results and specific content, could this activity be among the conditions that make men abstain from evil-doing or even actually "condition" them against it?[30]

The same question recurs in her essay of 1971, "Thinking and Moral Considerations," written during the same period she was composing the volume on *Thinking*, where she asked: "Is our ability to judge, to tell right from wrong, beautiful from ugly, dependent upon our faculty of thought? Do the inability to think and a disastrous failure of what we commonly call conscience coincide?"[31]

Arendt attempted a reply by connecting the activity of thinking to that of judging in a twofold manner. First, thinking – the silent dialogue of me and myself – dissolves our fixed habits of thought and the accepted rules of conduct, and thus prepares the way for the activity of judging particulars without the aid of pre-established universals. It is not that thinking provides judgment with new rules for subsuming the particular under the universal. Rather, it loosens the grip of the universal over the particular, thereby releasing judgment from ossified categories of thought and conventional standards of behavior. Indeed, thinking

does not create values, it will not find out, once and for all, what "the good" is, and it does not confirm but rather dissolves accepted rules of conduct. Its political and moral significance comes out only in those rare moments in history when "Things fall apart; the centre cannot hold; Mere anarchy is loosed upon the world," when "The best lack all conviction, while the worst are full of passionate intensity."[32]

It is in times of historical crisis that thinking ceases to be a marginal affair, because by undermining all established criteria and values, it prepares the individual to judge for him or herself instead of being carried away by the actions and opinions of the majority. As Arendt puts it:

When everybody is swept away unthinkingly by what everybody else does and believes in, those who think are drawn out of hiding because their refusal to join is conspicuous and thereby becomes a kind of action. The purging element in thinking, Socrates' midwifery, that brings out the implications of unexamined opinions and thereby destroys them – values, doctrines, theories, and even convictions – is political by implication. For this destruction has a liberating effect on another human faculty, the faculty of judgment, which one may call, with some justification, the most political of man's mental abilities. It is the faculty to judge *particulars* without subsuming them under those general rules which can be taught and learned until they grow into habits that can be replaced by other habits and rules.[33]

The second way in which Arendt connected the activity of thinking with that of judging is by showing that thinking, by actualizing the dialogue of me and myself which is given in consciousness, produces conscience as a by-product. This conscience, unlike the voice of God or what later thinkers called *lumen naturale*, gives no positive prescriptions; it only tells us what *not* to do, what to avoid in our actions and dealings with others, as well as what to repent of. Arendt notes in this context that Socrates' dictum "It is better to suffer wrong than to do wrong," and his proposition that "It would be better for me that my lyre or a chorus I directed should be out of tune and loud with discord, and that multitudes of men should disagree with me, rather than that I, *being one*, should be out of harmony with myself and contradict me," derive their validity from the idea that there is a silent partner within ourselves to whom we render account of our actions.[34] What we fear most is the anticipation of the presence of this partner (i.e., our conscience) who awaits us at the end of the day. Thus, as Arendt puts it,

a person who does not know that silent intercourse (in which we examine what we say and what we do) will not mind contradicting himself, and this means he will never be either able or willing to account for what he says or does; nor will he mind committing any crime, since he can count on its being forgotten the next moment. Bad people . . . are *not* "full of regrets."[35]

She goes on to note that thinking, as the actualization of the difference given in consciousness, "is not a prerogative of the few but an ever-present faculty in everybody; by the same token, inability to think is not a failing of the many who lack brain power, but an ever-present possibility for everybody."[36] For those who do engage in thinking, however, conscience emerges as an inevitable by-product, since the self

> must take care not to do anything that would make it impossible for the two-in-one to be friends and live in harmony . . . Its criterion for action will not be the usual rules, recognized by multitudes and agreed upon by society, but whether I shall be able to live with myself in peace when the time has come to think about my deeds and words.[37]

Conscience as the side-effect of thinking has its counterpart in judgment as the by-product of the liberating activity of thought. If conscience represents the inner check by which we evaluate our actions, judgment represents the outer manifestation of our capacity to think critically. Both faculties relate to the question of right and wrong, but while conscience directs attention to the self, judgment directs attention to the world.[38] In this respect, judgment makes possible what Arendt calls "the manifestation of the wind of thought" in the sphere of appearance. As she put it:

> If thinking – the two-in-one of the soundless dialogue – actualizes the difference within our identity as given in consciousness, and thereby results in *conscience* as its by-product, then *judging*, the by-product of the liberating effect of thinking, realizes thinking, makes it manifest in the world of appearances, where I am never alone and always too busy to be able to think. The manifestation of the wind of thought is not knowledge; it is the ability to tell right from wrong, beautiful from ugly.[39]

## JUDGMENT AND KANT'S AESTHETICS

The foregoing account has explored the way in which Arendt attempted to connect the activity of thinking to our capacity to judge. To be sure, this connection of thinking and judging seems to operate only in emergencies, in those exceptional moments where individuals, faced with the collapse of traditional standards, must come up with new ones and judge according to their own autonomous values. There is, however, a second, more elaborated view of judgment which does not restrict it to moments of crisis, but which identifies it with the capacity to think representatively, that is, from the standpoint of everyone else. Arendt called this capacity to think representatively an "enlarged mentality," adopting the same terms that Kant employed in his Third Critique to characterize aesthetic judgment. It is to this work that we must now turn our attention, since Arendt based her theory of political judgment on Kant's aesthetics rather than on his moral philosophy. At first sight this might seem a puzzling choice, since Kant himself based his moral and political philosophy on practical reason and not on our aesthetic faculties. Arendt, however, claimed that the *Critique of Judgment* contained Kant's unwritten political philosophy, and that the first part of it, the "Critique of Aesthetic Judgment," was the most fruitful basis on which to build a theory of political judgment, since it dealt with the world of appearances from the point of view of the judging spectator and took as its starting point the faculty of taste, understood as a faculty of concrete and embodied subjects.[40] "The *Critique of Judgment*," she argued

> is the only of [Kant's] great writings where his point of departure is the World and the senses and capabilities which made men (in the plural) fit to be inhabitants of it. This is perhaps not yet political philosophy, but it certainly is its condition *sine qua non*. If it could be found that in the capacities and regulative traffic and intercourse between men who are bound to each other by the common possession of a world (the earth) there exists an *a priori* principle, then it would be proved that man is essentially a political being.[41]

For Arendt the capacity to judge is a specifically political ability insofar as it enables individuals to orient themselves in the public realm and to judge the phenomena that are disclosed within it from a standpoint that is relatively detached and impartial. She credits Kant with having dislodged the prejudice that judgments of taste lie altogether outside the political realm, since they supposedly concern only aesthetic matters. She believes, in fact, that by linking taste to that wider manner of thinking which Kant called an "enlarged mentality" the way was opened to a revaluation of judgment as a specific political ability, namely, as the ability to think in the place of everybody else. As she put it in one of the early essays devoted to this topic:

> Kant expounds two political philosophies which differ sharply from one another – the first being that which is generally accepted as such in his *Critique of Practical Reason* and the second that contained in his *Critique of Judgment*. That the first part of the latter [i.e., the "Critique of Aesthetic Judgment"] is, in reality, a political philosophy is a fact that is seldom mentioned in works on Kant; on the other hand, it can, I think, be seen from all his political writings that for Kant himself the theme of "judgment" carried more weight

than that of "practical reason." In the *Critique of Judgment* freedom is portrayed as a predicate of the power of imagination and not of the will, and the power of imagination is linked most closely with that wider manner of thinking which is political thinking par excellence, because it enables us to "put ourselves in the minds of other men."[42]

Moreover, as Arendt noted in her *Lectures on Kant's Political Philosophy*, it is only in Kant's *Critique of Judgment* that we find room for the idea that judgment is not the faculty of noumenal selves legislating for mankind as a whole, but the faculty of concrete subjects operating in a worldly space of appearances. "In neither of the two parts [of the *Critique of Judgment*]," she writes, "does Kant speak of man as an intelligible or a cognitive being . . . The first part speaks of men in the plural, as they really are and live in societies; the second part speaks of the human species." Thus

> the most decisive difference between the *Critique of Practical Reason* and the *Critique of Judgment* is that the moral laws of the former are valid for all intelligible beings, whereas the rules of the latter are strictly limited in their validity to human beings on earth.[43]

Lastly, it is only in Kant's *Critique of Judgment* that we find a conception of judgment as the ability to deal with particulars in their particularity, that is, without subsuming them under a pre-given universal, but actively searching the universal out of the particular.[44] Kant formulated this distinction as that between *determinant* and *reflective* judgments. For him judgment in general is the faculty of thinking the particular as contained under the universal. If the universal (the rule, principle, or law) is given, then the judgment which subsumes the particular under it is determinant. If, however, only the particular is given and the universal has to be found for it, then the judgment is reflective.[45] For Kant determinant judgments were cognitive, while reflective judgments were non-cognitive. Kant then distinguished two kinds of reflective judgment, aesthetic and teleological: the former are dealt with in the "Critique of Aesthetic Judgment" and concern objects to which we attribute the property of beauty, the latter are dealt with in the "Critique of Teleological Judgment" and concern the attribution of finality to nature. In neither type of judgment is the universal given in advance or general rules provided under which to subsume the particular. Rather, in the case of aesthetic judgment the particular object is estimated as beautiful by virtue of the feeling that it arouses in us (Kant in fact defines taste as "the faculty of estimating what makes our feeling in a given representation universally communicable *without the mediation of a concept"*),[46] while in the case of teleological judgment, since the understanding provides no general concepts or laws under which to subsume the purposeless variety of nature, it is reason with its regulative ideas that comes to the help of judgment, allowing us to impute purposiveness or finality to nature. For Kant, therefore, reflective judgment is seen as the capacity to ascend from the particular to the universal without the mediation of determinate concepts or of general rules given in advance; it is reasoning about particulars in their relation to the universal rather than reasoning about universals in their relation to the particular. In the case of aesthetic judgment this means that I can understand and apply the universal predicate of beauty only through experiencing a particular object that exemplifies it. Thus, upon encountering a flower, a unique landscape, or a particular painting, I am able to say that it is an example of beauty, that it possesses "exemplary validity."

It is important to note in this context that this notion of examples – or of the exemplary validity that a particular may possess – strikes Arendt as the most fruitful solution to the problem of mediating the particular and the universal. "Examples," she says quoting Kant, "are the go-cart of judgments."[47] They permit us to discover the universal in and through the particular, insofar as they embody a universal meaning while retaining their particularity. Thus

> one may encounter or think of some table that one judges to be the best possible table and take this table as the example of how tables actually should be: the *exemplary table* ("example" comes from *eximere*, "to single out some particular"). This exemplar is and remains a particular that in its very particularity reveals the generality that otherwise could not be defined.[48]

For Arendt this notion of exemplary validity is not restricted to aesthetic objects or to individuals who exemplified certain virtues (she uses the figure of Achilles as an example of courage). Rather, she wants to extend this notion to events in the past that carry a meaning beyond their sheer happening, that is to say, to events that could be seen as exemplary for those who came after. It is here that aesthetic judgment joins with the retrospective judgment of the historian or spectator. The American and French Revolutions, the Paris Commune, the Russian Soviets, the German Revolutionary Councils of 1918–19, the Hungarian uprising of 1956, all these events possess the kind of exemplary validity that makes them of universal significance, while still retaining their own specificity and uniqueness. Thus, by attending to these events in their particularity the historian or judging spectator is able to illuminate their universal import and thereby preserve them as "examples" for posterity.

Arendt refers in this context to Kant's attitude to the French Revolution, an event which he praised for arousing a universal yet disinterested sympathy on the part of the spectators, although from the standpoint of the actors it was an illegitimate act. "We are here concerned only with the attitude of the onlookers," Kant writes,

> as it reveals itself *in public* while the drama of great political changes is taking place; for they openly express universal yet disinterested sympathy for one set of protagonists against their adversaries, even at the risk that their partiality could be of great disadvantage to themselves.[49]

The sympathy that the French Revolution evoked in the spectators indicates for Kant a "moral disposition" shared by mankind to establish a civil constitution of a republican form (i.e., governed by the principle of right) and to strive for the realization of perpetual peace and a universal cosmopolitan existence. Thus, even if unsuccessful, the French Revolution *"can never be forgotten*, since it has revealed in human nature an aptitude and power for improvement of a kind which no politician could have thought up by examining the course of events in the past."[50] Indeed,

> the occurrence in question is too momentous, too intimately interwoven with the interests of humanity, and too widespread in its influence upon all parts of the world for nations not to be reminded of it when favourable circumstances present themselves, and to rise up and make renewed attempts of the same kind as before.[51]

Arendt interprets this passage as an affirmation that the importance of the French Revolution lies for Kant exclusively in the opinions of the spectators rather than in the deeds of the actors. The spectators, because they are not involved, can perceive the ultimate meaning of the event, a meaning that the actors are not aware of, blinded as they are by their partiality and their lack of disinterestedness.

> Only the spectator occupies a position that enables him to see the whole; the actor, because he is part of the play, must enact his part — he is partial by definition. The spectator is impartial by definition — no part is assigned to him.

Hence, she concludes, "withdrawal from direct involvement to a standpoint outside the game is a condition *sine qua non* of all judgment."[52] Furthermore,

> what the actor is concerned with is *doxa*, fame – that is, the opinion of others . . . For the actor, the decisive question is thus how he appears to others . . . the actor is dependent on the opinion of the spectator; he is not autonomous (in Kant's language) . . . The standard is the spectator. And this standard is autonomous.[53]

By viewing judgment as the capacity to be impartial and disinterested, Arendt locates it on the side of the spectators rather than that of the actors. Only the spectators can produce judgments which are free, autonomous, disinterested, and impartial. They can thus understand the meaning of events better than the actors.

> What counted in the French Revolution, what made it a world-historical event, a phenomenon not to be forgotten, were not the deeds and misdeeds of the actors but the opinions, the enthusiastic approbation, of spectators, of persons who themselves were not involved.[54]

Therefore "what constituted the appropriate public realm for this particular event were not the actors but the acclaiming spectators."[55]

It would be a mistake, however, to take these passages as indicating an absolute separation of the actors from the spectators. Arendt in fact seeks to reconcile their different perspectives by noting that the "critic and spectator sits in every actor and fabricator; without this critical, judging faculty the doer or maker would be so isolated from the spectator that he would not even be perceived."[56] Moreover, as we shall see in the next section, in her essay "The Crisis in Culture" she assimilates judgment to *phronesis* on the grounds that both are capacities of political actors, and claims that the "wooing" or persuading character of judging "corresponds closely to what the Greeks called *peitein*, the convincing and persuading speech which they regarded as the typically political form of people talking with one another."[57]

We shall look into these claims later. For now it is sufficient to note that it is the spectators who have the privilege to judge impartially and disinterestedly. For Arendt this is due not simply to the fact that they are detached from the doings of actors, but also because in their judgment the spectators have to appeal to two crucial faculties, *imagination* and *common sense*.

Imagination is the faculty of representing in one's mind that which has already appeared to one's senses. Through the imagination one can represent objects that are no longer present and thus establish the distance necessary for an impartial judgment. Once this distancing has occurred, one is in a position to reflect upon these representations from a number of different perspectives, and thereby to reach a judgment about the proper value of an object. As Arendt says:

> Only what touches, affects, one in representation, when one can no longer be affected by immediate presence . . . can be judged to be right or wrong, important or irrelevant, beautiful or ugly, or something in between. One then speaks of judgment and no longer of taste because, though it still affects one like a matter of taste, one now has, by means of representation, established the proper distance, the remoteness or uninvolvedness or disinterestedness, that is requisite for approbation and disapprobation, for evaluating something at its proper worth. By removing the object, one has established the conditions for impartiality.[58]

The faculty of judgment thus depends upon two mental operations: there is the operation of the *imagination*, in which one represents objects that are removed from immediate sense perception and therefore no longer affect one directly, and then there is the operation of *reflection*, in which one judges these representations. This twofold operation establishes the most important condition for judgment, the condition of impartiality, or of "disinterestedness." As Arendt puts it:

> By closing one's eyes one becomes an impartial, not a directly affected, spectator of visible things . . . Also: by making what one's external senses perceived into an object for one's inner sense . . . one is in a position to "see" by the eyes of the mind, i.e., to see the whole that gives meaning to the particulars. The advantage the spectator has is that he sees the play as a whole, while each of the actors knows only his part or, if he should judge from the perspective of acting, only the part of the whole that concerns him.[59]

The other faculty that spectators have to appeal to is common sense or *sensus communis*, since without it they could not share their judgments or overcome their individual idiosyncrasies. Kant himself declared that "In matters of taste we must renounce ourselves in favour of others . . . In taste egoism is overcome."[60] By this he meant that for our judgments to be valid (i.e., publicly recognized and accepted) we must transcend our private or subjective conditions in favor of public and intersubjective ones, and we are able to do this by appealing to our community sense, our *sensus communis*. In this respect, Arendt notes

> Judgment, and especially judgments of taste, always reflects upon others and their taste, takes their possible judgments into account. This is necessary because I am human and cannot live outside the company of men. I judge as a member of this community and not as a member of a supersensible world.[61]

The criterion for judgment, then, is *communicability*, and the standard for deciding whether our judgments are indeed communicable is to see whether they could fit with the *sensus communis* of others. The term *sensus communis* is used by Kant to indicate not merely the common sense we expect everybody to have, but a special sense that fits us into a human community. It is a specifically *community* sense because communication and speech depend upon it, and without communication we could neither constitute nor enter into a community. Arendt remarks that in Kant this community sense or *sensus communis* is contrasted to the *sensus privatus* that every individual, in his or her singularity, possesses; whenever the latter takes precedence, the individual is unable to communicate his or her judgments. She quotes Kant's view that "the only general symptom of insanity is the loss of the *sensus communis* and the logical stubborness in insisting on one's own sense (*sensus privatus*)."[62] Kant's own definition of *sensus communis* is given in paragraph 40 of the *Critique of Judgment*, entitled "Taste as a kind of *sensus communis*." Here, after having distinguished it from mere common sense, he writes that

> By the name *sensus communis* is to be understood the idea of a *public* sense, i.e. a critical faculty which in its reflective act takes account (*a priori*) of the mode of representation of everyone else, in order, *as it were*, to weigh its judgment with the collective reason of mankind . . . This is accomplished by weighing the judgment, not so much with actual, as rather with the merely possible, judgments of others, and by putting ourselves in the position of everyone else, as the result of a mere abstraction from the limitations which contingently affect our own estimate.[63]

Kant then offers three maxims of "common human understanding": (1) think for oneself (the maxim of *unprejudiced* thought); (2) think from the standpoint of everyone else (the maxim of *enlarged* thought); (3) always think consistently (the maxim of *consistent* thought). Kant calls the first the maxim of understanding, the second that of judgment, the third that of reason. Arendt notes that these are not maxims of cognition, strictly speaking, since "truth compels, one doesn't need any 'maxims.' Maxims apply and are needed only for matters of opinion and in judgments."[64] In the case of the second maxim, that of enlarged thought, it indicates for Arendt one's quality of thought "in the worldly matters that are ruled by the community sense."[65] Or as Kant put it:

> However small the range and degree to which a man's natural endowments extend, still [it] indicates a man of *enlarged mind* if he detaches himself from the subjective personal conditions of his judgment, which cramp the minds of so many others, and reflects upon his own judgment from a *universal standpoint* (which he can only determine by shifting his ground to the standpoint of others).[66]

Immediately after this passage Kant says that "taste can with more justice be called a *sensus communis* than can sound understanding [i.e., common sense]" and that "aesthetic . . . judgment can bear the name of a *public sense*"; he then concludes his discussion by saying that "we might even define taste as the faculty of estimating what makes our feeling in a given representation *universally communicable* without the mediation of a concept."[67] In Arendt's view this means that judgments of taste always appeal to our *sensus communis*, and it is this appeal that gives them their specific validity. They are neither merely subjective nor entirely objective (that is, they are neither judgments of sense nor cognitive judgments), and their validity rests on the consent they elicit from the community within which one judges. As she puts it:

> The validity of these judgments never has the validity of cognitive or scientific propositions, which are not judgments, properly speaking . . . Similarly, one can never compel anyone to agree with one's judgments – "This is beautiful" or "This is wrong" (Kant does not believe that moral judgments are the product of reflection and imagination, hence they are not judgments strictly speaking); one can only "woo" or "court" the agreement of everyone else. And in this persuasive activity one actually appeals to the "community sense." In other words, when one judges, one judges as a member of a community.[68]

Arendt also notes that it is this community sense that enables individuals to acquire an "enlarged mentality" and thus to be in a position to judge impartially:

An "enlarged mentality" is the condition *sine qua non* of right judgment; one's community sense makes it possible to enlarge one's mentality. Negatively speaking, this means that one is able to abstract from private conditions and circumstances, which, as far as judgment is concerned, limit and inhibit its exercise. Private conditions condition us; imagination and reflection enable us to *liberate* ourselves from them and to attain that relative impartiality that is the specific virtue of judgment.[69]

The validity of judgment thus depends on its degree of impartiality (or what Kant calls "disinterestedness") and to achieve such impartiality what is required is the active employment of our capacities for imagination and reflection and an "enlarged mentality" that incorporates the standpoints of others.

In her concluding reflections on Kant's aesthetics Arendt remarks that the emphasis on the communicability of judgments of taste, and the correlative notion of an enlarged mentality, link up effortlessly with Kant's idea of a united mankind living in eternal peace. After quoting Kant's insistence that "a regard to universal communicability is a thing which everyone expects and requires from everyone else, just as if it were part of an original compact dictated by humanity itself,"[70] she goes on to argue that:

It is by virtue of this idea of mankind, present in every single man, that men are human, and they can be called civilized or humane to the extent that this idea becomes the principle not only of their judgments but of their actions. It is at this point that *actor* and *spectator* become united; the maxim of the actor and the maxim, the "standard," according to which the spectator judges the spectacle of the world, become one. The, as it were, categorical imperative for action could read as follows: Always act on the maxim through which this original compact can be actualized into a general law.[71]

In other words, both judgment and action are inspired by the same principle – universal communicability or publicness – which it is our duty to pursue just as if it were part of an original compact of mankind. In this sense, Arendt concludes, "When one judges and when one acts in political matters, one is supposed to take one's bearings from the idea, not the actuality, of being a world citizen and, therefore, also a *Weltbetrachter*, a world spectator."[72] Here it would appear that Arendt once again acknowledges the links between the standpoint of the actor and that of the spectator. Let us then look at the way in which judgment operates from the standpoint of the actor.

## JUDGMENT AND THE *VITA ACTIVA*

As I remarked at the beginning of this chapter, Arendt presented a model of judgment in the essays "The Crisis in Culture" and "Truth and Politics" which could be characterized as far more "political" than the one presented so far. In these essays, in fact, she treated judgment as a faculty that enables political actors to decide what courses of action to undertake in the public sphere, what kind of objectives are most appropriate or worth pursuing, as well as who to praise or blame for past actions or for the consequences of past decisions. In this model judgment is viewed as a specifically *political* ability, namely, as "the ability to see things not only from one's own point of view but in the perspective of all those who happen to be present," and as being "one of the fundamental abilities of man as a political being insofar as it enables him to orient himself in the public realm, in the common world."[73] Indeed, in this model Arendt identifies judgment with *phronesis* on the grounds that both are capacities of political actors, and that both are rooted in *sensus communis*. She says that

> the Greeks called this ability [to judge] *phronesis*, or insight, and they considered it the principal virtue or excellence of the statesman in distinction from the wisdom of the philosopher. The difference between this judging insight and speculative thought lies in that the former has its roots in what we usually call common sense, which the latter constantly transcends. Common sense . . . discloses to us the nature of the world insofar as it is a common world; we owe to it the fact that our strictly private and "subjective" five senses and their sensory data can adjust themselves to a nonsubjective and "objective" world which we have in common and share with others. Judging is one, if not the most, important activity in which this sharing-the-world-with-others comes to pass.[74]

Moreover, in discussing the non-coercive character of judgment, the fact that it can only appeal to but never force the agreement of others (the judging person can in fact only "woo the consent of everyone else in the hope of coming to an agreement with him eventually") she claims that "this 'wooing' or persuading corresponds closely to what the Greeks called *peitein*, the convincing and persuading speech which they regarded as the typically political form of people talking with one another."[75] She then goes on to claim that

> culture and politics . . . belong together because it is not knowledge or truth which is at stake, but rather *judgment* and *decision*, the

judicious exchange of opinion about the sphere of public life and the
common world, and the decision what manner of action is to be
taken in it, as well as to how it is to look henceforth, what kind of
things are to appear in it.[76]

Now, all these statements would seem to indicate that for Arendt
judgment is the ability most closely associated with political action,
with the judicious assessment of alternative proposals as to what a
political community should do. The identification of judgment with
*phronesis* would seem to confirm this, since what is required in matters
affecting the political community is precisely that form of practical
reasoning that Aristotle sought to discriminate from both *episteme* and
*sophia*, as well as from *techne*. Arendt's treatment of political judgment,
however, constantly makes reference to Kant's ideas, in particular
those discussed in the previous section under the heading of aesthetic
judgment. She claims that both aesthetic and political judgment are
concerned with particulars, that they can only claim a subjective-
universal validity (since they are reflective and not determinant), and
that they rest ultimately on the potential agreement with others.
Interestingly, Arendt also claims that Kant was the *first* philosopher to
discover the importance of judgment, and underlines the fact that

> what . . . is quite new and even startlingly new in Kant's
> propositions in the *Critique of Judgment* is that he discovered this
> phenomenon in all its grandeur precisely when he was examining
> the phenomenon of taste and hence the only kind of judgments
> which, since they concern merely aesthetic matters, have always
> been supposed to lie outside the political realm as well as the
> domain of reason.[77]

What becomes clear, therefore, is that even in her discussion of
judgment from the standpoint of political action Arendt appeals far
more to Kant's ideas than to those of Aristotle. The appeal, however
qualified, to the latter has nevertheless puzzled some commentators.
Both Christopher Lasch and Richard Bernstein have claimed that there
is a contradiction in Arendt's employment of the Aristotelian notion of
*phronesis* alongside Kant's idea of an "enlarged mentality," since they
supposedly pull in opposite directions, the former toward a concern
with the particular, the latter toward universality and impartiality.[78] I
would argue, however, that this contradiction is more apparent than
real, since Kant's theory of aesthetic judgment is a theory of *reflective*
judgment, that is, of those judgments where the universal is not given
but must be searched out of the particular. In this respect the theory of

aesthetic judgment to which Arendt appeals does have close affinities with Aristotle's notion of *phronesis*. Both are concerned with the judgment of particulars *qua* particulars, not with their subsumption under universal rules. If a distinction is to be made, it has more to do with the mode of *asserting validity*. In Aristotle, *phronesis* is in fact the privilege of a few experienced individuals (the *phronimos*) who, over time, have shown themselves to be wise in practical matters; the only criterion of validity is their experience and their past record of judicious actions. In the case of judgments of taste, on the other hand, individuals have to appeal to the judgments and opinions of others, and thus the validity of their judgments rests on the consent they can elicit from a community of differently situated subjects. If Arendt's references to *phronesis* are not as extensive or as important as those she makes to Kant's theory of aesthetic judgment, it is probably due to the fact that only in the latter do we find a conception of judgment which could be called democratic. In this conception judgment is no longer seen as the privilege of a few experienced individuals, but is instead a capacity available to all; everybody, by exercising his or her imagination and thinking "representatively," can acquire an "enlarged mentality." I would therefore argue that the stress on impartiality and universality should not be seen as a flight from the judicious assessment of particulars, but as a concern that our particular judgments be submitted to the assessment of others, that their validity be made subject to the consent of everyone else.

There is, however, another problem that needs to be addressed before proceeding further with Arendt's theory of political judgment, and it has to do with the fact that Arendt appealed to Kant's theory of aesthetic judgment to characterize the operation of this faculty *both* from the standpoint of the spectator *and* from the standpoint of the actor. This is not just the problem highlighted by Bernstein, Beiner, and others, that there are two distinct models of judgment in Arendt, one dealing with judgment as a feature of political life as such, as the faculty through which citizens decide how to act in the public sphere, the other dealing with judgment as a component in the life of the mind, the faculty through which the privileged spectators can recover meaning from the past and reconcile us to what has happened. Rather, the problem is that both these models appeal to the same philosophical source, namely, Kant's theory of aesthetic judgment, and this theory, as we have seen, was developed from the point of view of the spectator. How, then, could Arendt use Kant's aesthetics to formulate her theory of judgment from the viewpoint of the actor?

One possible answer to this problem is to argue that in her earlier "political" conception of judgment Arendt emphasized to a greater extent the *representative* nature of judgment, the fact that it always has to take into account the opinions of others, and that as a *political* faculty it can only be exercised and tested in public, in the free and open exchange of opinions in the public sphere. This emphasis is particularly evident in her treatment of Kant's notion of an "enlarged mentality," which he saw as the ability to think from the standpoint of everyone else. Arendt elaborates this notion as follows:

> The power of judgment rests on a potential agreement with others, and the thinking process which is active in judging something is not, like the thought process of pure reasoning, a dialogue between me and myself, but finds itself always and primarily, even if I am quite alone in making up my mind, in an anticipated communication with others with whom I know I must finally come to some agreement. From this potential agreement judgment derives its specific validity. This means, on the one hand, that such judgment must liberate itself from the "subjective private conditions," that is, from the idiosyncrasies which naturally determine the outlook of each individual in his privacy and are legitimate as long as they are only privately held opinions, but which are not fit to enter the market place, and lack all validity in the public realm. *And this enlarged way of thinking*, which as judgment knows how to transcend its own individual limitations, on the other hand, *cannot function in strict isolation or solitude*; it needs the presence of others in whose place it must think, whose perspectives it must take into consideration, and without whom it never has the opportunity to operate at all. As logic, to be sound, depends on the presence of the self, *so judgment, to be valid, depends on the presence of others.*[79]

For Arendt, therefore, the validity of political judgment depends on our ability to think "representatively," that is, from the standpoint of everyone else, so that we are able to look at the world from a number of different perspectives. And this ability, in turn, can only be acquired and tested in a public forum where individuals have the opportunity to exchange their opinions on particular matters and see whether they accord with the opinions of others. In this respect the process of opinion formation is never a solitary activity; rather, it requires a genuine encounter with different opinions so that a particular issue may be examined from every possible standpoint until, as she puts it, "it is flooded and made transparent by the full light of human comprehension."[80] Debate and discussion, and the capacity to enlarge one's perspective, are indeed crucial to the formation of opinions that can claim more than subjective validity; individuals may hold personal opinions on many subject matters, but they can form *representative* opinions only by enlarging their standpoint to incorporate those of others. As Arendt says:

> Political thought is representative. I form an opinion by considering a given issue from different viewpoints, by making present to my mind the standpoints of those who are absent; that is, I represent them. This process of representation does not blindly adopt the actual views of those who stand somewhere else, and hence look upon the world from a different perspective; this is a question neither of empathy . . . nor of counting noses and joining a majority, but of being and thinking in my own identity where actually I am not. The more people's standpoints I have present in my mind while I am pondering a given issue, and the better I can imagine how I would feel and think if I were in their place, the stronger will be my capacity for representative thinking and the more valid my final conclusions, my opinion.[81]

Opinions, in fact, are never self-evident. In matters of opinion, but not in matters of truth, "our thinking is truly discursive, running, as it were, from place to place, from one part of the world to another, through all kinds of conflicting views, until it finally ascends from these particularities to some impartial generality."[82] In this respect one is never alone while forming an opinion; as Arendt notes,

> even if I shun all company or am completely isolated while forming an opinion, I am not simply together only with myself in the solitude of philosophical thought; I remain in this world of universal interdependence, where I can make myself the representative of everybody else.[83]

## JUDGMENT AND VALIDITY

The representative character of judgment and opinion has important implications for the question of validity. Arendt always stressed that the formation of valid opinions requires a public space where individuals can test and purify their views through a process of mutual debate and enlightenment. She was, however, quite opposed to the idea that opinions should be measured by the standard of truth, or that debate should be conducted according to strict scientific standards of validity. In her view, truth belongs to the realm of cognition, the realm of logic, mathematics, and the strict sciences, and carries always an element of coercion, since it precludes debate and must be accepted by every individual in possession of his or her rational faculties. Set against the plurality of opinions, truth has a despotic character: it compels universal assent, leaves the mind little freedom of movement, eliminates the diversity of views and reduces the richness of human discourse. In this respect, truth is anti-political, since by eliminating debate and diversity it eliminates the very principles of political life. As Arendt writes:

> The trouble is that factual truth, like all other truth, peremptorily claims to be acknowledged and precludes debate, and debate constitutes the very essence of political life. *The modes of thought and communication that deal with truth, if seen from the political perspective, are necessarily domineering*; they don't take into account other people's opinions, and taking these into account is the hallmark of all strictly political thinking.[84]

For Arendt, a truth "whose validity needs no support from the side of opinion strikes at the very roots of all politics and all governments."[85] She cites the famous statement of Jefferson in the Declaration of Independence that says "We hold these truths to be self-evident, that all men are created equal, that they are endowed by their Creator with certain unalienable rights," and argues that by saying "*We hold* these truths to be self-evident" Jefferson acknowledged that these truths were not self-evident, that they stood in need of agreement and consent, and therefore that the statement "All men are created equal" was a matter of opinion and not of truth. "That all men are created equal," writes Arendt,

> is not self-evident nor can it be proved. We hold this opinion because freedom is possible only among equals, and we believe that the joys and gratifications of free company are to be preferred to the doubtful pleasures of holding dominion . . . *these are matters of opinion and not of truth* – as Jefferson, much against his will, admitted. *Their validity depends upon free agreement and consent*; they are arrived at by discursive, representative thinking; and they are communicated by means of persuasion and dissuasion.[86]

Arendt also quotes the remark by Lessing – "Let each man say what he deems truth, and let truth itself be commended unto God" – and interprets it as saying "Let us thank God that we don't know *the* truth."

For Arendt this expressed the insight that "for men living in company, the inexhaustible richness of human discourse is infinitely more significant and meaningful than any One Truth could ever be."[87] Lessing's greatness for Arendt consisted not merely in having reached

> a theoretical insight that there cannot be one single truth within the human world, but in his *gladness* that it does not exist and that, therefore, the unending discourse among men will never cease so long as there are men at all. *A single absolute truth*, could there have been one . . . *would have spelled the end of humanity.*[88]

Arendt's defense of opinion is motivated not just by her belief that truth leaves no room for debate or dissent, or for the acknowledgment of difference, but also by her conviction that our reasoning faculties can only flourish in a dialogic or communicative context. She cites Kant's remark that "the external power that deprives man of the freedom to communicate his thoughts publicly deprives him at the same time of his freedom to think," and underlines the fact that for Kant the only guarantee of the correctness of our thinking is that " 'we think, as it were, in community with others to whom we communicate our thoughts as they communicate theirs to us.' Man's reason, being fallible, can function only if he can make 'public use' of it."[89] She also quotes Madison's statement that "the reason of man, like man himself, is timid and cautious when left alone, and acquires firmness and confidence in proportion to the number with which it is associated."[90] It follows, therefore, that

> the shift from rational truth to opinion implies a shift from man in the singular to men in the plural, and this means a shift from a domain where, Madison says, nothing counts except the "solid reasoning" of one mind to a realm where "strength of opinion" is determined by the individual's reliance upon "the number which he supposes to have entertained the same opinion" − a number, incidentally, that is not necessarily limited to one's contemporaries.[91]

The appeal to Lessing, Kant, and Madison is meant to vindicate the power and dignity of opinion against those thinkers, from Plato to Hobbes, who saw it as mere illusion, as a confused or inadequate grasp of the truth. For Arendt opinion is not a defective form of knowledge that should be transcended or left behind as soon as one is in possession of the truth. Rather, it is a distinct form of knowledge which arises out of the collective deliberation of citizens, and which requires the use of the imagination and the capacity to think "representatively." By deliberating in common and engaging in "representative thinking" citizens are in fact able to form opinions that can claim intersubjective validity. It is important to stress in this context that Arendt does not want to dismiss the philosophers' attempt to find universal or absolute standards of knowledge and cognition, but to check their desire to impose those standards upon the sphere of human affairs, since they would eliminate its plurality and essential relativity, that is, the fact that it is composed of a plurality of individuals who view it from different perspectives which are all relative to each other.[92] The imposition of a single or absolute standard into the domain of *praxis* would do away with the need to persuade others of the relative merits of an opinion, to elicit their consent to a specific proposal, or to obtain their agreement with respect to a particular policy. Indeed, for Arendt the imposition of such a standard would mean that individuals would no longer be required to exercise their judgment, develop their imagination, or cultivate an "enlarged mentality," since they would no longer need to deliberate in common. Strict demonstration, rather than persuasive argumentation, would then become the only legitimate form of discourse.[93]

Now we must be careful not to impute to Arendt the view that truth has no legitimate role to play in politics or in the sphere of human affairs. She does indeed assert that "All truths — not only the various kinds of rational truth but also factual truth — are opposed to opinion in their mode of asserting validity,"[94] since they all carry an element of compulsion. However, she is only preoccupied with the negative consequences of the former (i.e., rational truth) when applied to the sphere of politics and collective deliberation, while she defends the importance of factual truth for the preservation of an accurate account of the past and for the very existence of political communities. Factual truth, she writes, "is always related to other people: it concerns events and circumstances in which many are involved; it is established by witnesses and depends upon testimony . . . It is political by nature."[95] It follows, therefore, that

> facts and opinions, though they must be kept apart, are not antagonistic to each other; they belong to the same realm. Facts inform opinions, and opinions, inspired by different interests and passions, can differ widely and still be legitimate as long as they respect factual truth. Freedom of opinion is a farce unless factual information is guaranteed and the facts themselves are not in

dispute. In other words, *factual truth informs political thought just as rational truth informs philosophical speculation.*[96]

The relationship between facts and opinions is thus one of mutual entailment: if opinions were not based on correct information and the free access to all relevant facts they could scarcely claim any validity. And if they were to be based on fantasy, self-deception, or deliberate falsehood, then no possibility of genuine debate and argumentation could be sustained. Both factual truth and the general habit of truth-telling are therefore basic to the formation of sound opinions and to the flourishing of political debate.[97] Moreover, if the record of the past were to be destroyed by organized lying, or be distorted by an attempt to rewrite history (as was the case of Stalinist historiography), political life would be deprived of one of its essential and stabilizing elements. As Arendt writes:

> The liar, who may get away with any number of single falsehoods, will find it impossible to get away with lying on principle. This is one of the lessons that could be learned from the totalitarian experiments and the totalitarian rulers' frightening confidence in the power of lying – in their ability, for instance, to rewrite history again and again to adapt the past to the "political line" of the present moment or to eliminate data that did not fit their ideology ... The results of such experiments when undertaken by those in possession of the means of violence are terrible enough, but lasting deception is not among them. There always comes a point beyond which lying becomes counterproductive. This point is reached when the audience to which the lies are addressed is forced to disregard altogether the distinguishing line between truth and falsehood in order to be able to survive ... truth that can be relied on disappears entirely from public life, and with it the chief stabilizing factor in the ever-changing affairs of men.[98]

In this respect, Arendt notes,

> Not the past – and all factual truth, of course, concerns the past – or the present, insofar as it is the outcome of the past, but the future is open to action. If the past and present are treated as part of the future – that is, changed back into their former state of potentiality – the political realm is deprived not only of its main stabilizing force but of the starting point from which to change, to begin something new.[99]

In sum, both factual truth and the practice of truth-telling are essential to political life. The antagonism for Arendt is between *rational* truth and well-grounded opinion, since the former does not allow for debate and dissent, while the latter thrives on it. Arendt's defense of opinion must therefore be understood as a defense of *political deliberation*, and of the role that persuasion and dissuasion play in all matters affecting the political community. Against Plato and Hobbes, who denigrated the role of opinion in political matters, Arendt reasserts the value and importance of political discourse, of *deliberation* and *persuasion*, and thus of a politics that acknowledges difference and the plurality of opinions.[100]

## CRITICAL REFLECTIONS

Having reconstructed the various aspects of Hannah Arendt's theory of judgment, I would like to examine a number of important criticisms with respect to the following issues: first, whether judgment is to be located in the *vita activa* or whether it is to be confined to the *vita contemplativa*; second, whether Kant's model of aesthetic judgment is the best source for a theory of political judgment rather than, say, Aristotle's notion of *phronesis* or practical reason; third, whether Arendt's theory of judgment rests on an adequate theory of knowledge and a plausible conception of rationality.

### 1

With respect to the first issue Ronald Beiner has argued that Arendt formulated two distinct conceptions of judgment, one from the standpoint of the *vita activa*, the other from the standpoint of the *vita contemplativa*. In her earlier formulation, he writes, "we find discussions of the relation of judgment to 'representative thinking' and opinion, leading one to suppose that judgment is a faculty exercised by actors in political deliberation and action."[101] But this approach is implicitly denied in her later formulation, in which judgment is made the prerogative of spectators who seek retrospectively the meaning of human affairs. The problem, therefore, is whether and to what extent judgment participates in the *vita activa* or whether it is confined to the *vita contemplativa*. Beiner maintains that

> this fundamental uncertainty as to where judgment fits within the overall perspective is finally resolved by Arendt only by negating some of her own broader insights into judgment. On the one hand,

she is tempted to integrate judgment into the *vita activa*, seeing it as a function of the representative thinking and enlarged mentality of political actors, exchanging opinions in public while engaged in common deliberation. On the other hand, she wants to emphasize the contemplative and disinterested dimension of judgment, which operates retrospectively, like aesthetic judgment. Judgment in the latter sense is placed exclusively within the ambit of the life of the mind. Arendt achieves a final resolution by abolishing this tension, opting wholly for the latter conception of judgment. This resolution ultimately produces consistency, but it is a strained consistency, achieved at the price of excluding any reference to the *vita activa* within the revised concept of judgment. The only point at which the exercise of judgment becomes practically efficacious, or even practically relevant, is in times of crisis or emergency ... aside from these rare moments, judgment pertains only to the life of the mind, the mind's communion with itself in solitary reflection.[102]

There are several things to be said in response to this passage. First, though it is true that Arendt formulated two distinct conceptions of judgment, their opposition is not as strong as Beiner claims. Even in the later "contemplative" conception, judgment does not withdraw from the world of appearances, nor is it reduced to the reflection of solitary individuals. In the *Life of the Mind* Arendt, in fact, claims that

the withdrawal of judgment is obviously very different from the withdrawal of the philosopher. It does not leave the world of appearances but retires from active involvement in it to a privileged position in order to contemplate the whole. Moreover ... [the] spectators are members of an audience and therefore quite unlike the philosopher who begins his *bios theoretikos* by leaving the company of his fellow-men and their uncertain opinions ... hence the spectator's verdict, while impartial ... is not independent of the view of others – on the contrary, according to Kant, an "enlarged mentality" has to take them into account. The spectators, although disengaged from the particularity characteristic of the actor, are not solitary.[103]

Similarly, in the Kant Lectures Arendt declares that the "spectators exist only in the plural. The spectator is not involved in the act, but he is always involved with fellow spectators."[104] Arendt, therefore, did not abandon her earlier insights into the nature of judgment; even in her later conception she retained the link between judgment and the world of human affairs, and stressed the intersubjective and public dimensions of this faculty (e.g., the spectators always judge as members of a community and have to appeal to the opinions of their fellow-spectators). In this respect the opposition between the two conceptions is not as sharp as Beiner maintains.

In the second place, Arendt attempted to reconcile the standpoint of the *vita activa* with that of the *vita contemplativa* by arguing that in every actor and fabricator there sits a critic and a spectator; the spectator, she says,

> does not share the faculty of genius, originality, with the maker or the faculty of novelty with the actor; the faculty they have in common is the faculty of judgment ... without this critical, judging faculty the doer or maker would be so isolated from the spectator that he would not even be perceived.[105]

Finally, even in her later formulation Arendt continued to emphasize the political character of judgment, calling it "the most political of man's mental abilities,"[106] and identifying it with the faculty of "telling right from wrong" as well as beautiful from ugly.[107] I therefore find it difficult to accept Beiner's view that Arendt ultimately adhered to "a firm disjunction between mental and worldly activities" and that she was forced to "expel judging from the world of the *vita activa*."[108] Arendt did indeed articulate a theory of judgment from the standpoint of the *vita contemplativa*, but this theory was not meant to exclude the concerns of the *vita activa*; rather to approach them from a more detached and impartial perspective.

## 2

The second issue raised by Arendt's theory of judgment is whether she was right to appeal to Kant's aesthetics rather than to Aristotle's theory of practical reason. Beiner, in particular, has argued that Kant's theory of aesthetic judgment is too formal and abstract to provide an adequate basis for a theory of *political* judgment. His argument is as follows:

> Kant offers a highly formalized account of what it is to judge because he is concerned not with substantive features of this or that judgment but, rather, with universal conditions of the possible validity of our judgments ... Nowhere in Kant's discussion of judgment do we find a concern with the qualities of experience, maturity, and sound habituation that have traditionally been observed as the mark of practical wisdom in a man of action.

Prudence was explicitly excluded by Kant from practical reason, for reasons deeply bound up with his moral philosophy . . . He conceived of prudence as a species of technical-practical rules of art and skill – in particular, rules governing the skill involved in exercising an influence over men and subordinating their will to one's own . . . In Kant's terms, this is a quasi-theoretical, not a genuinely practical capacity, and it serves to reduce prudence to a *techne*, in Aristotle's sense.[109]

Moreover, Kant

regards aesthetic judgment as purely contemplative, divorced from any practical interest. Accordingly, a judgment of taste must abstract from any consideration of *ends*; aesthetic judgment must make no reference to teleology. But can *political* judgments abstract from practical ends, and is a strictly nonteleological conception of political judgment coherent? This, in turn, gives rise to further questions. For instance, what is the status of rhetoric within political judgment, and are the two necessarily related? Because Kant expels teleology from judgments of taste, he condemns rhetoric, since it corrupts aesthetics with the pursuit of ends. But if the pursuit of ends is inseparable from, and indeed constitutive of, political as opposed to aesthetic judgment, is not rhetoric, too, in a constitutive relation to political judgment?[110]

Similarly, can judgment be formulated in terms of a purely formal appeal to the opinions of mankind as such, rather than to the substantive ends and purposes of a community?[111] Without addressing these questions, Beiner argues, Arendt's appropriation of a theory of judgment from Kant's aesthetics

runs the risk of turning from a genuine appreciation of political appearances *qua* appearances into an unwarranted aestheticization of politics. It is at this juncture that Arendt would have done well to consult Aristotle, for he situates judgment firmly within the context of the substantive ends and purposes of political deliberation, rhetoric, and community.[112]

Beiner is indeed correct to highlight the deficiencies of a too strict appropriation of Kantian aesthetics for a theory of political judgment. He does not seem aware, however, of the problems that arise in appealing to the Aristotelian notion of *phronesis* for a democratic theory of political judgment. Two problems in particular stand out. The first has to do with the question of validity. As I have already pointed out, Aristotle restricts the capacity for prudent judgment or *phronesis* to a few individuals, the *phronimos*; as such, the validity of judgment does not depend on the potential agreement with other judging subjects, but on the experience and insight of a few privileged individuals. From a democratic standpoint, a judgment of this kind lacks the criteria of equality, impartiality, and universality.[113] The second and related problem has to do with the appeal to community. Can community, in its Aristotelian sense of a congruence of *ethos* and *polis*, provide an adequate standard for judgment? Should we accept the substantive ends and purposes of our community as the sole criteria for guiding our moral and political judgments? I doubt that these questions could be answered in the affirmative without relapsing either into a pre-modern conception of politics or into a narrow and particularistic conception of judgment. As Wellmer has aptly observed:

> Judgment for Arendt is intrinsically related to the essential plurality of human beings, to our living in a common world, which as a common world is opened up by speech. Matters of praxis, which belong to this common world, are not susceptible to scientific proof, they are not matters of knowledge but of opinion. At this point a theory of *phronesis* could have been expected to emerge, analyzing the peculiar rationality related to the field of human praxis and explaining the difference between good and bad judgment in terms of this peculiar rationality. Neo-Aristotelians at this point usually rediscover Hegel's conception of "ethical life" (*Sittlichkeit*) and/or move toward a theory of institutions. Arendt, in contrast, seems to move rather in the opposite direction. She proves to be a decidedly modern thinker in that she denies the existence of anything like an ethical community which could provide the basis for the exercise of *phronesis*. The common world of human beings, to which the faculty of judgment appeals, turns out not to be an existing ethical totality, but a regulative idea, the *sensus communis* showing its reality above all in those rare moments when autonomous judgment breaks through the crust of established opinions and established generalities.[114]

In a similar vein, David Ingram has argued that

> for a civilization whose identity has become so abstract as to verge on total disintegration, the only community capable of serving as touchstone for judgment may well be that disinterested ideal mentioned by Kant. Despite formalistic shortcomings, the "aes-

theticization" and concomitant "depoliticization" of *sensus communis* for which Gadamer rebukes Kant is possibly a better gauge of how things really stand with us than he or any other neo-Aristotelian would care to admit.[115]

## 3

The third issue I would like to address is whether Arendt's theory of judgment rests on an adequate theory of knowledge and a plausible conception of rationality. Habermas and Bernstein, on the one hand, have claimed that Arendt subscribed to an antiquated conception of knowledge which prevented her from appreciating the role of rational argumentation in practical affairs. Albrecht Wellmer, on the other hand, has argued that she subscribed to an overly formalistic conception of rationality and that she was never able to free herself from the presuppositions of Kantian epistemology. Let us look at each of these claims in turn, which, to my mind, are the most pertinent and valid of all the ones we have examined so far.

With respect to the first claim Habermas has argued that Arendt, although she was highly critical of Plato's political philosophy, retained in part his theory of knowledge and the classical distinctions between *episteme* and *doxa* and between *theoria* and *praxis*. As Habermas says:

> Arendt sees a yawning abyss between knowledge and opinion that cannot be closed with arguments . . . She holds fast to the classical distinction between theory and practice; practice rests on opinions and convictions that cannot be true or false in the strict sense . . . [Thus] an antiquated concept of theoretical knowledge that is based on ultimate insights and certainties keeps Arendt from comprehending the process of reaching agreement about practical questions as *rational discourse*. If, by contrast, "representative thought" – which examines the generalizability of practical standpoints, that is, the legitimacy of norms – is not separated from argumentation by an abyss, then a *cognitive* foundation can also be claimed for the power of common convictions. In this case, such power is anchored in the *de facto* recognition of validity claims that can be discursively redeemed and fundamentally criticized.[116]

Similarly, Bernstein has argued that Arendt, in endeavoring to exclude rational truth from the realm of human affairs, and in drawing a sharp distinction between opinion and truth, risked downplaying the importance of rational argumentation. As he writes:

In stressing the gap between opinion and truth she tends to underestimate the importance of a concept that is most essential for her own understanding of judgment – argumentation. Argumentation does not make any sense unless there is some common acceptance of what is to count in support of, or against, an opinion. Without the possibility of a potential agreement that can be backed by reasons, argumentation, as the positivists and emotivists have claimed, is "pseudo argumentation." Arendt failed to realize that in exaggerating the differences between truth and opinion and between the validity tests for each of them, she was leading us down the slippery slope of "noncognitivism," where all argumentation about practical affairs is "pseudo argumentation".[117]

In fact, it might be argued that one of the reasons that led Arendt to draw such a sharp distinction between truth and opinion was her acceptance of the Kantian distinction between the *cognitive* judgments of the intellect or understanding and the *non-cognitive* judgments of taste. Kant argued that the former were cognitive judgments because they were based on an objective principle or law, while the latter, being based on the feelings of pleasure or displeasure evoked in the subject, were non-cognitive. Since Arendt based her theory of political judgment on Kant's theory of taste, she was bound to stress the non-cognitive dimensions of judgment and, more specifically, its non-cognitive criteria of validity. In doing so, however, she severed the links between judgment and argumentation, and produced what Wellmer has aptly termed a "mythology of judgment." As Wellmer writes:

Arendt, in her attempt to uncover Kant's unwritten political philosophy ... could only refer to the critique of aesthetic judgment as the only place in the Kantian system which allows for judgments which are neither arbitrary nor compelling for every rational being, and where the idea of the validity of judgments is explicitly tied to the idea of an intersubjective agreement among a plurality of sensuous and worldly beings. Given the contextual presuppositions of Kant's notion of aesthetic judgment, however, there remains a gulf between "logical" and aesthetic judgments: the former, whose intersubjective validity springs from concepts, are susceptible to rational argument; the latter, which are not based on definite concepts, are not open to argument, but only to "contention." Now it is this very distinction between conceptual or objective and non-conceptual or subjective general validity, and the corresponding distinction between judgments open to argument or dispute . . . and judgments which are only open to "contention," which might be put into question. Since Arendt, however, did not really question these distinctions, her attempt to take the problematic of political and moral judgment out of the context of Kant's practical philosophy and assimilate it to the problematic of aesthetic judgment, was bound to result in what I would call a *mythology* of judgment; a mythology of judgment, because the faculty of judgment now begins to emerge as the somewhat mysterious faculty to hit upon the truth when there is no context of possible arguments by which truth claims could be redeemed. Of course, Arendt would not speak of "truth" here; however, the word does not matter as long as it is clear that what is at stake is a claim to intersubjective validity; and *this* certainly belongs to the very notion of reflective judgment. Because of presuppositions Arendt shared with Kant, there was no place in her thought for a broader conception of rationality which would have allowed her to tie reflective judgment to rational argument.[118]

Such a broader conception of rationality, Wellmer argues, would allow us to recognize the internal relationship between different kinds of intersubjective validity claims, and their corresponding forms of argumentation, as well as the internal relationship between the different spheres of validity, for example, between the cognitive, the moral, and the aesthetic. Arendt, however, adhered too rigidly to Kant's epistemological framework, in particular, to his monological conception of cognition and his formalistic notion of rationality. As Wellmer says:

As far as moral judgment is concerned, she was too clearly aware that Kant's formal-monological conception of moral judgment cannot work as it stands; and I think she had good reasons to read Kant's conception of reflective judgment back, as it were, into his moral philosophy. But then she stuck to Kant's *monological* concept of cognition and his *formal* conception of rationality, i.e., to the conceptual presuppositions in terms of which Kant's notion of reflective judgment is articulated. Therefore Arendt could not use the notion of reflective judgment to uncover a suppressed dialogical dimension of Kant's conception of practical reason, but only assimilate moral and political judgment to aesthetic judgment. Arendt remains entrapped within an epistemological framework from the perspective of which physical science must appear as the paradigm of knowledge, physical facts as the paradigm of factuality, and logical demonstration as the paradigm of rational argument; correlatively, the activities of thinking and judging must appear as lying outside the sphere of cognition, truth, and rational argument proper.[119]

If, however, we abandon the formal and monological presuppositions of Kantian epistemology, and conceive rationality in terms of the argumentative redemption of validity claims, then, Wellmer maintains,

we can begin to redefine the role of the faculty of judgment, since now a broader conception of rationality will provide us with the missing link between the notion of judgment and the idea of intersubjective agreement . . . If the validity of judgments could be explained in the Habermasian sense by the possibility of a consensus brought about by arguments, then the faculty of judgment would just be the faculty to hit upon what also could be agreed to in a rational consensus; and this faculty would certainly be inexplicable without some internal relationship to an ability to argue and deliberate well.[120]

The faculty of judgment would then lose its mysterious or mythological character; it would just be a faculty

to hit upon the truth in situations where it is not easy to do so, or where – depending on the situation – experience, or character, or imagination, or courage is needed to do so, although the *goodness* of judgment could only prove itself by . . . being confirmed through either experience, or arguments, or – connected with these two – the independent judgment of others.[121]

In this respect, Wellmer concludes, "a well developed faculty of judgment is certainly of immense importance in moral as well as political matters. But it is not an addition to, but rather an expression of what we might call the faculty of discursive rationality."[122]

# Chapter 4

# Hannah Arendt's conception of citizenship

In the preceding chapters I have examined three central themes of Arendt's political philosophy, namely, her conception of modernity, her theory of action, and her reflections on judgment. In this fourth and final chapter I would like to examine her conception of citizenship and to link it to certain issues explored in each of the preceding chapters. Specifically, I would like to frame my discussion of citizenship in relation to the notion of the public sphere, to the idea of political agency and collective identity, and to the question of political culture. Each of these issues has been addressed in the context of larger discussions about modernity, action, and judgment. To briefly recall these discussions, in Chapter 1 we saw that the loss or decline of the public sphere was one of the consequences of world alienation, of that "loss of the world" which for Arendt characterizes the rise of modernity. In Chapter 2 the questions of the identity of the actors, of the constitution of collective identity, and of the capacities for political agency were established to be central to Arendt's theory of action. And lastly, in Chapter 3, we saw that the possibility of reactivating the public capacity for impartial and responsible judgment depended upon the creation and cultivation of political spaces for collective deliberation and on the constitution of an active political culture. It will be my aim, therefore, to articulate Arendt's conception of citizenship around these three issues: (1) the public sphere; (2) political agency and collective identity; and (3) political culture. I hope in this way to show that, notwithstanding certain problematic features of Arendt's political philosophy, many of her insights are worth preserving and can become the basis of a democratic, participatory, and egalitarian conception of citizenship. I shall begin with an examination of the relationship between citizenship and the public sphere.

## CITIZENSHIP AND THE PUBLIC SPHERE

As we saw in Chapter 1, one of the major concerns arising out of Arendt's analysis of modernity was the loss or decline of the public sphere, of that sphere of appearance where *freedom* and *equality* reign, and where individuals as *citizens* interact through the medium of speech and persuasion, disclose their unique identities, and decide through collective deliberation about matters of common concern. The loss of the public sphere is in turn related to that wider phenomenon that Arendt calls the "loss of the world" or *world alienation*. With this term Arendt refers to the loss of a common world of humanly created artifacts, institutions, and settings that separates us from nature and provides a relatively permanent or durable context for our activities. With the loss or erosion of this common world we lose that stable framework from which we partly derive our sense of reality and our conception of personal identity; moreover, we also lose that background of institutions and settings from which a public space for political action and deliberation can arise. For Arendt, therefore, the reactivation of the public sphere, of the sphere within which the activity of citizenship can flourish, depends upon *both* the recovery of a common, shared world (i.e., the overcoming of world alienation), and the creation of numerous spaces of appearance in which individuals can disclose their identities and establish relations of reciprocity and solidarity

Now, if we look at Arendt's definition of the public realm we see that it already articulates these two dimensions, in that it refers both to the *space of appearance* and to the *world we hold in common*. According to the *first* meaning, the public realm is that space where everything that appears

> can be seen and heard by everybody and has the widest possible publicity. For us, appearance — something that is being seen and heard by others as well as by ourselves — constitutes reality. Compared with the reality which comes from being seen and heard, even the greatest forces of intimate life — the passions of the heart, the thoughts of the mind, the delights of the senses — lead an uncertain, shadowy kind of existence unless and until they are transformed, deprivatized and deindividualized, as it were, into a shape to fit them for public appearance . . . Each time we talk about things that can be experienced only in privacy or intimacy, we bring them out into a sphere where they will assume a kind of reality which . . . they never could have had before. The presence of others

who see what we see and hear what we hear assures us of the reality of the world and of ourselves.[1]

Within this space of appearance, therefore, experiences can be shared, actions evaluated, and identities disclosed. Indeed, Arendt maintains that

> since our feeling for reality depends utterly upon appearance and therefore upon the existence of a public realm into which things can appear out of the darkness of sheltered existence, even the twilight which illuminates our private and intimate lives is ultimately derived from the much harsher light of the public realm.[2]

And as she remarked in the preface to *Men in Dark Times*, addressing the question of whether in certain periods of history it is not better to say that "The light of the public obscures everything" (*Das Licht der Oeffentlichkeit verdunkelt alles*):

> If it is the function of the public realm to throw light on the affairs of men by providing a space of appearances in which they can show in deed and word, for better and worse, who they are and what they can do, then darkness has come when this light is extinguished by "credibility gaps" and "invisible government," by speech that does not disclose what is but sweeps it under the carpet, by exhortations, moral and otherwise, that, under the pretext of upholding old truths, degrade all truth to meaningless triviality.[3]

In sum, the public realm as a space of appearance provides the light and the publicity which are necessary for the establishment of our public identities, for the recognition of a common reality, and for the assessment of the actions of others.

For Arendt the space of appearance is created every time individuals gather together politically, which is to say, "wherever men are together in the manner of speech and action," and in this respect it "predates and precedes all formal constitution of the public realm and the various forms of government."[4] It is not restricted to a set of institutions or to a specific location; rather, it comes into existence whenever action is coordinated through speech and persuasion and is oriented toward the attainment of collective goals.

The *second* meaning that Arendt assigns to the public realm, that which supports the space of appearance and provides action with its proper concerns, is the world, or more precisely, the world that we hold in common. This is the world which "is common to all of us and distinguished from our privately owned place in it."[5] It is not identical with the earth or with nature; it is related, rather, "to the human artifact, the fabrication of human hands, as well as to the affairs which go on among those who inhabit the man-made world together."[6] Thus

> to live together in the world means essentially that a world of things is between those who have it in common, as a table is located between those who sit around it; the world, like every in-between, relates and separates men at the same time.[7]

In this respect the public realm, as the common world,

> gathers us together and yet prevents our falling over each other, so to speak. What makes mass society so difficult to bear is not the number of people involved . . . but the fact that the world between them has lost its power to gather them together, to relate and to separate them.[8]

By establishing a space between individuals, an in-between which connects and separates them at the same time, the world provides the physical context within which political action can arise. Moreover, by virtue of its permanence and durability, the world provides the temporal context within which individual lives can unfold and, by being turned into narratives, acquire a measure of immortality. As Arendt writes:

> The common world is what we enter when we are born and what we leave behind when we die. It transcends our life-span into past and future alike; it was there before we came and will outlast our brief sojourn in it. It is what we have in common not only with those who live with us, but also with those who were here before and with those who will come after us. But such a common world can survive the coming and going of the generations only to the extent that it appears in public.[9]

It is this capacity of human artifacts and institutions – that is, the world we have in common – to endure through time and to become the common heritage of successive generations, that enables individuals to feel at home in the world and to transcend, however partially, the fleetingness of their existence.[10] Indeed, without a measure of permanence and durability provided by the world, "life would never be human."[11] "Permanence and durability [are what] human beings need precisely because they are mortals – the most unstable and futile beings we know of."[12] For Arendt, therefore, the transitoriness of life can be overcome by constructing a lasting and stable world that allows for human remembrance and anticipation, that is, for both memory and a measure of trust in the future. As she expressed it:

> Life in its non-biological sense, the span of time each man has between birth and death, manifests itself in action and speech, both of which share with life its essential futility. The "doing of great deeds and the speaking of great words" will leave no trace, no product that might endure after the moment of action and the spoken word has passed . . . [unless] the man-made world of things, the human artifice erected by *homo faber*, becomes a home for mortal men.[13]

It is for this reason, Arendt continues, that

> If the *animal laborans* needs the help of *homo faber* to ease his labor and remove his pain, and if mortals need his help to erect a home on earth, acting and speaking men need the help of *homo faber* in his highest capacity, that is, the help of the artist, of poets and historiographers, of monument-builders and writers, because without them the only product of their activity, the story they enact and tell, would not survive at all.[14]

Human mortality can thus be partly transcended by the durability of the world and the public memory of individuals' deeds. By building and preserving a world that can link one generation to the next and that makes possible forms of collective memory, we are able, in Arendt's words, "to absorb and make shine through the centuries whatever men may want to save from the natural ruin of time."[15]

Arendt's notion of the public realm, then, refers both to a durable common world and to something much more fragile and transitory, the space of appearance which arises every time individuals interact through the medium of speech and persuasion. Arendt emphasizes that the world and the activities that take place in the public sphere are necessary for the constitution of a vibrant political life; moreover, the world and these public activities always stand in need of each other. As she puts it :

> Without being talked about by men and without housing them, the world would not be a human artifice but a heap of unrelated things . . . without the human artifice to house them, human affairs would be as floating, as futile and vain, as the wanderings of nomad tribes. The melancholy wisdom of *Ecclesiastes* – "Vanity of vanities; all is vanity" . . . is certainly unavoidable wherever and whenever trust in

the world as a place fit for human appearance, for action and speech, is gone."[16]

## THE PUBLIC REALM: THREE FEATURES

I would like now to turn to an examination of three features of the public realm and of the sphere of politics that are closely connected to Arendt's conception of citizenship. I will rely for this on an interesting essay by Margaret Canovan entitled "Politics as Culture: Hannah Arendt and the Public Realm," in which she argues that Arendt's conception of the public realm is based on an implicit analogy between politics and culture.[17] For the purpose of exploring Arendt's conception of citizenship, there are three features of the public-political realm identified by Canovan that deserve our attention: first, the artificial or constructed quality of politics and of public life in general; second, its spatial quality; third, the distinction between public and private interests.

### The artificiality of public life

As regards the first feature, Arendt always stressed the artificiality of public life and of political activities in general, the fact that they are man-made and constructed, rather than natural or given. She regarded this artificiality as something to be celebrated rather than deplored. Politics for her was not the result of some natural predisposition, or the realization of the inherent traits of human nature.[18] Rather, it was a cultural achievement of the first order, enabling individuals to transcend the necessities of life and to fashion a world within which free political action and discourse could flourish. It is for this reason, we might note, that Arendt's political philosophy cannot be easily located within the neo-Aristotelian tradition, notwithstanding their common emphasis on the importance of the *vita activa*. Indeed, if we take Michael Oakeshott's distinction between the tradition of political thought based on Reason and Nature and that based on Will and Artifice (characterizing respectively the ancient and the modern conception of politics), it would appear that Arendt fits more easily into the latter, since for her politics was always an artificial creation, a product of action and speech, and not the result of some natural or innate trait shared by all human beings.[19]

The stress on the artificiality of politics has a number of important consequences. For example, Arendt emphasized that the principle of political equality among citizens is not the result of some natural condition that precedes the constitution of the political realm. Political equality for Arendt is not a natural human attribute, nor can it rest on a theory of natural rights; rather, it is an artificial attribute which individuals acquire upon entering the public realm and which is secured by democratic political institutions.[20] As she remarked in *The Origins of Totalitarianism*, those who had been deprived of civil and political rights by the Nazi regime were not able to defend themselves by an appeal to their natural rights; on the contrary, they discovered that, having been excluded from the body politic, they had no rights whatsoever.[21] Political equality and the recognition of one's rights (what Arendt called "a right to have rights") can thus be secured only by membership in a democratic political community.[22]

A further consequence of Arendt's stress on the artificiality of political life is evident in her rejection of all neo-romantic appeals to the *volk* and to ethnic identity as the basis for political community. She maintained that one's ethnic, religious, or racial identity was irrelevant to one's identity as a *citizen*, that it should never be made the basis of membership in a *political* community, and praised the American Constitution for having excluded in principle any connection between one's ethnic or religious identity and one's political status as a citizen.[23] Similarly, at the time of establishment of the state of Israel, she advocated a conception of citizenship based not on race or religion, but on the formal political rights of freedom and equality that would have extended to both Arabs and Jews.[24]

Finally, it is worth pointing out that Arendt's emphasis on the formal qualities of citizenship made her position rather distant from those advocates of participation during the 1960s who saw it in terms of recapturing a sense of intimacy, of community, of warmth, and of authenticity.[25] For Arendt political participation was important because it permitted the establishment of relations of civility and solidarity among citizens. In the essay "On Humanity in Dark Times" she wrote that the search for intimacy is characteristic of those groups excluded from the public realm, as were the Jews during the Nazi period, but that such intimacy is bought at the price of worldlessness, which "is always a form of barbarism."[26] Since they represent "psychological substitutes . . . for the loss of the common, visible world,"[27] the ties of intimacy and warmth can never become political; the only truly political ties are those of civic friendship and solidarity, since they "make political demands and preserve reference to the world."[28] In other words, for Arendt the danger of trying to recapture a sense of intimacy and warmth, of authenticity and communal feelings, is that one loses the public values of impartiality, civic friendship, and solidarity. As Canovan has put it:

> [Arendt's] conception of the public realm is opposed not only to society but also to community: to *Gemeinschaft* as well as to *Gesellschaft*. While greatly valuing warmth, intimacy and natural-ness in private life, she insisted on the importance of a formal, artificial public realm in which what mattered was people's actions rather than their sentiments; in which the natural ties of kinship and intimacy were set aside in favour of a deliberate, impartial solidarity with other citizens; in which there was enough space between people for them to stand back and judge one another coolly and objectively.[29]

## The spatial quality of public life

The second feature stressed by Arendt has to do with the spatial quality of public life, with the fact that political activities are located in a public space where citizens are able to meet one another, to exchange their opinions and debate their differences, and to search for some collective solution to their problems. Politics, in this respect, is a matter of people sharing a common world and a common space of appearance in which public concerns can emerge and be articulated from different perspectives. For politics to occur it is not enough to have a collection of private individuals voting separately and anonymously according to their private opinions.[30] Rather, these individuals must be able to see and talk to one another in public, to meet in a public space so that their differences as well as their commonalities can emerge and become the subject of democratic debate.[31]

This notion of a common public space helps us to understand how political opinions can be formed which are neither reducible to private, idiosyncratic preferences, on the one hand, nor to a unanimous collective opinion, on the other. Arendt herself distrusted the term "public opinion," since it suggested the mindless unanimity of mass society.[32] In her view representative opinions could arise only when citizens actually confronted one another in a public space, so that they could examine an issue from a number of different perspectives, modify their views, and enlarge their standpoint to incorporate that of others.[33] Political opinions, she claimed, can never be formed in private; rather, they are formed, tested, and enlarged only within a public context of argumentation and debate. "Opinions will rise wherever men communicate freely with one another and have the right to make their views public; but these views, in their endless variety, seem to stand also in need of purification and representation."[34] Where an appropriate public space exists (the example chosen by Arendt is the US Senate, at least in its original conception, but we can extend her example to all those spaces of relatively formal and structured debate that are located within civil society), these opinions can be shaped and elaborated into a sophisticated political discourse, rather than remaining the expression of arbitrary preferences or being molded into a unanimous "public opinion."

Another implication of Arendt's stress on the spatial quality of politics has to do with the question of how a collection of distinct individuals can be united to form a political community. For Arendt the unity that may be achieved in a political community is neither the result of religious or ethnic affinity, nor the expression of some common value system. Rather, the unity in question can be attained by sharing a public space and a set of political institutions, and engaging in the practices and activities which are characteristic of that space and those institutions. As Christopher Lasch has remarked in an essay clearly indebted to Arendt, the assumption that "shared values, not political institutions or a common political language, provide the only source of social cohesion . . . represents a radical break from many of the republican principles on which this country was founded."[35] What unites people in a political community is therefore not some set of common values, but the world they set up in common, the spaces they inhabit together, the institutions and practices which they share as citizens. As Canovan puts it, individuals can be united "by the *world* which lies between them. All that is necessary is that they should have amongst them a common political world which they enter as citizens, and which they can hand on to their successors. It is the space between them that unites them, rather than some quality inside each of them,"[36] or some set of common values and beliefs.

A further implication of Arendt's conception of the spatial quality of politics is that since politics is a public activity, one cannot be part of it without in some sense being present in a public space. To be engaged in politics means actively participating in the various public forums where the decisions affecting one's community are taken. Arendt's insistence on the importance of direct participation in politics has sometimes been interpreted to imply that individuals have an existential need for participation which they can only satisfy by engaging in public affairs. This actually represents a misunderstanding of Arendt's commitment to participatory politics, since it is based on what Canovan aptly calls a subjective or *person-centered*, rather than a public or *world-centered*, conception of politics. Although people may engage in political activity to fulfill their needs for involvement and participation, for Arendt it is not so much these personal needs as the *concerns* about the common world that constitute the substance and value of political action. Thus, as Canovan notes,

> while Arendt certainly did maintain that political participation was personally fulfilling, her fundamental argument for it was not only less subjectivist but also more simple . . . it was that, since politics is something that needs a worldly location and can only happen in a public space, then if you are not present in such a space you are simply not engaged in politics.[37]

## Public and private interests

This public or world-centered conception of politics lies also at the basis of Arendt's distinction between public and private interests. According to Arendt, political activity is not a means to an end, but an end in itself; one does not engage in political action simply to promote one's welfare, but to realize the principles intrinsic to political life, such as freedom, equality, justice, solidarity, courage, and excellence. Politics is a world with its own values and ends that are realized in public action and deliberation; it is, as Arendt says, "concerned with the *world as such* and not with those who live in it."[38] In a late essay entitled "Public Rights and Private Interests" she discusses the difference between one's life as an individual and one's life as a citizen, between the life spent on one's own and the life spent in common with others. As she writes:

> Throughout his life man moves constantly in two different orders of existence: he moves within what is his *own* and he also moves in a sphere that is common to him and his fellow men. The "public good," the concerns of the citizen, is indeed the common good because it is located in the *world* which we have in common *without owning it*. Quite frequently, it will be antagonistic to whatever we may deem good to ourselves in our private existence.[39]

What Arendt is claiming is that our *public* interests as citizens are quite distinct from our *private* interests as individuals. The public interest cannot be automatically derived from our private interests: indeed, it is not the sum of private interests, nor their highest common denominator, nor even the total of enlightened self-interests.[40] In fact, it has little to do with our private interests, since it concerns the world that lies beyond the self, that was there before our birth and that will be there after our death, and that finds its embodiment in activities and institutions with their own intrinsic purposes which may be often at odds with our short-term and private interests.[41] As Arendt says, "the self *qua* self cannot reckon in terms of long-range interest, i.e. the interest of a world that survives its inhabitants."[42] The interests of the world are not the interests of individuals: they are the interests of the public realm which we share as citizens and which we can pursue and enjoy only by going beyond our own self-interest. As citizens we share that public realm and participate in its interests: but the interests belong to the public realm, to the realm that we have in common "without owning it," to that realm which transcends our limited life-span and our limited private purposes.

Arendt provides an example of such public interests by examining the activity of serving on a jury. As jurors, the interests we are asked to uphold are the public interests of justice and fairness. These are not the interests of our private selves, nor do they coincide with our enlightened self-interest. They are the interests of a political community that regulates its affairs by means of constitutional laws and procedures. They are *public* interests, transcending and outlasting the private interests that we may have as individuals. Indeed, the fairness and impartiality demanded of the citizens, Arendt notes, "is resisted at every turn by the urgency of one's self-interests, which are always more urgent than the common good."[43] The public interest in impartial justice which we share as jurors may interfere with our private affairs: it often involves inconvenience, and could sometimes involve greater risks, as when one is asked to testify against a group of criminals who have threatened retribution. According to Arendt, the only compensation for the risks and sacrifices demanded by the public interest lies in what she calls the "public happiness" of acting in concert as citizens in the public realm. Indeed, it is only through acting in the public realm and enjoying the freedom and happiness of common deliberation that we are able to discover our public interests and to transcend, when needed, our more limited private interests.[44]

A further illustration of Arendt's distinction between public and private interests is provided by her discussion of the question of civil disobedience. At the time of the protest movement against the Vietnam War and the struggle for Civil Rights for blacks in the 1960s, the legitimacy of civil disobedience was often discussed in terms drawn from exemplary cases of conscience, in particular, Socrates' refusal to escape from prison after being condemned to death by the Athenians, and Thoreau's refusal to pay taxes to a government that tolerated slavery and engaged in an expansionist war against Mexico. Arendt maintained that these examples of action undertaken for the sake of one's conscience were inappropriate to characterize the struggles and protests of the 1960s, since the latter were motivated not by a concern with the integrity of one's conscience, but by a concern with the injustices taking place in the world. Thoreau's stance, as set out in his famous essay "On the Duty of Civil Disobedience," was to avoid being implicated in the actions of the US Government, rather than fighting actively for the abolition of slavery and foreign aggression. "It is not a man's duty" – he writes – "to devote himself to the eradication of any, even the most enormous, wrong; he may still properly have other concerns to engage him; but it is his duty, at least, to wash his hands of it."[45] Thoreau's concern, in other words, was to avoid self-reproach, to avoid being implicated in something he considered wrong, rather than fighting for the redress of injustice. Arendt's comment is the following:

> Here, as elsewhere, conscience is unpolitical. It is not primarily interested in the world where the wrong is committed or in the consequences that the wrong will have for the future course of the world. It does not say, with Jefferson, "I tremble *for my country* when I reflect that God is just; that His justice cannot sleep forever," because it trembles for the individual self and its integrity.[46]

The rules of conscience are unpolitical, they concern the self's integrity and not the integrity of the world. They say: "Beware of doing something that you will not be able to live with."[47] As such, they may be effective during emergencies or when a particular atrocity is being committed, but they cannot serve as political standards; they are too much concerned with the self to serve as a basis for collective action aiming at the redress of injustice in the world.[48] One of the comments Arendt made about Rosa Luxemburg was that she "was very much concerned with the *world* and not at all concerned with herself." She had engaged in political action because "she could not stand the injustice *within the world*." Thus, for Arendt, "the decisive thing is whether your own motivation is clear – for the world – or for yourself, by which I mean for your soul."[49] To be sure, Arendt did not dismiss the role of conscience altogether; in her lecture "Thinking and Moral Considerations" and in *The Life of the Mind* she argued that conscience, as the inner dialogue of me and myself, can prevent individuals from committing or participating in atrocities.[50] Conscience, however, gives no positive prescriptions; it only tells us what *not* to do, what to avoid in our actions and dealings with others; its criterion for action is "whether I shall be able to live with myself in peace when the time has come to think about my deeds and words."[51] It is not something that can be taken for granted — many people lack it or are unable to feel self-reproach. It cannot be generalized — what I cannot live with may not bother another person's conscience, with the result that one person's conscience will stand against another person's conscience. And, as we have seen, it directs attention to the self rather than to the world. The counsels of conscience are therefore unpolitical. They can only be expressed in purely individual, subjective form. As Arendt writes :

> When Socrates stated that "it is better to suffer wrong than to to do wrong," he clearly meant that it was better *for him*, just as it was better for him "to be in disagreement with multitudes than, being one, to be in disagreement with himself." Politically, on the contrary, what counts is that a wrong has been done.[52]

In sum, for Arendt there was a clear distinction to be made between the private, unpolitical stand of conscience and the public, political stance of actively caring for the affairs of the political community. Those who struggled for the extension of civil rights and the termination of the war in Vietnam were not trying to save their conscience; rather, they were struggling to improve their polity, to establish standards of universal justice and respect for national self-determination. They were acting as citizens rather than as individuals concerned with their own private integrity.[53]

Before closing this section, it is worth noting that Arendt's conception of the public interest escapes the traditional dichotomy between individualism and collectivism, and helps us to find a way out of the debate between liberals and communitarians on the issue of the "common good." Her conception of the public interest does not in fact reduce it either to the sum of individual preferences or to the idea of an undifferentiated common good. Since *plurality* is considered by her as the political principle *par excellence*, the good that a community tries to attain is always a *plural* good, that is, a good that reflects both the differences among persons, that is, their distinct interests and opinions, and the commonality that binds them together as citizens, that is, the solidarity and reciprocity they cultivate as political equals. When individuals come together to discuss and decide matters of public concern, they bring with them their own distinct views and opinions which are shaped and transformed, tested and enlarged in the encounter, but which are never eliminated nor transfigured into a unanimous agreement. The substantive common interest is only discovered through mutual persuasion and debate, but as Pitkin and Shumer point out, "it remains contested as much as shared."[54] The public interest of the citizens can thus only arise in a context of political argumentation and collective deliberation, where there is room for disagreement on what the interests of the community actually are. There is no vision of the common good or of a General Will to which individuals have to subscribe; what unites the citizens is instead their common world and their willingness to create a political space where their differences can be articulated, contested, and hopefully resolved in a democratic fashion.[55]

## THE PUBLIC SPHERE: DRAMATIC SETTING OR DISCURSIVE SPACE?

Our discussion so far of Arendt's conception of citizenship has focused on a number of issues. The first was the notion of the public realm, which comprises both the sphere of appearance and the durable world we hold in common. We saw in this context that for Arendt the reactivation of the public realm, of the realm within which the activity of citizenship can flourish, depends upon *both* the recovery of a common, shared world (i.e., the overcoming of world alienation), and the creation of numerous spaces of appearance in which individuals can disclose their identities and establish relations of reciprocity and solidarity. In the second place, we have examined three features of the public-political realm which have a number of important implications for Arendt's conception of citizenship: (1) its artificiality; (2) its spatial quality; and (3) the distinction between public and private interests. In this section I would like to focus on an unresolved tension at the heart of Arendt's political theory, a tension which finds expression in two opposing conceptions of the public-political sphere and in two distinct conceptions of citizenship. Let us look first at the two conceptions of the public-political sphere.

According to the first conception, the public sphere is a *dramatic setting* for the performance of noble and courageous deeds and the utterance of memorable words, that is to say, for the display of the excellence of political actors. Here action is viewed in terms of an expressive model, as the disclosure of one's unique identity and the recognition of one's distinctive qualities. According to the second conception, the public sphere is a *discursive space* that arises whenever people act together in concert, establish relations of equality and solidarity, and engage in processes of collective deliberation mediated by speech and persuasion. Here action is viewed in terms of a communicative model, that is, in terms of the consensual generation and testing of the norms of social interaction.[56]

Arendt was never able to resolve the tension between these two conceptions of the public sphere, and the reason for this, I would argue, lies in the fundamental duality of her theory of action. As we saw in Chapter 2, Arendt articulated her theory of action along two dimensions, an *expressive* and a *communicative* one, and was never able to integrate the two in a satisfactory manner. According to the first conception, action is that mode of human activity in which individuals are able to disclose their unique identities, their distinctive "who" as against their shared "what," and to overcome the futility and mortality of their lives through the performance of exemplary deeds. Both the disclosure of one's identity and the attainment of earthly immortality depend, in turn, upon a community of interpreters who are able to ascertain and to preserve for posterity the unique identity of the actors.[57] Although a communicative dimension is present in this conception of action, it is clear that the emphasis is on the expressive dimension, that is, on the articulation and confirmation of the unique qualities and capacities of actors. On the other hand, Arendt elaborated a conception of action as a mode of human togetherness in which individuals are able to establish relations of reciprocity and solidarity. In this conception what matters is not so much the uniqueness of the self, or the overcoming of one's mortality, but the establishment of communicative relations based on mutuality, symmetry, and per-suasion. Here action is characterized by the "sharing of words and deeds," by processes of collective deliberation and mutual accom-modation, rather than by the striving for glory and immortality.[58]

My argument, then, is that Arendt's theory of action was developed along two distinct dimensions, an expressive and a communicative one, and that her inability to integrate the two lies at the basis of her two opposing conceptions of the public sphere. When action is conceptualized in terms of an expressive model, the public sphere is viewed as a dramatic setting where actors compete for recognition and glory; conversely, when action is conceptualized in terms of a communicative model, the public sphere is viewed as a discursive space of action and unconstrained deliberation for the establishment of relations of mutuality and solidarity.[59]

The tension between these two models of action can, in turn, be related to two distinct conceptions of citizenship. As Peter Fuss and Bhikhu Parekh have pointed out, Arendt oscillated between an agonal or heroic conception of citizenship, and an accommodational or participatory one. These two conceptions correspond rather closely to the opposition between the expressive and the communicative models of action. According to Fuss, when Arendt looked back to the Greek *polis*, and particularly to the Athens portrayed by Pericles' Speech, she articulated the *agonal* conception; on the other hand, when she turned to the American Revolution, she praised its institutionalization of the arts of *persuasion* and *accommodation*. In his view, Arendt's works published after *The Human Condition* have tended to accentuate the latter conception; in this respect, he writes,

> her laudatory assessment of the roots of the American political experience in *On Revolution* is, in the final analysis, a tribute to a politics of persuasion and mutual accommodation, rather than to a *polis* dedicated to the manifestation of individual excellence.[60]

Similarly, Parekh has argued that Arendt in *The Human Condition* formulated a *heroic* view of citizenship, while in her subsequent writings she developed a more realistic *participatory* view. In these later writings, he says, Arendt

> argues that politics . . . involves cooperation rather than contest and that a "politically minded" citizen is motivated by *amor mundi* rather than a desire to express his individuality and attain glory. She justifies political participation and the political way of life not in terms of glory and historical immortality, but [in terms of] public freedom and happiness. Not surprisingly, she takes persuasion to be the paradigmatic form of political speech, emphasizes the "relativity" of opinion, insists on the importance of compromise and consensus, and explores new institutions upon which a participatory community could be constructed.[61]

Both Fuss and Parekh suggest ways of reconciling these two conceptions of citizenship. For Fuss it is a question of reconciling its substantive and its procedural dimensions: citizenship is substantially the taking of personal initiatives which are "individually enacted and plurally responded to," and procedurally the persuasion and accommodation required in the decision-making process with respect to the best way to preserve the substance of those initiatives.[62] For Parekh it is a question of recognizing the connection between the participatory and the heroic conceptions, in the sense that "participatory politics creates and sustains the climate necessary for heroic politics, and the latter inspires and encourages men to take active interest in public life."[63] Both Fuss and Parekh, however, recognize that Arendt failed in the end to integrate these two conceptions of citizenship, a failure which I have argued can be traced back to the tension in Arendt's theory between an expressive and a communicative model of action.

## CITIZENSHIP, AGENCY, AND COLLECTIVE IDENTITY

In the light of the preceding discussion, I would like now to turn to an examination of the connection between Arendt's conception of citizenship and the questions of political agency and collective identity. As we have seen, Arendt oscillated between a heroic and a participatory conception of citizenship, and was unable to integrate these two conceptions because of the fundamental duality of her theory of action. My aim in what follows is not to argue that the tension between the two conceptions of citizenship, or between the two models of action, can be resolved; rather, I wish to argue that Arendt's participatory conception of citizenship and her communicative model of action provide the best starting points for addressing both the question of the constitution of collective identity and that concerning the conditions for the exercise of effective political agency.

### Citizenship and collective identity

Let us then examine first the question of collective identity. In her book *Wittgenstein and Justice* Hanna Pitkin argues that one of the crucial questions at stake in political discourse is the creation of a collective identity, a "we" to which we can appeal when faced with the problem of deciding among alternative courses of action. In addressing the question "What shall we do?" the "we," she notes, is not given but must be constantly negotiated. Indeed, since in political discourse there is always disagreement about the possible courses of action, the identity of the "we" that is going to be created through a specific form of collective action becomes the central question. As Pitkin puts it:

> In political discourse's problem of "what shall we do?" the "we" is
> always called into question. Part of the issue becomes, if we pursue

this or that course of action open to us, who could affirm it, who could regard it as done in his name? Who will still be with "us" if "we" take this course of action?[64]

Thus "Part of the knowledge revealed in political discourse is the scope and validity of the claim entered in saying 'we': i.e., who turns out to be willing and able to endorse that claim."[65] Whenever we engage in action and political discourse we are thereby also engaging in the constitution of our collective identity, in the creation of a "we" with which we are able to identify both ourselves and our actions. This process of identity-construction is never given once and for all, and is never unproblematic. Rather, it is a process of constant renegotiation and struggle, a process in which actors articulate and defend competing conceptions of cultural and political identity, and competing conceptions of political legitimacy. As Habermas has noted, if a collective identity emerges in complex societies,

> its form would be an identity, non-prejudiced in its content and independent of particular organizational types, of the community of those who engage in the *discursive* and *experimental* formation of an identity-related knowledge on the basis of a critical appropriation of tradition, as well as of the inputs from science, philosophy and the arts."[66]

In political terms this means that a collective identity under modern conditions can arise out of a process of public argumentation and debate in which competing ideals of identity and political legitimacy are articulated, contested, and refined.[67] From this standpoint, Arendt's participatory conception of citizenship assumes a particular relevance, since it articulates the conditions for the establishment of collective identities. I would argue, in fact, that once citizenship is viewed as the process of active deliberation about competing identity projections, its value would reside in the possibility of establishing forms of collective identity that can be acknowledged, tested, and transformed in a discursive and democratic fashion.

Such a conception of citizenship would also be able to articulate what Nancy Fraser has called "the standpoint of the *collective concrete other*." By this term Fraser refers to the standpoint from which specific collective identities are constructed on the basis of the specific narrative resources and vocabularies of particular groups, such as women, blacks, and members of oppressed classes. The standpoint of the collective concrete other, Fraser writes, focuses on "the specificity of the vocabularies available to individuals and groups for the interpretation of their needs and for the definitions of situations in which they encounter one another." It would also focus on the "specificity of the narrative resources available to individuals and groups for the construction of individual life-stories [and of] group identities and solidarities."[68] From such a standpoint people are encountered

> less as unique individuals than as members of groups or collect-
> ivities with culturally specific identities, solidarities and forms of life
> . . . here one would abstract *both* from unique individuality *and* from
> universal humanity to focalize the intermediate zone of group
> identity.[69]

The norms that would govern the interactions among such groups or collectivities would be "neither norms of intimacy such as love and care, nor those of formal institutions such as rights and entitlements. Rather, they would be norms of collective solidarities as expressed in shared but non-universal social practices."[70] The value of autonomy could then be formulated in terms that would not pit it against solidarity; rather, to be autonomous would mean

> to be a member of a group or groups which have achieved a degree
> of collective control over the means of interpretation and
> communication sufficient to enable one to participate on a par with
> members of other groups in moral and political deliberation."[71]

The achievement of autonomy could then be considered as one of the conditions necessary to the establishment of relations of equality, mutuality, and solidarity.

This formulation of the norms and values of citizenship from the standpoint of the "collective concrete other" can be interpreted in my view as a fruitful extension of many of the themes articulated by Arendt's participatory conception of citizenship. The stress on *solidarity* rather than on care or compassion, on *respect* rather on love or sympathy, and on *autonomy* as a precondition of solidarity, seems to express the same concerns that animated Arendt's conception of citizenship.[72] Indeed, as Fraser remarks, an ethic of solidarity elaborated from the standpoint of the collective concrete other

> is superior to an ethic of care as a *political* ethic. It is the sort of ethic
> which is attuned to the contestatory activities of social movements
> struggling to forge narrative resources and vocabularies adequate
> to the expression of their self-interpreted needs. It is attuned also to
> collective struggles to deconstruct narrative forms and vocabularies

of dominant groups and collectivities so as to show these are partial rather than genuinely shared, and are incapable of giving voice to the needs and hopes of subordinated groups. In short, an ethic of solidarity elaborated from the standpoint of the collective concrete other is more appropriate than an ethic of care for a feminist ethic, if we think of a feminist ethic as the ethic of a *social and political movement*.[73]

In this respect, Fraser concludes, an ethic of solidarity is "just as appropriate as a *political* ethic for movements of lesbians, gays, blacks, hispanics, other people of color and subordinated classes."[74] An ethic of solidarity is therefore not the prerogative of any specific group; rather, it is an ethic that can develop out of the struggles of all those groups who have been silenced or marginalized in the past, and who are now attempting to articulate new conceptions of cultural and political identity.[75]

Before closing this section, I would like to mention one of the most interesting attempts to demonstrate the connection between citizenship and the construction of collective identity. In the article "On the Rationality of Democratic Choice,"[76] and subsequently in an essay entitled "Some Other Kind of Otherness,"[77] Alessandro Pizzorno has developed a number of arguments to show that political action and discourse cannot be explained in terms of a logic of *utility*, that is, in terms of the maximization of individual interests, but only in terms of a logic of *identity*, that is, as activities whose principal objective is the constitution of collective identities. In order to substantiate this claim Pizzorno first examines the argument made by neo-utilitarian theorists that political action can be explained as the outcome of the rational pursuit of individual interests. "In order to evaluate his own interest in a certain objective," he writes,

the subject has to assume that his criteria of evaluation (or, in the language of economics, the order of his preferences) will be identical when he appraises the costs and when he enjoys the benefits. This is plausible either if the two moments are simultaneous, or if there exists a conversion formula to determine their worth (which, in economics, is money) that is relatively constant or whose variations can be predicted. In other words, the subject has to assume his own identity through time – but after Hume there can be no doubt that this is logically impossible on the basis of what is given solely to the individual. The identity of an individual can only be secured through a process of identification with other individuals (a group, a public, a collective entity, a system of relations). In order to evaluate interests — that is, to calculate costs and benefits — the calculating subject has to be assured of an *identifying collectivity*. From this he will obtain the criteria that allow him to define interests — the criteria, in other words, that permit him to give meaning to actions. It follows, therefore, that a comprehensive theory of politics must be able to give an account of the activity that establishes identifying collectivities; in effect, an account of politics.[78]

Pizzorno then goes on to provide a number of examples, such as voting, the relation between citizens and their representatives, and the competition betwen political parties, and shows that in each case they can be explained as activities directed at the establishment of collective identities, rather than as purely instrumental or utilitarian activities. In the case of voting he shows that it is an act of collective identification, a way to demonstrate one's membership in the political community, and to a particular collectivity within that community. In the case of the relation between citizens and their political representatives, Pizzorno argues that it cannot be explained in terms of the expected utility that will flow to the citizens from the actions of their representatives. This explanation assumes that the role of the politician is merely to *re-present* interests, and that these interests are already formed before the politician is able to articulate them. "In reality," Pizzorno notes, "political action . . . is aimed at defining and continually redefining interests."[79] The major function of politics is, in fact, "to define the long-term interests and in so doing to construct a collective identity."[80] As he puts it:

> The definition of long-term interest itself is the work of a social process in which the individual participates, always with others, in a way more or less conscious and active, throughout his life . . . It is an open-ended process and certainly it involves politics in any case; or, better, that aspect of political activity that we have defined as constitutive of collective identity — from which come long-term interests.[81]

In stressing the constitutive function of politics Pizzorno does not belittle or overlook its more instrumental or utilitarian functions. He recognizes that politics comprises both, that to some extent they are complementary, but argues, nonetheless, that

> one can speak of a pre-eminence of identification over instrumentality. A group with strong identification can last a long time

even if it doesn't gain power or achieve victory in confrontations with its adversaries. (Think of the socialist and communist parties for long periods of their history.) The inverse situation isn't imaginable: How can power be conquered without identification? For whom? We seem to be drawing nearer to the possibility of an administrative government, but this is illusory. If this does occur, it will only mean collective identification with the state.[82]

The last example discussed by Pizzorno is that of party competition. Utilitarian theories of politics maintain that the presence of conflicting parties allows citizens to choose the better policy, defined as the one more likely to procure their utility. According to a theory of identification, however, "party competition in democratic governments isn't over who has the best policies, but is used, instead, to strengthen collective identities."[83] Pizzorno elaborates this point as follows:

If it is characteristic of politics to define the long-term interests and in so doing to construct a collective identity, why isn't this function wholly assumed by the national collectivity, that is, by the state? In certain cases this is exactly what happens, but not in democratic-liberal states. Why? The traditional answer is that, in the latter, there exist social forces – essentially those based on private property and religion – that were not compatible with the individual's complete identification with the state. But if this were the whole story, it would follow that the political parties would have to represent economic and religious interests, which they do not. Even when there might be a partial correspondence with these interests, a party, in its discourse and even more in its decisions, will never be the simple expression of certain interests. The political collective identity, as we have seen, doesn't simply gather pre-existing social interests; it selects them, it molds them, it invents them, it ignores them."[84]

The conclusion to Pizzorno's arguments is that a theory based on the logic of identity provides a much better explanation of political action than a theory based on the logic of utility. This identity-based theory is not presented as a symmetrical alternative to a theory based on utility. Rather, it explains

in a consistent manner facts that the other theory cannot, and it describes in a generalizable manner the citizen's motivation and that of the politician. Both those who vote and those who struggle for political power aim . . . at securing for themselves recognition by a collective identity.[85]

Indeed, from the standpoint of such a theory, one is able to appreciate how,

by means of discourse, the inducement of trust, persuasion, and conversion, and finally by decisions of the authorities, political action mobilizes, constructs new identities, and binds individuals together, in ways strong or tenuous, long-lasting or fleeting.[86]

## Citizenship and political agency

The foregoing discussion has stressed the importance that political action and discourse have for the constitution of collective identities. In this section I would like to focus on a related theme, namely, the connection between political action, understood as the active engagement of citizens in the public realm, and the exercise of effective political agency. This connection represents in my view one of the central contributions of Arendt's theory of action, and underlies what I have called her "participatory" conception of citizenship. According to Arendt, the active engagement of citizens in the determination of the affairs of their community provides them not only with the experience of public freedom and the joys of public happiness, but also with a sense of *political agency and efficacy*, the sense, in Jefferson's phrase, of being "participators in government." The importance of participation for political agency and efficacy is brought out clearly in the following passage from *On Revolution*. Commenting on Jefferson's proposal to institute a system of wards or local councils in which citizens would be able to have an effective share in political power, Arendt remarks that:

Jefferson called every government degenerate in which all powers were concentrated "in the hands of the one, the few, the well-born or the many." Hence, the ward system was not meant to strengthen the power of the many but the power of *"every one"* within the limits of his competence; and only by breaking up "the many" into assemblies where *every one* could count and be counted upon "shall we be as republican as a large society can be." In terms of the safety of the citizens of the republic, the question was how to make everybody feel "that he is a *participator* in the government of affairs, not merely at an election one day in the year, but every day."[87]

In Arendt's view only the sharing of power that comes from civic engagement and common deliberation can provide each citizen with a sense of effective political agency. Arendt's strictures against representation must be understood in this light. She saw representation as a substitute for the direct involvement of the citizens, and as a means whereby the distinction between rulers and ruled could reassert itself. When representation becomes the substitute for direct democracy, the citizens can exercise their powers of political agency only at election day, and their capacities for deliberation and political insight are correspondingly weakened. Moreover, by encouraging the formation of a political elite, representation means that

> the age-old distinction between ruler and ruled ... has asserted itself again; once more, the people are not admitted to the public realm, once more the business of government has become the privilege of the few, who alone may "exercise their virtuous dispositions" ... The result is that the people must either sink into lethargy ... or preserve the spirit of resistance to whatever government they have elected, since the only power they retain is the "reserve power of revolution."[88]

As an alternative to a system of representation based on bureaucratic parties and state structures, Arendt proposed a federated system of councils where citizens could be actively engaged at various levels in the determination of their affairs. I have already examined the limits of this proposal in Chapter 2, and will not repeat the objections raised there.[89] The relevance of Arendt's proposal for direct democracy lies, rather, in the connection it establishes between *active citizenship* and *effective political agency*. It is only by means of direct political participation, by engaging in common action and in public deliberation, that citizenship can be reaffirmed and political agency effectively exercised. As Pitkin and Shumer have remarked,

> even the most oppressed people sometimes rediscover within themselves the capacity to act. Democrats today must seek out and foster every opportunity for people to experience their own *effective agency* ... dependency and apathy must be attacked wherever people's experience centers. Yet such attacks remain incomplete unless they relate personal concerns to public issues, extend individual initiative into shared political action.[90]

In a similar vein, Sara Evans and Harry Boyte have highlighted the ways in which the dispossessed and powerless have again and again sought simultaneously to revive and remember older notions of democratic participation . . . and . . . given them new and deeper meanings and applications. Democracy, in these terms, means more than changing structures so as to make democracy possible. It means, also, schooling citizens in *citizenship* – that is, in the varied skills and values which are essential to sustaining effective participation.[91]

Viewed in this light, Arendt's conception of participatory democracy represents an attempt to reactivate the experience of citizenship and to articulate the conditions for the exercise of effective political agency. It is worth noting, moreover, that such conception does not imply value homogeneity or value consensus, nor does it require the de-differentiation of social spheres. Insofar as Arendt's participatory conception is based on the principle of *plurality*, it does not aim at the recovery or revitalization of some coherent value scheme, nor at the reintegration of different social spheres. As Benhabib has noted, on Arendt's participatory conception,

the public sentiment which is encouraged is not reconciliation and harmony, but rather *political agency and efficacy*, namely, the sense that we have a say in the economic, political, and civic arrangements which define our lives together, and that what one does makes a difference. This can be achieved without value homogeneity among individuals, and without collapsing the various spheres into one another.[92]

Arendt's conception of participatory democracy does not, therefore, aim at value integration or at the de-differentiation of social spheres; rather, it aims at reactivating the conditions for active citizenship and democratic self-determination. As she put it in a passage of *On Revolution*:

If the ultimate end of the Revolution was freedom and the constitution of a public space where freedom could appear . . . then the elementary republics of the wards, the only tangible place where everyone could be free, actually were the end of the great republic . . . The basic assumption of the ward system, whether Jefferson knew it or not, was that no one could be called happy without his share in public business, that no one could be called free without his experience in public freedom, and that no one could be called either happy or free without participating and having a share in public power.[93]

## CITIZENSHIP AND POLITICAL CULTURE

The foregoing discussion has articulated Arendt's conception of citizenship around the issues of political agency and collective identity. In this last section I would like to explore the connection between Arendt's conception of participatory citizenship and the constitution of an active and democratic political culture. In her book *On Revolution* and in two essays contained in *Between Past and Future*[94] Arendt claimed that the possibility of reactivating the political capacity for impartial and responsible judgment depended upon the creation of public spaces for collective deliberation in which citizens could test and enlarge their opinions. As Arendt puts it:

> Opinions will rise wherever men communicate freely with one another and have the right to make their views public; but these views in their endless variety seem to stand also in need of purification and representation ... Even though opinions are formed by individuals and must remain, as it were, their property, no single individual . . . can ever be equal to the task of sifting opinions, of passing them through the sieve of an intelligence which will separate the arbitrary and the merely idiosyncratic, and thus purify them into public views.[95]

Where an appropriate public space exists, these opinions can in fact be tested, enlarged, and transformed through a process of democratic debate and enlightenment. Democratic debate is indeed crucial to the formation of opinions that can claim more than subjective validity; individuals may hold personal opinions on many subject matters, but they can form *representative* opinions only by enlarging their standpoint to incorporate those of others. In the words of Arendt:

> Political thought is representative. I form an opinion by considering a given issue from different viewpoints, by making present to my mind the standpoints of those who are absent; that is, I represent them . . . The more people's standpoints I have present in my mind while I am pondering a given issue, and the better I can imagine how I would feel and think if I were in their place, the stronger will be my capacity for representative thinking and the more valid my final conclusions, my opinion.[96]

The capacity to form valid opinions requires therefore a public space where individuals can test and purify their views through a process of public argumentation and debate. The same holds true for the formation of valid judgments: as "the most political of man's mental abilities,"[97] judgment can only be exercised and tested in public, in the free and open exchange of opinions in the public sphere. As Arendt says, judgment

> cannot function in strict isolation or solitude; it needs the presence of others "in whose place" it must think, whose perspectives it must take into consideration, and without whom it never has the opportunity to operate at all. As logic, to be sound, depends on the presence of the self, so judgment, to be valid, depends on the presence of others.[98]

As in the case of opinion, the validity of judgment depends on the ability to think "representatively," that is, from the standpoint of everyone else, so that we are able to look at the world from a number of different perspectives. And this ability, in turn, can only be acquired and tested in a public setting where individuals have the opportunity to exchange their opinions and to articulate their differences through democratic discourse. As Benhabib has put it:

> To think from the standpoint of everyone else entails sharing a public culture such that everyone else can articulate indeed what they think and what their perspectives are. The cultivation of one's moral imagination flourishes in such a culture in which the self-centered perspective of the individual is constantly challenged by the multiplicity and diversity of perspectives that constitute public life.[99]

In this respect, she argues, the cultivation of enlarged thought "politically requires the creation of institutions and practices whereby the voice and the perspective of others, often unknown to us, can become expressed in their own right."[100] The creation and cultivation of a public culture of democratic citizenship that guarantees to everyone the right to opinion and action is therefore essential to the flourishing of the capacity to articulate and acknowledge the perspectives of others.

## CONCLUSION

In this chapter I have argued that Arendt's conception of citizenship can be articulated around three major themes, namely, the public sphere, political agency and collective identity, and political culture.

With respect to the first theme, after having analyzed Arendt's understanding of the public sphere, I highlighted three of its major features: its artificial or constructed quality, its spatiality, and the distinction between public and private interests. I then examined the tension at the heart of Arendt's political theory between a dramaturgical and a discursive conception of the public sphere, and showed its connection to the fundamental duality of her theory of action. I argued that insofar as Arendt never integrated the expressive and the communicative models of action in her theory, she was bound to present two distinct and opposed conceptions of the public sphere, and to articulate two opposed conceptions of citizenship.

With respect to the second theme, I argued that Arendt's participatory conception of citizenship provides the best starting point for addressing both the question of the constitution of collective identity and that concerning the conditions for the exercise of effective political agency. I drew for this purpose on the writings of Pitkin, Habermas, Fraser, and Pizzorno, and showed the connection between the practice of citizenship and the constitution of collective identities. I then examined Arendt's conception of participatory democracy and stressed the links between active citizenship and effective political agency. I also argued that Arendt's conception of participatory democracy does not imply value homogeneity or the de-differentiation of social spheres.

Finally, with respect to the third theme, I explored the connection between citizenship and political culture, and argued that the ability of citizens to enlarge their opinions and to test their judgments can only flourish in a public culture of democratic participation that guarantees to everyone the right to opinion and action.

# Notes

The following abbreviations of Hannah Arendt's writings will be used:

BPF:    *Between Past and Future*, New York: Viking Press, 1968.
CR:     *Crises of the Republic*, New York: Harcourt Brace Jovanovich, 1972.
HC:     *The Human Condition*, Chicago: The University of Chicago Press, 1958.
LKPP:   *Lectures on Kant's Political Philosophy*, ed. R. Beiner, Chicago: The University of Chicago Press, 1982.
LM:     *The Life of the Mind*; vol. 1, *Thinking*; vol. 2, *Willing*, New York: Harcourt Brace Jovanovich, 1978.
MDT:    *Men in Dark Times*, New York: Harcourt Brace Jovanovich, 1968.
OR:     *On Revolution*, New York: Viking Press, 1965.
OT:     *The Origins of Totalitarianism*, New York: Harcourt Brace Jovanovich, 1973.
RPW:    *Hannah Arendt: The Recovery of the Public World*, ed. M. A. Hill, New York: St Martin's Press, 1979.

## 1 Hannah Arendt's conception of modernity

1 M. Riedel, "Hegels Begriff der burgerlichen Gesellschaft und das Problem seines geschichtlichen Ursprungs," in *Materialien zu Hegels Rechtsphilosophie*, Frankfurt: Suhrkamp, 1974, pp. 247 ff.
2 Cf. Marx's criticism of the opposition between abstract citizen and bourgeois man, of concrete and abstract labor, of use value and exchange value, and Tönnies' distinction of *Gemeinschaft* and *Gesellschaft*, of organic face-to-face community and artificial contractual association. K. Marx, *Early Writings*, Harmondsworth: Penguin Books, 1975; F. Tönnies, *Community and Association*, London: Routledge & Kegan Paul, 1963.
3 J. Habermas, *The Philosophical Discourse of Modernity*, trans. F. G. Lawrence, Cambridge, Mass.: MIT Press, 1987, p. 43.
4 ibid., p. 41.
5 ibid., p. 20.
6 M. Weber, "Science as a Vocation", in *From Max Weber*, trans. and ed. H. H. Gerth and C. W. Mills, London: Routledge & Kegan Paul, 1948, p. 155.

7  M. Weber, "Objectivity in Social Science and Social Policy," in *The Methodology of the Social Sciences*, trans. and ed. E. A. Shils and H. A. Finch, New York: Free Press, 1949, p. 57.

8  M. Weber, *The Protestant Ethic and the Spirit of Capitalism*, trans. T. Parsons, London: George Allen & Unwin, 1976, pp. 181–2.

9  M. Weber, "Politics as a Vocation," in *From Max Weber*, op. cit., p. 120.

10  See S. Benhabib, "Modernity and the Aporias of Critical Theory," *Telos*, 49, Fall 1981, pp. 39–49.

11  Cf. J. Habermas, *Communication and the Evolution of Society*, Boston: Beacon Press, 1979, chaps 3 and 4; *The Theory of Communicative Action*, vol. I, Boston: Beacon Press, 1984, chap. 2.

12  Cf. Habermas, *The Theory of Communicative Action*, vol. II, Boston: Beacon Press, 1987, chap. 6.

13  Cf. Habermas, *The Philosophical Discourse of Modernity*, op. cit.

14  Cf. J. Habermas, "The Dialectics of Rationalization: An Interview," *Telos* 49, Fall 1981, p. 28; "Modernity versus Postmodernity," *New German Critique* 22, Winter 1981, pp. 11–13.

15  See *LKPP*, pp. 3–85; *BPF*, pp. 219–26, 227–64; Cf. J. Habermas, "Hannah Arendt's Communications Concept of Power," *Social Research*, vol. 44, no. 1, 1977.

16  Cf. J. Habermas, "Consciousness-Raising or Redemptive Criticism – The Contemporaneity of Walter Benjamin," *New German Critique* 17, Spring 1979.

17  This distinction between future-oriented fulfillment and past-oriented redemption is indebted to Seyla Benhabib's distinction of the poles of *norm* and *utopia*, of fulfillment and transfiguration, within which the discourse of Critical Theory has unfolded. Fulfillment refers to the idea that the society of the future executes and carries out the unfinished task of the present, without necessarily forging new imaginative constellations out of its cultural heritage. Transfiguration, by contrast, means that the future envisaged by a theory entails a radical rupture with the present, and that in such a rupture a new and imaginative constellation of the values and meanings of the present takes place. Habermas' future-oriented thinking belongs more to the normative pole of the distinction, in the sense that it operates on the assumption that modernity is an incomplete project in need of fulfillment. Arendt's past-oriented thinking, by contrast, would appear to belong to the utopian pole, to the idea that the redemption of modernity requires a transfiguration of its cultural heritage. In the case of Arendt, however, the redemption of modernity is made possible by a critical reappropriation of the past, by a rescuing of its forgotten treasures, rather than by a radical rupture with the present constellation of values. The importance of memory and of the narrative recollection of the past (cf. Arendt's essay on Isak Dinesen in *MDT*, pp. 95–109) precludes the clear location of Arendt on the utopian side of Benhabib's distinction. See S. Benhabib, *Critique, Norm, and Utopia*, New York: Columbia University Press, 1986, pp. 327 ff.

18  *LM, Thinking*, p. 212.

19  *BPF*, p. 5.

20  *BPF*, p. 13.

21  *BPF*, p. 5.

22 *OT*, p. ix.
23 *OT*, p. viii.
24 *RPW*, p. 336.
25 "Thinking Without a Ground: Hannah Arendt and the Contemporary Situation of Understanding," in *RPW*, pp. 214–15.
26 *MDT*, pp. 205–6.
27 Arendt recalls a memorable phrase of Tocqueville – "The past has ceased to throw its light onto the future, and the mind of man wanders in darkness" – to highlight the importance of a critical reappropriation of the past. See *RPW*, p. 337.
28 Cf. W. Benjamin, "Theses on the Philosophy of History," in *Illuminations*, New York: Harcourt Brace Jovanovich, 1968, p. 255:

   To articulate the past historically does not mean to recognize it "the way it really was" (Ranke). It means to seize hold of a memory as it flashes up at a moment of danger . . . Only that historian will have the gift of fanning the spark of hope in the past who is firmly convinced that *even the dead* will not be safe from the enemy if he wins. And this enemy has not ceased to be victorious.

29 Cf. M. Bakan, "Hannah Arendt's Critical Appropriation of Heidegger's Thought as Political Philosophy," in D. Ihde and H. J. Silverman (eds), *Descriptions*, New York: SUNY Press, 1985, pp. 224–47; *idem*, "Arendt and Heidegger: The Episodic Intertwining of Life and Work," *Philosophy and Social Criticism*, vol. 12, no. 1, 1987, pp. 71–98.
30 Cf. M. Heidegger, *Being and Time*, New York: Harper & Row, 1962, pp. 43–4.
31 H. Arendt, "Martin Heidegger at Eighty," in M. Murray (ed.), *Heidegger and Modern Philosophy*, New Haven: Yale University Press, 1978, p. 296.
32 M. Heidegger, *Being and Time*, op. cit., p. 44.
33 *MDT*, p. 201.
34 H. Arendt, "Martin Heidegger at Eighty," op. cit., p. 295.
35 *BPF*, p. 94.
36 *BPF*, pp. 28–9; cf. *BPF*, p. 204:

   And the task of preserving the past without the help of tradition, and often even against traditional standards and interpretations, is the same for the whole of Western civilization. Intellectually, though not socially, America and Europe are in the same situation: the thread of tradition is broken, and we must discover the past for ourselves – that is, read its authors as though nobody had ever read them before.

37 In her last book Arendt provides some fruitful insights as to how this standpoint could be reconstituted. In her view the activity of thought and the exercise of judgment can re-establish a link between the past and the future, the former by operating in the *nunc stans* of the present, the latter by reconciling us to time and, retrospectively, to tragedy. See *LM*, *Thinking*, pp. 209–10. Cf. *BPF*, p. 262; *LKPP, passim*.
38 Genuineness is established by the "deadly impact of new thoughts" which liberate phenomena from the incrustation of tradition. The lost or forgotten treasures are redeemed by the saving power of remembrance and by the

retrospective judgment of the historian. See *MDT*, pp. 198–201; *LM, Thinking*, p. 216; *LKPP*, p. 77. Cf. D. Luban, "Explaining Dark Times: Hannah Arendt's Theory of Theory," *Social Research*, vol. 50, no. 1, 1983.

39  The same attention to language and the etymology of words to be found in Arendt's work can be traced back to her attempt to evoke the original experience out of which certain concepts arose, an experience now distorted or even silenced by the dominant traditions of thought. As she wrote:

Any period to which its own past has become as questionable as it has to us must eventually come up against the phenomenon of language, for in it the past is contained ineradicably, thwarting all attempts to get rid of it once and for all. The Greek *polis* will continue to exist at the bottom of our political existence – that is, at the bottom of the sea – for as long as we use the word "politics."

(*MDT*, p. 204).

40  *HC*, p. 11.

41  *HC*, p. 10.

42  Arendt argues that questions about the nature of man cannot be answered, since only a god could know and define our essence. She distinguishes between the questions of "Who am I?" and "What am I?" (a distinction credited to St Augustine) and says that the answer to the question "Who am I?" is simply "You are a man – whatever that may be," and the answer to the question "What am I?" can be given only by God who made man. Thus the question about the nature of man turns out to be a theological question which can be settled only "within the framework of a divinely revealed answer," that is to say, outside the framework of secular categories. See *HC*, pp. 10–11, n. 2.

43  *HC*, pp. 7–9.

44  *HC*, pp. 8–9.

45  *HC*, p. 17.

46  Arendt's intent, as we saw in our opening section, is to bring back to life the original experience out of which certain categories emerged, and to use this reactualization as a standpoint from which to evaluate the various modifications (and distortions) that such categories underwent in time. See E. Young-Bruehl, *Hannah Arendt: For Love of the World*, New Haven: Yale University Press, 1982, p. 325.

47  Cf. Michael Oakeshott's review of *Between Past and Future* in *Political Science Quarterly*, vol. 77, 1962, p. 90.

48  This account draws on *The Human Condition*, especially chaps 2 and 6, as well as on her essays in *Between Past and Future*, particularly chaps 1, 3, 6, 8.

49  Cf. *HC*, pp. 248–57.

50  Cf. G. Kateb, *Hannah Arendt: Politics, Conscience, Evil*, Oxford: Martin Robertson, 1984, p. 158.

51  Arendt associates the loss of faith in the senses and in reason with the rise of Cartesian doubt, with its attempt to ground certainty in a systematic doubting of everything that is given or self-evident. This doubting led to introspection, since only by concentrating on the self could certainty be achieved, and to the loss of common sense, since experience was now radically privatized. See *HC*, pp. 273–84.

52  *HC*, pp. 254–5.

53  *HC*, p. 132.

54  *HC*, p. 257. It is important to remember that for Arendt property is opposed to wealth, and is thus not to be identified with the conventional meaning of the term. For her, property stands for location, for a privately held place. It is a privately owned share of a common world, the necessary counterpart to the public realm, enabling individuals to find refuge and shelter from the glare and activity of the public sphere. In her view, without a proper establishment and protection of this private space there can be no free public realm. See *HC*, pp. 58–67.

55  Arendt's reflections are here indebted to the writings of A. Koyrè, *From the Closed World to the Infinite Universe*, Baltimore: Johns Hopkins University Press, 1957; E. A. Burtt, *The Metaphysical Foundations of Modern Science*, London: Routledge & Kegan Paul, 1932, 2nd edn; A. N. Whitehead, *Science and the Modern World*, Cambridge: Cambridge University Press, 1926.

56  "Modern natural science owes its great triumphs to having looked upon and treated earth-bound nature from a truly universal viewpoint, that is, from an Archimedean standpoint taken, wilfully and explicitly, outside the earth" (*HC*, p. 11).

57  *HC*, p. 264.

58  *HC*, p. 2.

59  G. Kateb, *Hannah Arendt: Politics, Conscience, Evil*, op. cit., p. 162.

60  *BPF*, p. 277.

61  *BPF*, p. 278.

62  *HC*, p. 288. Cf. *HC*, p. 3; *BPF*, p. 269.

63  *HC*, p. 276. The concept of truth that Arendt here employs is based on Heidegger's notion of *aletheia*, of truth as disclosure, as unconcealment. It is a notion that Heidegger claims to find in pre-Socratic thinkers, before the rise of Western metaphysics and Platonic philosophy occluded the original sense of being. It is a conception of truth that has been the subject of deep controversy, and that modern philosophers, particularly in the analytic tradition, have tended to reject. For them truth is a property of sentences, not of reality, of language, not of being. I do not wish to enter at present into a discussion of this topic, since I will address it more extensively in the chapter on Arendt's theory of judgment. I wanted to raise it only for the purpose of showing that the cogency of Arendt's understanding of modern science is dependent upon this Heideggerian conception of truth, and that, consequently, any criticism of it would need to address the validity of Heidegger's notion of *aletheia*.

64  *HC*, p. 10; cf. *BPF*, pp. 279–80, where Arendt speaks of the possibility of a mutation of the human race and claims that

under these circumstances, speech and everyday language would indeed be no longer a meaningful utterance that transcends behavior even if it only expresses it, and it would much better be replaced by the extreme and in itself meaningless formalism of mathematical signs.

65  *BPF*, pp. 17–18; *HC*, pp. 14–17. This characterization of the role of the philosopher bears resemblance to the one given by Leo Strauss, with the crucial difference that for Arendt the philosopher introduces extraneous

schemes (such as ruling, derived from the realm of fabrication) into the realm of public affairs, while for Strauss he brings – reluctantly – a degree of order and justice to an otherwise corrupt world. See L. Strauss, *The City and Man*, Chicago: University of Chicago Press, 1964.

66 *HC*, p. 314.

67 "It was not reason but a man-made instrument, the telescope, which actually changed the physical world-view; it was not contemplation, observation, and speculation which led to the new knowledge, but the active stepping in of *homo faber*, of making and fabricating." (*HC*, p. 274).

68 *HC*, p. 297.

69 "Processes, therefore, and not ideas, the models and shapes of the things to be, become the guide for the making and fabricating activities of *homo faber* in the modern age" (*HC*, p. 300).

70 *HC*, p. 296.

71 *HC*, p. 301 (emphasis mine). Cf. *HC*, p. 304, where Arendt says:

This framework [of contemplation and fabrication] was forced wide open ... when in the understanding of fabrication itself the emphasis shifted entirely away from the product and from the permanent, guiding model to the fabrication process, away from the question of what a thing is and what kind of thing was to be produced to the question of how and through which means and processes it had come into being and could be reproduced.

72 *HC*, p. 307.

73 See *HC*, pp. 308, where Arendt claims that:

When this happened it was manifest that the conviction of the age that man can know only what he makes himself – which seemingly was so eminently propitious to a full victory of *homo faber* – would be overruled and eventually destroyed by the even more modern principle of process, whose concepts and categories are altogether alien to the needs and ideals of *homo faber*.

74 *HC*, p. 316.

75 *HC*, p. 321.

76 Daniel Bell's recent call for a renewal of public philosophy formulated in terms of the values of the "public household" is, in this respect, indicative of a semantic confusion, since the household is by definition private. Nonetheless, it is an example of those modern terminological shifts highlighted by Arendt, among which she included "political economy" and "national housekeeping," which accompany the emergence of the social and the predominance of economic concerns and activities. For D. Bell, see "The Public Household: On Fiscal Sociology and the Liberal Society," in *The Cultural Contradictions of Capitalism*, London: Heinemann, 1976.

77 "With the rise of society, that is, the rise of the 'household' (*oikia*) or of economic activities to the public realm, housekeeping and all matters pertaining formerly to the private sphere of the family have become a 'collective' concern" (*HC*, p. 33).

78 *HC*, p. 73.

79 *HC*, p. 69; cf. *HC*, p. 45, where Arendt claims that:

Since the rise of society, since the admission of household and housekeeping activities to the public realm, an irresistible tendency to grow, to devour the older realms of the political and private as well as the more recently established sphere of intimacy, has been one of the outstanding characteristics of the new [social] realm. This constant growth . . . derives its strength from the fact that through society it is the life process itself which in one form or another has been channeled into the public realm.

80  *HC*, pp. 70–3; cf. *HC*, p. 121: "Man cannot be free if he does not know that he is subject to necessity, because his freedom is always won in his never wholly successful attempts to liberate himself from necessity."

81  *HC*, pp. 50–8.

82  See the last chapter of *The Origins of Totalitarianism* entitled "Ideology and Terror," where Arendt maintains that:

Totalitarian government, like all tyrannies, certainly could not exist without destroying the public realm of life, that is, without destroying, by isolating men, their political capacities. But totalitarian domination as a form of government is new in that it is not content with this isolation and destroys private life as well. It bases itself on loneliness, on the experience of not belonging to the world at all, which is among the most radical and desperate experiences of men.

*(OT*, p. 475).

83  *HC*, p. 40.

84  *HC*, pp. 44–5.

85  *HC*, p. 41.

86  *HC*, p. 46.

87  *HC*, p. 135.

88  *HC*, p. 56.

89  *HC*, p. 197.

90  *HC*, p. 19.

91  *HC*, p. 198.

92  As argued, for example, by N. O'Sullivan, "Hellenic Nostalgia and Industrial Society," in A. de Crespigny and K. Minogue (eds), *Contemporary Political Philosophers*, London: Methuen, 1976; R. N. Berki, *On Political Realism*, London: J. M. Dent, 1981; P. P. Portinaro, "Hannah Arendt e l'Utopia della Polis," *Comunità*, vol. 35, 1981.

93  *BPF*, pp. 89–90.

94  *OT*, p. 475.

95  *BPF*, p. 26.

96  *HC*, p. 100.

97  *BPF*, p. 89.

98  *HC*, pp. 2–3.

99  *BPF*, p. 277.

100  Aquinas' formulation that grace completes or perfects nature (*gratia non tollit naturam, sed perficit*) was judged by Alessandro Passerin d'Entrèves to be "a genial insight." Its success with humanist scholars stemmed from the fact that nature and grace were made to stand in a complementary relation. See *Aquinas: Selected Political Writings*, ed. and introduced A. P. d'Entrèves, Oxford: Basil Blackwell, 1948, p. xiii.

101  See *HC*, p. 307; cf. also "The Concept of History," where Arendt claims that "the common origin of both nature and history in the modern age . . . lies indeed in the concept of process" (*BPF*, p. 62).

102  *BPF*, pp. 41–90.

103  *BPF*, p. 88.

104  *BPF*, pp. 86–7.

105  *BPF*, pp. 87–8.

106  Cf. *HC*, pp. 301–4.

107  Cf. *HC*, pp. 305–7.

108  *BPF*, p. 62.

109  *BPF*, p. 85.

110  *BPF*, p. 168.

111  *BPF*, p. 170.

112  Cf. *BPF*, p. 62.

113  *HC*, p. 232.

114  *HC*, p. 233.

115  The capacity for action, at least in the sense of the releasing of processes, is still with us, although it has become the exclusive prerogative of the scientists . . . But the action of the scientists, since it acts into nature from the standpoint of the universe and not into the web of human relationships, lacks the revelatory character of action as well as the ability to produce stories and become historical, which together form the very source from which meaningfulness springs into and illuminates human existence. (*HC*, pp. 323–4)

116  Without being forgiven, released from the consequences of what we have done, our capacity to act would, as it were, be confined to one single deed from which we could never recover; we would remain the victims of its consequences forever, not unlike the sorcerer's apprentice who lacked the magic formula to break the spell. (*HC*, p. 237)

117  *HC*, p. 104.

118  It could be argued that Arendt's ambivalence as regards the understanding of the relation between freedom and necessity is a result of her indebtedness to Kant's theory of freedom. As Ronald Beiner has argued, Arendt derives from Kant an absolute dichotomy between freedom and nature and an appreciation of the pure spontaneity of action. In this sense, the opposition of action (characterized by freedom and spontaneity) and process (characterized by necessity and automatism) reproduces the Kantian opposition of freedom and necessity with all its aporias. See R. Beiner, review of E. Young-Bruehl, *Times Higher Educational Supplement*, 16 July 1982, p. 14.

119  *HC*, p. 33.

120  *HC*, p. 28.

121  *HC*, p. 45.

122  *HC*, p. 47.

123  *HC*, p. 46.

124  Arendt says in this context that "society expects from each of its members a certain kind of behavior, imposing innumerable and various rules, all of which tend to 'normalize' its members, to make them behave, to exclude spontaneous action or outstanding achievement" (*HC*, p. 40).

125 For an interesting collection of essays dealing with the liberal distinction between public and private, see S. I. Benn and G. F. Gaus (eds), *Public and Private in Social Life*, New York: St Martin's Press, 1983; for a critique and reformulation of such distinction, see J. B. Elshtain, *Public Man, Private Woman*, Princeton: Princeton University Press, 1981.

126 S. Wolin, "Hannah Arendt: Democracy and the Political," *Salmagundi*, no. 60, 1983, pp. 9–10.

127 H. Pitkin, "Justice: On Relating Private and Public," *Political Theory*, vol. 9, no. 3, 1981, pp. 327–52, esp. pp. 338–42.

128 The French Revolution was an example for Arendt of what happens when social questions (i.e., questions about justice) are allowed to enter into the public sphere. She claimed that the terror and dictatorship to which it fell prey were a result of trying to solve the "social question" by political means. See *OR*, pp. 59–114. The implausibility of this account has been shown by many authors. See, among others, E. J. Hobsbawm, *Revolutionaries*, London: Quartet Books, 1977, pp. 201–8; J. Habermas, *Kultur und Kritik*, Frankfurt: Suhrkamp, 1973, pp. 365–70; F. Fehér, "Freedom and the Social Question: Hannah Arendt's Theory of the French Revolution," *Philosophy and Social Criticism*, vol. 12, no. 1, 1987, pp. 1–30; J. Miller, "The Pathos of Novelty: Hannah Arendt's Image of Freedom in the Modern World," in *RPW*, p. 177–208.

129 And in any political practice as well. Richard Bernstein has emphasized this point in the essay "Rethinking the Social and the Political," where he writes:

Arendt is right in seeing that the demand for social liberation is not to be identified with the demand for political freedom; and that social liberation does not automatically lead to positive political freedom. But it is just as true to assert that any attempt to found political freedom in the modern age that neglects or forgets its origin in fighting and eliminating social injustice is in danger of betraying itself.

(*Philosophical Profiles*, Cambridge: Polity Press, 1986, pp. 255–6)

130 See "Reflections on Little Rock," *Dissent*, vol. 6, no. 1, 1959, pp. 45–56; "A Reply to Critics," *Dissent*, vol. 6, no. 2, 1959, pp. 179–181. Cf. *OR*, pp. 272–5, and the discussion between Mary McCarthy, Richard Bernstein, Albrecht Wellmer, and Arendt in *RPW*, pp. 315–22.

131 R. Bernstein, "Rethinking the Social and the Political, in *Philosophical Profiles*, op. cit., p. 252.

132 This last distinction is a reformulation of that offered by C. W. Mills between "personal troubles of milieu" and "public issues of social structure." See *The Sociological Imagination*, Harmondsworth: Penguin, 1970, pp. 14–17.

133 The challenge of the feminist movement has been precisely that of redefining the boundaries between the two spheres, to argue for the political nature of the relations between the sexes and to stress the politically oppressive (i.e., patriarchal) character of relations within the family. See, among others, K. Millett, *Sexual Politics*, New York: Doubleday, 1970; J. Mitchell, *Woman's Estate*, Harmondsworth: Penguin, 1971; S. Rowbotham, *Woman's Consciousness, Man's World*, Harmondsworth: Penguin, 1973; M. Barrett, *Women's Oppression Today*, London: Verso, 1980; Z. R. Eisenstein, *The Radical Future of Liberal Feminism*, New York: Longman, 1981; M. O'Brien,

*The Politics of Reproduction*, London: Routledge & Kegan Paul, 1981; A. M. Jaggar, *Feminist Politics and Human Nature*, Totowa: Rowman & Allanheld, 1983; N. Hartsock, *Money, Sex, and Power*, New York: Longman, 1983; J. Grimshaw, *Philosophy and Feminist Thinking*, Minneapolis: University of Minnesota Press, 1986; S. M. Okin, *Women in Western Political Thought*, Princeton: Princeton University Press, 1979; C. Pateman, *The Sexual Contract*, Cambridge: Polity, 1988; I. M. Young, *Justice and the Politics of Difference*, Princeton: Princeton University Press, 1990.

134 C. Pateman, "Feminist Critiques of the Public/Private Dichotomy," in S. I. Benn and G. F. Gaus (eds), *Public and Private in Social Life*, op. cit., p. 299.

135 I have in mind here T. H. Marshall's theory of citizenship, in which he distinguishes three forms of citizenship, the civil, the political, and the social. The first refers to legal rights (life, liberty, expression, etc.); the second to rights to participate or be represented in the political process; the third to rights to a minimum standard of welfare and economic security. Arendt's theory of citizenship would, in the light of this schema, be restricted only to the first two. See T. H. Marshall, *Citizenship and Social Class*, London: Pluto Press, 1992.

136 See the final chapter of her book *Public Man, Private Woman*, op. cit.

137 ibid., pp. 346–7.

138 Nancy Fraser, "The French Derrideans: Politicizing Deconstruction or Deconstructing the Political?" *New German Critique* 33, Fall 1984; "What's Critical About Critical Theory? The Case of Habermas and Gender," *New German Critique* 35, Spring–Summer 1985, both reprinted in *Unruly Practices*, Cambridge: Polity Press, 1989.

139 N. Fraser, "The French Derrideans," op. cit., p. 150.

140 ibid., pp. 151–2.

## 2 Hannah Arendt's theory of action

1 *HC*, p. 7.

2 *HC*, pp. 7–11, 175–88.

3 The most instructive contrast may be found in the theories of Leo Strauss and Eric Voegelin. Both subscribed to a Platonic conception of knowledge (in which *theoria* and *episteme* are privileged over *praxis* and *doxa*) which prevented them from developing a democratic theory of political action. See L. Strauss, *What is Political Philosophy?* Chicago: University of Chicago Press, 1988; E. Voegelin, *Anamnesis*, Notre Dame: University of Notre Dame Press, 1978. Among Anglo-Saxon political thinkers, Michael Oakeshott shows a deep understanding of the distinctive qualities of action (cf. his critique of behaviorism in *Rationalism in Politics*, London: Methuen, 1962), but fails ultimately to give action a central place in his theory of political association (cf. *On Human Conduct*, Oxford: Oxford University Press, 1975). One of the few political theorists to devote considerable attention to action and participation as modes of human togetherness, in which individuality as well as membership are affirmed, is Michael Walzer (cf. *Spheres of Justice*, New York: Basic Books, 1983).

4 Cf. *HC*, pp. 220–30, where Arendt accuses Plato of substituting the category of making (*poiesis*) for the category of action (*praxis*) and therefore of

imposing an alien standard upon the reality of human affairs. Arendt contends that as a result of this substitution, the Western tradition of political philosophy that originated with Plato understood politics on the model of fabrication, with the result that *ruling* – rather than action and participation – became the paradigm for political life.

5  *HC*, p. 177. Cf. *BPF*, p. 167.

6  *HC*, p. 9.

7  *HC*, pp. 177–8. Cf. *HC*, p. 246; *BPF*, pp. 169–70. In stressing the innovative character of action and conceiving freedom as the capacity to do the unexpected, Arendt is implicitly criticizing all those understandings of action which reduce it to the categories of "behavior," "role," or "function," which have in common the idea that individuals are predictable and adaptable units of a self-regulating system. Against these understandings Arendt sets her theory of action as the freedom to innovate, to break the continuum of automatic processes, to do that which is "infinitely improbable." It is also clear that Arendt's theory of action stands opposed to those understandings of human conduct, to be found in writers such as Burke and Oakeshott, which see it as the product of custom and conventions, of habit and circumstances beyond the control of the agent. By rooting the faculty of action in the phenomenon of natality Arendt is able to show that circumstances can never determine us absolutely, that each of us represents something new and distinctive, so that when we act we bring the unexpected to bear against that which is customary, the novel against that which is habitual.

8  *BPF*, p. 153. In the essay "What is Freedom?" – from which the quote has been taken – Arendt draws a distinction between the understanding of freedom articulated by the philosophical tradition and that which found expression in the political experience of Greek and Roman antiquity. The philosophical tradition understood freedom as an attribute of the will (*liberum arbitrium*), while in the Greek and Roman republican experience it was seen as a property of action, of appearing in public and deliberating among a community of peers. Against the idea of freedom as *liberum arbitrium* Arendt sets the notion of freedom as public, political intercourse with one's peers, as a reciprocal sharing of words and deeds, as the mutual endeavor to reach agreement on matters of collective concern. This participatory and communicative notion of freedom is among the most important contributions of Arendt, a contribution she summed up beautifully in her claim that "the *raison d'être* of politics is freedom, and its field of experience is action" (*BPF*, p. 146).

9  *HC*, p. 246.

10  *HC*, p. 247.

11  *OR*, p. 21.

12  *OR*, p. 119.

13  *OR*, p. 69.

14  *OR*, p. 124.

15  *HC*, pp. 181–8. Cf. *BPF*, pp. 154–5.

16  Arendt also makes the connection between speech and plurality and claims that speech is the *actualization* of the human condition of plurality, since through speech we are able to disclose our unique identities. As she puts it:

If action as beginning corresponds to the fact of birth, if it is the actualization of the human condition of natality, then speech corresponds to the fact of distinctness and is the actualization of the human condition of plurality, that is, of living as a distinct and unique being among equals.

(*HC*, p. 178)

17  *HC*, pp. 7–8.
18  *HC*, pp. 175–6.
19  *HC*, pp. 178–9, 184–6, 199–200.
20  *HC*, p. 200.
21  *HC*, p. 179.
22  *HC*, pp. 180–1.
23  *HC*, pp. 178–9.
24  *HC*, p. 180.
25  *HC*, p. 186.
26  *HC*, p. 184.
27  *HC*, p. 192.
28  *HC*, p. 192.
29  *HC*, pp. 192 ff.; *BPF*, pp. 63–75.
30  S. Wolin, "Hannah Arendt and the Ordinance of Time," *Social Research*, vol. 44, no. 1, Spring 1977, p. 97. For an elaboration of Wolin's idea of remembrance, see his "Contract and Birthright," *Political Theory*, vol. 14, no. 2, May 1986, pp. 179–93. See also Bruce James Smith, *Politics and Remembrance: Republican Themes in Machiavelli, Burke, and Tocqueville*, Princeton: Princeton University Press, 1985.
31  *HC*, pp. 197–8. Cf. *HC*, p. 56, where Arendt states that:

the *polis* was for the Greeks, as the *res publica* was for the Romans, first of all their guarantee against the futility of individual life, the space protected against this futility and reserved for the relative permanence, if not immortality, of mortals.

32  *HC*, p. 198.
33  *HC*, pp. 198–9.
34  *HC*, p. 199.
35  *HC*, p. 199.
36  Arendt defines *power* as "the human ability not just to act but to act in concert"; as such, it is never the property of an individual (like strength) but belongs to a group and remains in existence only so long as the group keeps together. *Strength* refers to the property inherent in an object or a person and, as such, is not something that can be shared. *Force* indicates the energy released by natural phenomena (as when we speak of the "force of nature") or the constraints imposed by the situation (as in the "force of circumstances"). *Violence* refers to the imposition of one's will upon others, that is, coercion; it requires implements such as weapons or tools of destruction and is therefore wholly instrumental in character; when exercised by a government it is called tyranny. Although violence can destroy power, it can never replace it, since it can never generate the support that arises out of common convictions. This explains the impotence of tyrannical regimes, based as they are on a monopoly of the means of violence and a lack of power at the same time. See *CR*, pp. 143–55.

37 *HC*, p. 201.
38 *HC*, p. 200.
39 *CR*, p. 151.
40 *CR*, p. 151.
41 Habermas has emphasized this grounding of legitimate power in un-constrained public deliberation in the essay "Hannah Arendt's Communications Concept of Power," *Social Research*, vol. 44, no. 1, Spring 1977. He argues in fact that:

> The public-political realm has also been conceived by others as a generator, if not of power, then of the legitimation of power; but Hannah Arendt insists that a public-political realm can produce legitimate power only so long as structures of nondistorted communication find their expression in it.
>
> (p. 9)

42 *HC*, p. 200.
43 *HC*, p. 200.
44 *CR*, p. 140; cf. J. Habermas, "On the German-Jewish Heritage," *Telos*, no. 44, 1980, where he makes the following comment in his discussion of Arendt's theory of action:

> It is this innovative potential which makes the domain of praxis vulnerable and dependent on protective institutions. Only when they originate through the power of common convictions of those who act in concert, these institutions take the form of a "constitution of liberty"; and liberty can be maintained only as long as political institutions in turn protect that source of unimpaired intersubjectivity from which a communicatively generated power springs.
>
> (p. 128)

45 In discussing the problem of civil disobedience, in particular the extent to which it is compatible with the spirit of American law and the principles embodied in the Constitution, Arendt makes the following observation:

> If Montesquieu was right – and I believe he was – that there is such a thing as "the spirit of the laws," which varies from country to country and is different in the various forms of government, then we might say that consent, not in the very old sense of mere acquiescence . . . but in the sense of active support and continuing participation in all matters of public interest, is the spirit of American law.
>
> (*CR*, p. 85)

Later in the same essay, however, she notes that:

> It is often argued that the consent to the Constitution, the *consensus universalis*, implies consent to statutory laws as well, because in representative government the people have helped to make them. This consent, I think, is indeed entirely fictitious; under the present circumstances, at any rate, it has lost all plausibility. Representative government itself is in a crisis today, partly because it has lost, in the course of time, all institutions that permitted the citizens' actual participation, and partly because it is now gravely affected by the disease from which the party system suffers:

bureaucratization and the two parties' tendency to represent nobody except the party machines.

(*CR*, pp. 88–9).

46 *HC*, p. 244.
47 *HC*, p. 184.
48 *HC*, p. 184. Cf. *HC*, p. 190:

Because the actor always moves among and in relation to other acting beings, he is never merely a "doer" but always and at the same time a "sufferer." To do and to suffer are like opposite sides of the same coin, and the story that an act starts is composed of its consequent deeds and sufferings.

49 *HC*, p. 233.
50 *HC*, p. 190; moreover, as Arendt notes, action,

no matter what its specific content, always establishes new relationships and therefore has an inherent tendency to force open all limitations and cut across all boundaries . . . this is why the old virtue of moderation, of keeping within bounds, is indeed one of the political virtues par excellence.

(*HC*, pp. 190–1)

51 *HC*, pp. 232–3.
52 *HC*, pp. 233–4.
53 *HC*, p. 237.
54 *HC*, p. 237.
55 *HC*, p. 237.
56 *HC*, pp. 241–3.
57 *HC*, p. 246.
58 *HC*, p. 240.
59 *HC*, p. 244. Cf. *HC*, p. 234, where Arendt notes that

if it were true that sovereignty and freedom are the same, then indeed no man could be free, because sovereignty, the ideal of uncompromising self-sufficiency and mastership, is contradictory to the very condition of plurality. No man can be sovereign because not one man, but men, inhabit the earth.

60 Seyla Benhabib has characterized this aspect of action in terms of its *interpretive indeterminacy*. "By the interpretive indeterminacy of action I mean that human actions and the intentions embedded in them can only be identified by a process of social interpretation and communication in the shared world." In this respect, "others can understand what we do and who we are insofar as our actions can be retold by them as a story, as a narrative. Action unfolds within a 'web of interpretations'" (*Critique, Norm, and Utopia*, New York: Columbia University Press, 1986, p. 136).

61 This emphasis is to be found in those passages of *The Human Condition* where Arendt claims that action needs for its full appearance "the shining brightness we once called glory" (p. 180), that it can be judged only by its "greatness" (p. 205), that politics is neither the pursuit of truth nor of goodness but of "excellence" (p. 13), and that the urge toward self-disclosure

may be seen as "the passionate drive to show one's self in measuring up against others" (p. 194). In these passages Arendt conceives action in terms of an expressive model and downplays its communicative dimension.

62 Peter Fuss, "Hannah Arendt's Conception of Political Community," in *RPW*, pp. 157–76; Bhikhu Parekh, *Hannah Arendt and the Search for a New Political Philosophy*, London: Macmillan, 1981.

63 Benhabib, *Critique, Norm, and Utopia*, op. cit., pp. 137–9.

64 H. Arendt, "What is Existenz Philosophy?" *Partisan Review*, vol. 13, no. 1, Winter 1946, pp. 34–56.

65 Martin Jay and Leon Botstein, "Hannah Arendt: Opposing Views," *Partisan Review*, vol. 45, no. 3, Summer 1978, p. 351.

66 ibid., pp. 352–3.

67 See her essay "What is Freedom?" in *BPF*, pp. 143–71.

68 ibid., pp. 151 ff.

69 Martin Jay and Leon Botstein, "Hannah Arendt: Opposing Views," op. cit., p. 379.

70 Contained in *BPF*, pp. 17–40.

71 For Arendt goodness loses its essential quality when it is made public, for it is clear, she says, "that the moment a good work becomes known and public, it loses its specific character of goodness, of being done for nothing but goodness' sake" (*HC*, p. 74). Similarly, love harbors an anti-political tendency, since it is by its very nature unworldly, and by reason of its passion "destroys the in-between which relates us to and separates us from others" (*HC*, p. 242).

72 *HC*, p. 182.

73 Martin Jay and Leon Botstein, "Hannah Arendt; Opposing Views," op. cit., p. 364 (emphases mine).

74 *HC*, p. 191; pp. 243 ff. Cf. *OT*, p. 465. With respect to this issue, see Leroy A. Cooper, "Hannah Arendt's Political Philosophy: An Interpretation," *Review of Politics*, vol. 38, no. 2, April 1976, pp. 161 ff.

75 *HC*, p. 191.

76 *HC*, p. 246.

77 Martin Jay and Leon Botstein, "Hannah Arendt: Opposing Views," op. cit., p. 353.

78 *BPF*, p. 154.

79 *HC*, p. 188.

80 Martin Jay and Leon Botstein, "Hannah Arendt: Opposing Views," op. cit., p. 363.

81 George Kateb, *Hannah Arendt: Politics, Conscience, Evil*, Oxford: Martin Robertson, 1984, p. 33.

82 ibid., p. 31.

83 ibid., pp. 6 ff.

84 ibid., p. 23.

85 ibid., p. 28.

86 ibid., p. 30.

87 ibid., p. 36.

88 ibid., p. 39.

89 *CR*, p. 130.

90 *CR*, p. 203.

91 *CR*, pp. 204–5.

92 G. Kateb, *Hannah Arendt: Politics, Conscience, Evil*, op. cit., p. 40.

93 ibid., p. 85.

94 For the relevant literature see: S. Cavell, *The Claim of Reason*, Oxford: Oxford University Press, 1979; P. Foot, *Virtues and Vices*, Berkeley: University of California Press, 1978; *idem*, *Moral Relativism* (The Lindley Lecture), Lawrence: University of Kansas Press, 1978; S. Hampshire, *Morality and Conflict*, Cambridge, Mass.: Harvard University Press, 1983; S. Lovibond, *Realism and Imagination in Ethics*, Minneapolis: University of Minnesota Press, 1983; A. MacIntyre, *After Virtue*, Notre Dame: University of Notre Dame Press, 1981; B. Williams, *Ethics and the Limits of Philosophy*, Cambridge, Mass.: Harvard University Press, 1985.

95 B. Williams, *Ethics and the Limits of Philosophy*, op. cit., p. 1.

96 G. Kateb, *Hannah Arendt: Politics, Conscience, Evil*, op. cit., p. 85 (emphases mine). Activist absolute morality refers to the Christian morality of love and goodness; abstentionist absolute morality refers to the Socratic morality of conscience.

97 *HC*, p. 74.

98 *HC*, p. 242.

99 See Arendt's reflections on Melville's *Billy Budd* in *On Revolution*. She claims that "absolute goodness is hardly any less dangerous than absolute evil" (p. 82) and that "the absolute . . . spells doom to everyone when it is introduced into the political realm" (p. 84). She maintained that politics, and the human relations characteristic of it, reside in the middle, in the sphere of ordinary virtue and vice, rather than in the sphere of absolute good and evil.

100 G. Kateb, *Hannah Arendt: Politics, Conscience, Evil*, op. cit., p. 29.

101 See for example, her praise of the "old virtue of moderation" (*HC*, p. 191) and her denunciation of ambition (*OR*, pp. 119–20).

102 See *HC*, pp. 236–47; "Thinking and Moral Considerations," *Social Research*, vol. 38, no. 3, Autumn 1971; "Truth and Politics," in *BPF*, pp. 227–64; "The Crisis in Culture," in *BPF*, pp. 197–226.

103 Cf. Fred Dallmayr's critique of Kateb in "Public or Private Freedom?" *Social Research*, vol. 54, no. 3, Autumn 1987, pp. 617–28.

104 Margaret Canovan, "The Contradictions of Hannah Arendt's Political Thought," *Political Theory*, vol. 6, no. 1, February 1978, pp. 5–26.

105 ibid., pp. 5–6.

106 ibid., p. 9.

107 ibid., p. 13.

108 See the last chapter of *On Revolution* and the essays contained in *Crises of the Republic*, especially "Civil Disobedience" and "Thoughts on Politics and Revolution."

109 Cf. J. Habermas, "Hannah Arendt's Communications Concept of Power," op. cit., pp. 10–11.

110 For Arendt politics should be separated from the management of economic affairs, which for her belonged to the sphere of "administration." For a critique of Arendt's understanding of the "social" see Chapter 1.

111 M. Canovan, "The Contradictions of Hannah Arendt's Political Thought," op. cit., p. 19. This criticism, however, seems inappropriate in the case of Arendt. She never thought that the public realm should exclude the interests and welfare of those who were unable or unwilling to participate. Her proposal of a federated council system was predicated on the idea that

everybody should be given the opportunity to voice their opinions; those who did not participate did not lose thereby their rights or their economic entitlements.

112  ibid., p. 20.
113  ibid., p. 21.
114  Arendt's theory of participatory democracy should be seen as the attempt to reactivate the experience of citizenship in the modern world, and not as a nostalgic or utopian return to the past. See my discussion of this question in Chapter 1, pp. 28–34.
115  Peter Fuss, "Hannah Arendt's Conception of Political Community," in RPW, p. 172.
116  Bhikhu Parekh, Hannah Arendt and the Search for a New Political Philosophy, op. cit., p. 177.
117  P. Fuss, "Hannah Arendt's Conception of Political Community," op. cit., p. 173.
118  B. Parekh, Hannah Arendt and the Search for a New Political Philosophy, op. cit., pp. 177–8.
119  J. Habermas, "Hannah Arendt's Communications Concept of Power," op. cit., p. 4.
120  ibid., p. 6.
121  ibid., p. 7.
122  ibid., pp. 15–16 (emphases mine).
123  Habermas formulates this distinction as follows:

The acquisition and maintenance of political power must be distinguished from both the employment of political power – that is, rule – and the generation of political power. In the last case, but only in the last case, the concept of praxis is helpful.

(ibid., p. 17)

124  ibid., pp. 17–18 (emphasis mine).

## 3  Hannah Arendt's theory of judgment

1  Michael Denneny, "The Privilege of Ourselves: Hannah Arendt on Judgment," in RPW, pp. 246–7.
2  LM, Thinking, p. 193.
3  LM, Thinking, pp. 5–6, 69–70, 76, 92–8, 111, 129–30, 140, 192–3, 207–9, 213–16; Willing, pp. 59–62, 217.
4  These lectures have been edited and introduced by Ronald Beiner under the title Lectures on Kant's Political Philosophy, Chicago: University of Chicago Press, 1982, hereafter cited as LKPP.
5  Hannah Arendt, "Thinking and Moral Considerations: A Lecture" appeared in Social Research, vol. 38, no. 3, Autumn 1971, and was reprinted in Social Research, vol. 51, no. 1, Spring 1984; all citations will be from the reprinted version.
6  "The Crisis in Culture" and "Truth and Politics" are included in BPF, at pp. 197–226 and pp. 227–64, respectively.
7  R. Beiner, "Interpretive Essay," in LKPP, p. 93.

8 Arendt also endows judgment with the capacity to reclaim human dignity against those theories that would posit a world-historical process whose only criterion is "success." In the Postscriptum to *Thinking* she claims that:

> If judgment is our faculty for dealing with the past, the historian is the inquiring man who by relating it sits in judgment over it. If that is so, we may reclaim our human dignity, win it back, as it were, from the pseudo-divinity named History of the modern age, without denying history's importance but denying its right to being the ultimate judge.

*(LM, Thinking*, p. 216).

9 Cf. R. Bernstein, "Judging – the Actor and the Spectator" in *Philosophical Profiles*, Cambridge: Polity Press, 1986.

10 Seyla Benhabib, "Judgment and the Moral Foundations of Politics in Hannah Arendt's Thought," in *Situating the Self*, Cambridge: Polity Press, 1992, p. 123.

11 For a related argument, see S. Benhabib, "Judgment and the Moral Foundations of Politics in Hannah Arendt's Thought," op. cit., p. 124.

12 *OT*, p. viii.

13 Hannah Arendt, "Understanding and Politics," *Partisan Review*, 20, 1953, p. 377.

14 ibid., p. 383.

15 ibid., p. 379. Cf. *BPF*, p. 26, where Arendt writes that:

> Totalitarian domination as an established fact, which in its unprecedentedness cannot be comprehended through the usual categories of political thought, and whose "crimes" cannot be judged by traditional moral standards or punished within the legal framework of our civilization, has broken the continuity of Occidental history. The break in our tradition is now an accomplished fact.

16 Indeed, as Arendt noted in her review of *The Black Book: The Nazi Crime Against the Jewish People*, in *Commentary*, vol. 2, September 1946, pp. 291–5, significantly entitled "The Image of Hell": "The attempt of the Nazis to fabricate a wickedness beyond vice did nothing more than establish an innocence beyond virtue. Such innocence and such wickedness have no bearing on the reality where politics exists."

17 Arendt, "Understanding and Politics," op. cit., p. 379.

18 ibid., p. 383.

19 ibid., p. 383.

20 ibid., p. 391.

21 ibid., p. 392.

22 ibid., p. 392.

23 ibid., p. 391.

24 *BPF*, p. 262.

25 Hannah Arendt, "Personal Responsibility under Dictatorship," *The Listener*, 6 August 1964, p. 187.

26 Hannah Arendt, *Eichmann in Jerusalem: A Report on the Banality of Evil*, New York: Viking Press, 1965, p. 294.

27 ibid., p. 295.

28 *LM, Thinking*, p. 3.

29  *LM, Thinking*, pp. 4–5.

30  *LM, Thinking*, p. 5.

31  Arendt, "Thinking and Moral Considerations," op. cit., p. 8.

32  ibid., p. 36; the last lines are from W. B. Yeats, who was one of Arendt's favorite modern poets.

33  ibid., p. 36. Cf. J. Glenn Gray "The Winds of Thought," *Social Research*, vol. 44, no. 1, Spring 1977, p. 47.

34  ibid., pp. 29–30, 35.

35  *LM, Thinking*, p. 191.

36  ibid., p. 191.

37  ibid., p. 191.

38  Cf. "Collective Responsibility," in James W. Bernauer (ed.), *Amor Mundi: Explorations in the Faith and Thought of Hannah Arendt*, Dordrecht: Martinus Nijhoff Publishers, 1987, pp. 43–50.

39  *LM, Thinking*, p. 193 (emphases mine).

40  See *BPF*, pp. 219–20.

41  Lecture course at the University of Chicago on "Kant's Political Philosophy," Fall 1964 (Hannah Arendt Papers, Library of Congress, Container 41, p. 032259), cited in R. Beiner, *Political Judgment*, London: Methuen, 1983, p. 15.

42  "Freedom and Politics," in A. Hunold (ed.), *Freedom and Serfdom: An Anthology of Western Thought*, Dordrecht: D. Reidel, 1961, p. 207. Cf. "The Crisis in Culture," where Arendt states that:

In order to see the faculty of judgment in its proper perspective and to understand that it implies a political rather than a merely theoretical activity, we must shortly recall what is usually considered to be Kant's political philosophy, namely, the *Critique of Practical Reason*, which deals with the lawgiving faculty of reason. The principle of lawgiving, as laid down in the "categorical imperative" – "always act in such a manner that the principle of your action can become a general law" – is based upon the necessity for rational thought to agree with itself . . . In the *Critique of Judgment*, however, Kant insisted upon a different way of thinking, for which it would not be enough to be in agreement with one's own self, but which consisted of being able to "think in the place of everybody else" and which he therefore called an "enlarged mentality."

(*BPF*, pp. 219–20)

In both essays the intersubjective nature of judgment is thus contrasted to the solitary character of thought; not agreement with oneself, but the capacity to expand one's point of view to encompass those of others marks the faculty of judgment.

43  *LKPP*, p. 13.

44  Arendt stresses that this capacity to judge the particular *qua* particular is not to be found in Kant's moral philosophy. As she puts it:

For judgment of the particular – *This* is beautiful, *This* is ugly; *This* is right, *This* is wrong – has no place in Kant's moral philosophy. Judgment is not practical reason; practical reason "reasons" and tells me what to do and what not to do; it lays down the law and is identical with the will, and the will utters commands; it speaks in imperatives. Judgment, on the contrary, arises from "a merely contemplative pleasure or inactive delight."

(*LKPP*, p. 15).

45 Immanuel Kant, *Critique of Judgment*, trans. with analytical index by J. C. Meredith, Oxford: Clarendon Press, 1952, p. 18.
46 ibid., p. 153 (emphasis mine).
47 *LKPP*, p. 76; I. Kant, *Critique of Pure Reason*, op. cit., B 173.
48 *LKPP*, p. 77.
49 Immanuel Kant, "The Contest of Faculties," in *Kant's Political Writings*, ed. Hans Reiss, Cambridge: Cambridge University Press, p. 182.
50 ibid., p. 184.
51 ibid., p. 185.
52 *LKPP*, p. 55.
53 *LKPP*, p. 55.
54 *LKPP*, p. 65.
55 *LKPP*, p. 61.
56 *LKPP*, p. 63.
57 *BPF*, p. 222.
58 *LKPP*, p. 67.
59 *LKPP*, pp. 68–9. See also *LM, Thinking*, pp. 94–6.
60 *LKPP*, p. 67 (cited from Kant's "Reflexionen zur Anthropologie," no. 767, in *Gesammelte Schriften*, Prussian Academy edn, 15: 334–5).
61 *LKPP*, p. 67.
62 *LKPP*, p. 70; the quote is taken from Kant's *Anthropology from a Pragmatic Point of View*, trans. Mary J. Gregor, The Hague: Martinus Nijhoff, 1974, para. 53.
63 I. Kant, *Critique of Judgment*, op. cit., p. 151.
64 *LKPP*, p. 71.
65 *LKPP*, p. 71.
66 I. Kant, *Critique of Judgment*, op. cit., p. 153.
67 ibid., p. 153.
68 *LKPP*, p. 72.
69 *LKPP*, p. 73.
70 *LKPP*, p. 74; I. Kant, *Critique of Judgment*, op. cit., p. 155.
71 *LKPP*, p. 75 (emphasis mine).
72 *LKPP*, pp. 75–6.
73 *BPF*, p. 221.
74 *BPF*, p. 221.
75 *BPF*, p. 222.
76 *BPF*, p. 223 (emphases mine).
77 *BPF*, p. 221. Cf. *LM, Thinking*, p. 95: "Kant was the first, and has remained the last, of the great philosophers to deal with judgment as one of the basic mental activities." ibid., p. 215: "Not till Kant's *Critique of Judgment* did this faculty become a major topic of a major thinker."
78 See C. Lasch, "Introduction," *Salmagundi*, no. 60, Spring-Summer 1983; R. Bernstein, "Judging – the Actor and the Spectator," in *Philosophical Profiles*, Cambridge: Polity Press, 1986; for a rejoinder, see S. Benhabib, "Judgment and the Moral Foundations of Politics in Hannah Arendt's Thought," in *Situating the Self*, Cambridge: Polity Press, 1992.

79 *BPF*, pp. 220–1 (emphases mine).

80 *BPF*, p. 242.

81 *BPF*, p. 241.

82 *BPF*, p. 242.

83 *BPF*, p. 242.

84 *BPF*, p. 241.

85 *BPF*, p. 233.

86 *BPF*, p. 247 (emphases mine).

87 *BPF*, pp. 233–4.

88 *MDT*, p. 27 (emphases mine).

89 *BPF*, pp. 234–5. For recent discussions on the Kantian themes of publicity and the free use of reason in public, see Onora O'Neill, "The Public Use of Reason," *Political Theory*, vol. 14, no. 4, November 1986, pp. 523–51; John Christian Laursen, "The Subversive Kant: The Vocabulary of Public and Publicity," *Political Theory*, vol. 14, no. 4, November 1986, pp. 584–603; John Rawls, "On the Idea of Free Public Reason," lecture delivered at the Conference for the Study of Political Thought, New York, 9 April 1988 (unpublished).

90 *BPF*, p. 234.

91 *BPF*, p. 235. On the role and importance of opinion in Madison, see E. Vollrath, "That All Governments Rest on Opinion," *Social Research*, vol. 43, no. 1, Spring 1976, pp. 46–61.

92 Arendt reproaches Kant for having proposed an absolute standard for morality in the form of the categorical imperative. This standard for Arendt is inhuman, because it "is postulated as absolute and *in its absoluteness introduces into the interhuman realm* – which by its nature consists of relationships – *something that runs counter to its fundamental relativity*" (*MDT*, p. 27, emphases mine).

93 It is important to note that for Arendt persuasion is the only truly *political* form of speech. It is that form of speech designed to "woo the consent of everyone else in the hope of coming to an agreement with him eventually" (*BPF*, p. 222). Because of this it is very different from demonstration or logical proof, which rests on compelling arguments that require the assent of every rational being. For the distinction between persuasive argumentation and strict demonstration, see Chaïm Perelman, *The Realm of Rhetoric*, Notre Dame: University of Notre Dame Press, 1982; Chaïm Perelman and Lucie Olbrechts-Tyteca, *The New Rhetoric: A Treatise on Argumentation*, Notre Dame: University of Notre Dame Press, 1969; Chaïm Perelman, *The Idea of Justice and the Problem of Argument*, London: Routledge & Kegan Paul, 1963. On the nature of argumentation, see also Bernard Manin, "On Legitimacy and Political Deliberation," *Political Theory*, vol. 15, no. 3, August 1987, pp. 338–68.

94 *BPF*, p. 239. The distinction between rational truth and factual truth is derived from Leibniz. In the *Monadology* he in fact distinguished *truths of reasoning* from *truths of fact* and stated that the former "are necessary and their opposite is impossible," while the latter "are contingent and their opposite is possible." G. W. Leibniz, *Philosophical Writings*, ed. by G. H. R. Parkinson, London: Dent, 1973, p. 184.

95 *BPF*, p. 238.

96 *BPF*, p. 238 (emphases mine). Arendt is fully aware that facts are theory-laden and that historical inquiry is always framed by interpretive categories. Nevertheless, she believes that facts cannot be changed at will and that the historian must always respect the line separating the interpretation of facts from their manipulation or distortion. See her comments on this issue in *BPF*, pp. 238–9.

97 Indeed, they are the basic preconditions for the establishment of self-identity and of an adequate sense of reality. As Arendt observes:

> The result of a consistent and total substitution of lies for factual truth is not that the lies will now be accepted as truth, and the truth be defamed as lies, but that the sense by which we take our bearings in the real world – and the category of truth vs. falsehood is among the mental means to this end – is being destroyed.
>
> (*BPF*, p. 257)

98 *CR*, p. 7. Cf. *BPF*, pp. 257–8.
99 *BPF*, p. 258.
100 On the importance of deliberation for a theory of democratic legitimacy, see B. Manin, "On Legitimacy and Political Deliberation," op. cit., pp. 351–9, and J. Cohen, "Deliberation and Democratic Legitimacy," in A. Hamlin and P. Pettit (eds), *The Good Polity*, Oxford: Blackwell, 1989, pp. 17–34. For the importance of persuasion and deliberation as ways to address the conflict arising out of the plurality of interests and opinions, see Hanna Pitkin and Sara Shumer, "On Participation," *Democracy*, vol. 2, no. 4, Fall 1982, pp. 43–54, esp. pp. 47–8. See also Hanna Pitkin, *Wittgenstein and Justice*, Berkeley: University of California Press, 1972, p. 208:

> In political discourse there is, characteristically, disagreement before, during, and after deliberation on what is to be done. What one hopes for is not the absence or the eradication of dissent, but its containment within the political association, the avoidance of dissent so severe that it leads to dissociation. What one hopes for is that, at the end of political deliberation, the polis will be affirmed by its membership, despite continuing dissent.

101 R. Beiner, "Interpretive Essay," *LKPP*, p. 138.
102 ibid., p. 139.
103 *LM, Thinking*, p. 94.
104 *LKPP*, p. 63.
105 *LKPP*, p. 63.
106 *LM, Thinking*, p. 192.
107 *LM, Thinking*, p. 193; Arendt, "Thinking and Moral Considerations: A Lecture," op. cit., p. 8.
108 R. Beiner, "Interpretive Essay," *LKPP*, p. 140.
109 ibid., pp. 134.
110 ibid., p. 135.
111 As Beiner puts it (ibid., pp. 135–6):

> Appealing to the judgment of one's fellows is, in the account Kant gives of it, a purely formal appeal, having nothing at all to do with any substantive relations of community . . . The substantive needs, purposes, and particular

ends of my own community are as strictly irrelevant to the judgment as those of any other.

112 ibid., p. 138.
113 Cf. David Ingram, "The Postmodern Kantianism of Arendt and Lyotard," *The Review of Metaphysics*, vol. 42, September 1988, pp. 51–77, at p. 68, where he claims that Aristotle's notion of *phronesis*

is quite opposed to Kant's notion of reflective judgment in its focus on the substantive qualifications of statesmanship – experience, cultivation of virtuous character, formation of sound habits, and so on – which, presupposing active membership within local political communities bound by common customs, cannot fulfill ideal conditions of impartiality, universalizability, and autonomy.

114 A. Wellmer, "Hannah Arendt on Judgment: The Unwritten Doctrine of Reason" (unpublished manuscript, 1985), pp. 2–3.
115 D. Ingram, "The Postmodern Kantianism of Arendt and Lyotard," op. cit., p. 69.
116 J. Habermas, "Hannah Arendt's Communications Concept of Power," *Social Research*, vol. 44, no. 1, Spring 1977, pp. 22–3 (emphases mine). For three important responses to Habermas' critique of Arendt's theory of judgment, see D. Luban, "On Habermas on Arendt on Power," *Philosophy and Social Criticism*, vol. 6, no. 1, Spring 1979, pp. 80–95; M. Canovan, "A Case of Distorted Communication: A Note on Habermas and Arendt," *Political Theory*, vol. 11, no. 1, February 1983, pp. 105–16; Ernst Vollrath, "Associational versus Communicative Rationality of Politics," in B. Parekh and T. Pantham (eds), *Political Discourse: Explorations in Indian and Western Political Thought*, New Delhi: Sage Publications, 1987, pp. 194–201.
117 R. Bernstein, *Beyond Objectivism and Relativism*, Philadelphia: University of Pennsylvania Press, 1983, pp. 221–2. For a critique directly opposed to that of Habermas and Bernstein, see F. Mechner Barnard, "Infinity and Finality: Hannah Arendt on Politics and Truth," *Canadian Journal of Political and Social Theory*, vol. 1, no. 3, Fall 1977, pp. 29–57, at p. 42, where he claims that

having drawn the line separating truth from opinion, Arendt herself succeeds – albeit unwittingly – in blurring it by elevating opinion to a degree of universality which makes it scarcely distinguishable from truth . . . Arendt, starting from a pluralistic and diversitarian base, shunning unanimity in the best Millian tradition, arrives at consensual unity strangely reminiscent of Rousseau's General Will.

This critique seems rather off the mark, since Arendt always acknowledged the existence of conflict over alternative conceptions of the common good and proposed modes of conflict-resolution based on persuasion, deliberation, and unconstrained political debate.

118 A. Wellmer, "Hannah Arendt on Judgment: The Unwritten Doctrine of Reason," op. cit., pp. 8–9.
119 ibid., pp. 16–17 (emphases mine). For a similar critique, see John Nelson, "Politics and Truth: Arendt's Problematic," *American Journal of Political Science*, vol. 22, no. 2, May 1978, pp. 270–301, esp. pp. 283–5.

120  A. Wellmer, "Hannah Arendt on Judgment," op. cit., p. 20.
121  ibid., p. 22.
122  ibid., p. 28 (emphasis mine).


## 4  Hannah Arendt's conception of citizenship

1  *HC*, p. 50.
2  *HC*, p. 51.
3  *MDT*, p. viii.
4  *HC*, p. 199.
5  *HC*, p. 52.
6  *HC*, p. 52.
7  *HC*, p. 52.
8  *HC*, pp. 52–3.
9  *HC*, p. 55.
10  Cf. *HC*, p. 173, where Arendt argues that:

> The man-made world of things, the human artifice erected by *homo faber*, becomes a home for mortal men, whose stability will endure and outlast the ever-changing movement of their lives and actions, only insomuch as it transcends both the sheer functionalism of things produced for consumption and the sheer utility of objects produced for use.

11  *HC*, p. 135.
12  *BPF*, p. 95.
13  *HC*, p. 173.
14  *HC*, p. 173.
15  *HC*, p. 55.
16  *HC*, p. 204. Cf. *MDT*, pp. 24–5 (emphasis mine), where Arendt maintains that discourse humanizes the world at the same time that it makes us human. "The common world," she writes,

> remains "inhuman" . . . unless it is constantly talked about by human beings. For the world is not humane just because it is made by human beings, and it does not become humane just because the human voice sounds in it, but only when it has become the object of discourse . . . Whatever cannot become the object of discourse – the truly sublime, the truly horrible or the uncanny – may find a human voice through which to sound into the world, but it is not exactly human. *We humanize what is going on in the world and in ourselves only by speaking of it, and in the course of speaking of it we learn to be human.*

17  M. Canovan, "Politics as Culture: Hannah Arendt and the Public Realm," *History of Political Thought*, vol. 6, no. 3, Winter 1985, pp. 617–42. In this essay Canovan argues that Arendt's conception of the public realm rests upon an implicit analogy between politics and high culture, in particular, between the values, activities, and ends of political life and those characteristic of cultural life.
18  For Arendt's rejection of the concept of human nature, see *HC*, pp. 10–11, and my comments in Chapter 1, pp. 34–5.
19  M. Oakeshott has characterized the main traditions of Western political philosophy in terms of three master-concepts, namely, Reason and Nature,

Will and Artifice, and Rational Will. He considered Plato's *Republic* as the representative text of the first tradition, Hobbes' *Leviathan* as representative of the second, and Hegel's *Philosophy of Right* as representative of the third. ("Introduction to *Leviathan*," in *Hobbes on Civil Association*, Oxford: Basil Blackwell, 1975, p. 7). Given the broad sweep of such typology, it is not surprising that Arendt's political philosophy does not fit neatly into one of the three traditions. Her political thought is in fact indebted to the civic republican tradition of Machiavelli, Montesquieu, Jefferson, and Tocqueville. For Arendt politics is neither the product of Reason and Nature, nor does it find embodiment in the Rational Will of a people. Rather, it is based on *artifice* and *speech*, that is, on durable political institutions that permit the formation of numerous spaces of appearance, and on the linguistically mediated actions and deliberations of a plurality of free and equal citizens.

20  See *HC*, p. 215; *OT*, p. 234; *OR*, pp. 30–1.

21  See *OT*, pp. 290–302, esp. pp. 295–6.

22  Arendt identified these rights as the *right to action* and the *right to opinion*. "People deprived of human rights . . . are deprived not of the right to freedom, but of the right to action; not of the right to think whatever they please, but of the right to opinion." Thus,

the fundamental deprivation of human rights is manifested first and above all in the deprivation of a place in the world which makes opinions significant and actions effective . . . We became aware of the existence of a right to have rights . . . and a right to belong to some kind of organized community, only when millions of people emerged who had lost and could not regain these rights because of the new global political situation.

(*OT*, pp. 296–7)

23  Cf. E. Young-Bruehl, *Hannah Arendt: For Love of the World*, New Haven: Yale University Press, 1982, p. xiv; L. Botstein, "Liberating the Pariah: Politics, The Jews, and Hannah Arendt," *Salmagundi*, no. 60, Spring–Summer 1983, pp. 73–106, esp. pp. 79–89; F. Fehér, "The Pariah and the Citizen: On Arendt's Political Theory," *Thesis Eleven*, no. 15, 1986, pp. 15–29, reprinted in G. T. Kaplan and C. S. Kessler (eds), *Hannah Arendt: Thinking, Judging, Freedom*, Sydney: Allen & Unwin, 1989, pp. 18–28.

24  Hannah Arendt, *The Jew as Pariah*, ed. R. Feldman, New York: Grove Press, 1978, esp. the essays "Creating a Cultural Atmosphere" and "To Save the Jewish Homeland," first published respectively in November 1947 and May 1948. For a discussion of Arendt's attitude to the "Jewish Question" see S. Benhabib, "Hannah Arendt and the Redemptive Power of Narrative," *Social Research*, vol. 57, no. 1, Spring 1990, pp. 167–96.

25  Cf. C. Pateman, *Participation and Democratic Theory*, Cambridge: Cambridge University Press, 1970; J. R. Pennock and J. W. Chapman (eds), *Participation in Politics*, New York: Atherton, 1975; B. Barber, *Strong Democracy: Participatory Politics for a New Age*, Berkeley: University of California Press, 1984. For a critique of the modern "ideology of intimacy" see R. Sennett, *The Fall of Public Man*, New York: Random House, 1978; for a related critique of the "myth of authenticity" see L. Trilling, *Sincerity and Authenticity*, Cambridge, Mass.: Harvard University Press, 1972.

26  *MDT*, p. 13.

27 *MDT*, p. 16.
28 *MDT*, p. 25.
29 M. Canovan, "Politics as Culture: Hannah Arendt and the Public Realm," op. cit., p. 632.
30 See *OR*, p. 253.
31 Cf. H. Pitkin and S. Shumer, "On Participation," *Democracy*, vol. 2, no. 4, Fall 1982, pp. 43–54, esp. pp. 47–8.
32 See *OR*, pp. 227–8, where Arendt writes that "public opinion is the death of opinions," because it is not the result of public deliberation among the body of citizens using their reason "coolly and freely," but the product of mass sentiments which are easily manipulated and molded into a "unanimous opinion" by those in authority.
33 See *BPF*, pp. 220–1. For a discussion of Arendt's notion of judgment and her use of the Kantian idea of an "enlarged mentality," see Chapter 3, pp. 111 ff.
34 *OR*, p. 227.
35 C. Lasch, "The Communitarian Critique of Liberalism," *Soundings*, vol. 69, nos. 1–2, Spring–Summer 1986, p. 64.
36 M. Canovan, "Politics as Culture : Hannah Arendt and the Public Realm," op. cit., p. 634 (emphasis mine).
37 ibid., p. 635.
38 H. Arendt, "Freedom and Politics," in A. Hunold (ed.), *Freedom and Serfdom: An Anthology of Western Thought*, Dordrecht: D. Reidel, 1961, p. 200 (emphasis mine).
39 H. Arendt, "Public Rights and Private Interests," in M. Mooney and F. Stuber (eds), *Small Comforts for Hard Times: Humanists on Public Policy*, New York: Columbia University Press, 1977, pp. 103–8, at p. 104.
40 In the essay "On Violence" Arendt provides an apt illustration of this point by contrasting the (public) interest we have in the preservation of good housing and the (private) interests of landlords and tenants. At first sight the "enlightened" self-interest of landlords and tenants might appear to be the same, that is, an interest in a well-maintained, habitable building. But in fact this is never the case: the landlord's interest is in making a profit and the tenant's interest is in keeping the rent low. The answer of an "enlightened" arbiter, Arendt notes,

> that *in the long run* the interest of the building is the *true* interest of both landlord and tenant, leaves out of account the time factor, which is of paramount importance for all concerned. Self-interest is interested in the self, and the self dies or moves out or sells the house; because of its changing condition, that is, ultimately because of the human condition of mortality, the self *qua* self cannot reckon in terms of long-range interest, i.e. the interest of a world that survives its inhabitants . . . Self-interest, when asked to yield to "true" interest – that is, the interest of the world as distinguished from that of the self – will always reply: Near is my shirt, but nearer is my skin.
>
> (*CR*, p. 175)

41 Cf. M. Markus, "The 'Anti-Feminism' of Hannah Arendt," *Thesis Eleven*, no. 17, 1987, pp. 76–87, at p. 85, where she argues that for Arendt

> action is genuinely political because it is led by the *concern with the world* and not with one's own particular interests . . . What Arendt is saying here is that

politics primarily is not about "making claims" but first of all about learning what it means to "share the world with others."

42  *CR*, p.175.
43  H. Arendt, "Public Rights and Private Interests," op. cit., p. 105.
44  ibid., p. 106.
45  H. D. Thoreau, "On the Duty of Civil Disobedience," quoted in Arendt, "Civil Disobedience," in *CR*, p. 60.
46  *CR*, pp. 60–1.
47  *CR*, p. 64.
48  Arendt believed that the morality of conscience was too private and subjective to serve as a valid standard for political action. Moreover, since it is often formulated in terms of absolute principles, she thought that it was bound to be distorted or to become destructive when introduced into the public realm. In place of conscience she advocated the political principle of *active citizenship*. See my discussion of this issue in Chapter 2, pp. 93–4.
49  *RPW*, p. 311.
50  H. Arendt, "Thinking and Moral Considerations: A Lecture," *Social Research*, vol. 51, no. 1, Spring 1984, pp. 7–37; *LM, Thinking*, pp. 190–3. See my discussion in Chapter 3, pp. 110–11.
51  *LM, Thinking*, p. 191. Cf. *CR*, p. 63:

> The rules of conscience . . . like those Thoreau announced in his essay, [are] entirely negative. They do not say what to do; they say what not to do. They do not spell out certain principles for taking action; they lay down boundaries no act should transgress. They say: Don't do wrong, for then you will have to live together with a wrongdoer.

52  *CR*, p. 62.
53  Canovan formulates this distinction as that between

> looking at a political issue from a private point of view, asking "what does my conscience demand of me," and looking at it from a public point of view, saying "what will become of the polity, and what action must I take to promote the public good?"

> She argues that for Arendt the important difference was between "living as a private individual with a conscience, and living together with others in a public world for which all are jointly responsible." ("Politics as Culture: Hannah Arendt and the Public Realm," op. cit., pp. 638–9).

54  Pitkin and Shumer, "On Participation," op. cit., p. 47.
55  Cf. M. Canovan, "A Case of Distorted Communication: A Note on Habermas and Arendt," *Political Theory*, vol. 11, no. 1, February 1983, pp. 105–16, at pp. 111–12, where Canovan argues that for Arendt

> the public world and its institutions are the only means of holding plural individuals together in freedom. Free people do not share common convictions or have a "common will" . . . What they can share is not convictions that are identical inside all their individual minds, but a common world of institutions that is outside them and that all support by their actions . . . They can be united . . . because outside in the world they all inhabit the

same public space, acknowledge its formal rules, and are therefore committed to achieving a working compromise when they differ . . . Where there is a mutual commitment to the continuance of the same public world, differences can be settled through purely political means.

56 I have discussed the tension between the expressive and the communicative model of action, which underlies the contrast between the dramaturgical and the discursive conception of the public sphere, in Chapter 2, pp. 83–5, and pp. 95–9.

57 In *The Human Condition* Arendt identifies this community with the institution of the *polis*. The *polis* in her view had a twofold function. First, it "was supposed to multiply the occasions to win 'immortal fame,' that is, to multiply the chances for everybody to distinguish himself, to show in deed and word who he was in his unique distinctness." Second, it "was to offer a remedy for the futility of action and speech, for the chances that a deed deserving fame would not be forgotten, that it actually would become 'immortal,' were not very good." The *polis*, therefore, "seemed to assure that the most futile of human activities, action and speech, and the least tangible and most ephemeral of man-made 'products,' the deeds and stories which are their outcome, would become imperishable" (*HC*, pp. 197–8).

58 See the last chapter of *On Revolution* and the essays contained in *Crises of the Republic*, especially "Civil Disobedience" and "Thoughts on Politics and Revolution."

59 Seyla Benhabib argues that the opposition between the two conceptions of the public sphere

corresponds to the tension between the Greek and the modern experiences of politics. For the moderns, the public space is essentially porous: the distinction between the "social" and the "political" makes no sense in the modern world, not because all politics has become administration and because the economy has become the quintessential "public" in modern societies, but primarily because the struggle to make something public is a struggle for justice. With the entry of every new group into the public space of politics after the French and American revolutions, the scope of the public gets extended.

("Hannah Arendt and the Redemptive Power of Narrative," op. cit., pp. 194–5)

For a discussion of this issue and a critique of Arendt's distinction between the "social" and the "political," and the related distinction between the "private" and the "public," see Chapter 1, pp. 58 ff.

60 P. Fuss, "Hannah Arendt's Conception of Political Community," in *RPW*, p. 172.

61 B. Parekh, *Hannah Arendt and the Search for a New Political Philosophy*, London: Macmillan, 1981, p. 177.

62 P. Fuss, "Hannah Arendt's Conception of Political Community," op. cit., p. 173.

63 B. Parekh, *Hannah Arendt and the Search for a New Political Philosophy*, op. cit., pp. 177–8.

64 H. Pitkin, *Wittgenstein and Justice*, Berkeley: University of California Press, 1972, p. 208.

65 ibid., p. 208.
66 J. Habermas, "On Social Identity," *Telos*, no. 19, Spring 1974, pp. 91–103, at p. 102.
67 Cf. C. Mouffe, "Rawls: Political Philosophy without Politics," *Philosophy and Social Criticism*, vol. 13, no. 2, Summer 1988, pp. 105–23, esp. pp. 116–17.
68 Nancy Fraser, "Toward a Discourse Ethic of Solidarity," *Praxis International*, vol. 5, no. 4, January 1986, pp. 425–9, at p. 428.
69 ibid., p. 428.
70 ibid., p. 428.
71 ibid., p. 428.
72 See Chapter 2, pp. 93–4; Chapter 4, pp. 145–6.
73 N. Fraser, "Toward a Discourse Ethic of Solidarity," op. cit., pp. 428–9 (last emphasis mine). For a number of recent attempts to formulate a feminist theory of citizenship, see Mary G. Dietz, "Citizenship with a Feminist Face: The Problem with Maternal Thinking," *Political Theory*, vol. 13, no. 1, February 1985, pp. 19–37; *idem*, "Context is All: Feminism and Theories of Citizenship," in C. Mouffe (ed.), *Dimensions of Radical Democracy*, London: Verso, 1992, pp. 63–85; Carole Pateman, *The Disorder of Women*, Cambridge: Polity Press, 1989; Iris M. Young, *Justice and the Politics of Difference*, Princeton: Princeton University Press, 1990; Anne Phillips, *Engendering Democracy*, Cambridge: Polity Press, 1991.
74 N. Fraser, "Toward a Discourse Ethic of Solidarity," op. cit., p. 429 (emphasis mine).
75 For a discussion of Arendt's attitude to the questions raised by the women's movement, see M. Markus, "The 'Anti-Feminism' of Hannah Arendt," op. cit. In this essay Markus argues that both Rosa Luxemburg and Hannah Arendt shared the conviction that

women's issues could not and should not be divorced from the larger range of political concerns, and the broader political struggle. It is not that either of them, and certainly not Arendt, expected these very real problems to be solved automatically as the result of other social-political transformations. They both, however, insisted that these issues should become part of explicitly political activity correlated and coordinated with the goals of other political groups.

(p. 82)

See also Mary G. Dietz, "Hannah Arendt and Feminist Politics," in M. L. Shanley and C. Pateman (eds), *Feminist Interpretations and Political Theory*, Cambridge: Polity Press, 1991, pp. 232–52.
76 A. Pizzorno, "On the Rationality of Democratic Choice," *Telos*, no. 63, Spring 1985, pp. 41–69.
77 A. Pizzorno, "Some Other Kind of Otherness," in A. Foxley, M. S. McPherson, and G. O'Donnell (eds), *Development, Democracy, and the Art of Trespassing*, Notre Dame: University of Notre Dame Press, 1986, pp. 355–73.
78 A. Pizzorno, "On the Rationality of Democratic Choice," op. cit., pp. 56–7. In the essay "Some Other Kind of Otherness" Pizzorno argues that any theory that explains human action in terms of rational choice must be self-defeating. A person who chooses "rationally" must be able to evaluate the

consequences of his choice in terms of his own interests. But the interests of his *present* self are not the same as those of his *future* selves. Since comparing utilities intertemporally is as arbitrary as comparing them interpersonally, normally a state of choice is a state of uncertainty about how a future self will evaluate the situation resulting from the choices made in the present. The special condition that allows a comparison of some sort to be made is the constitution of a state of identity that can persist through time. This state depends on the stability of what Pizzorno calls a "circle of recognition." What this "circle" is required to recognize are the values that a person is using in his choices, that is, the values that make him a certain recognizable identical agent. Social action can thus be explained not as the product of selves maximizing instantaneous satisfactions, nor of selves devising strategies aimed at procuring benefits for future selves. Rather, it is the product of selves aiming at securing *horizontal ties* with selves of other persons, or *vertical ties* with future selves.

79 A. Pizzorno, "On the Rationality of Democratic Choice," op. cit., p. 62.
80 ibid., p. 64.
81 ibid., p. 60.
82 ibid., p. 63.
83 ibid., p. 64.
84 ibid., p. 64.
85 ibid., pp. 66–7.
86 ibid., p. 68.
87 *OR*, p. 254 (emphases mine).
88 *OR*, pp. 237–8. In the essay "Hannah Arendt's Communications Concept of Power," Habermas suggests that it was Arendt's fear of mass apathy under modern representative democracy that made her into an advocate of the council system. As he puts it:

Whereas the theorists of democratic elitism (following Schumpeter) commend representative government and the party system as channels for the political participation of a depoliticized mass, Arendt sees the danger precisely in this situation. Mediatizing the population through highly bureaucratized administrations, parties, and organizations just supplements and fortifies those privatistic forms of life which provide the psychological base for mobilizing the unpolitical, that is, for establishing totalitarian rule.

See J. Habermas, "Hannah Arendt's Communications Concept of Power," *Social Research*, vol. 44, no. 1, Spring 1977, pp. 10–11.
89 See Chapter 2, pp. 96–7.
90 H. Pitkin and S. Shumer, "On Participation," op. cit., p. 52 (emphasis mine).
91 S. Evans and H. Boyte, *Free Spaces: The Sources of Democratic Change in America*, New York: Harper & Row, 1986, p. 17 (emphasis mine).
92 S. Benhabib, "Autonomy, Modernity and Community: Communitarianism and Critical Social Theory in Dialogue," in *Situating the Self* (Cambridge: Polity Press, 1992, p. 81 (emphasis mine).
93 *OR*, p. 255.
94 "The Crisis in Culture" and "Truth and Politics," in *BPF*, pp. 197–226, 227–64.
95 *OR*, p. 227.

96  *BPF*, p. 241.
97  H. Arendt, "Thinking and Moral Considerations," *Social Research*, vol. 51, no. 1, Spring 1984, p. 36. See also *BPF*, p. 221, where Arendt says that "the capacity to judge is a specifically political ability," and that "judgment may be one of the fundamental abilities of man as a political being insofar as it enables him to orient himself in the public realm."
98  *BPF*, pp. 220–1.
99  S. Benhabib, "Judgment and the Moral Foundations of Politics in Arendt's Thought," in *Situating the Self*, op. cit., p. 141.
100 ibid., p. 140.

# Bibliography

## Books by Hannah Arendt

Arendt, H. *Der Liebesbegriff bei Augustin* (Berlin: Springer, 1929).
—— *The Origins of Totalitarianism* (New York: Harcourt Brace Jovanovich, 1951, new edn 1973).
—— *The Human Condition* (Chicago: University of Chicago Press, 1958).
—— *Rahel Varnhagen* (New York: Harcourt Brace Jovanovich, 1958, new edn 1974).
—— *Between Past and Future* (New York: Viking Press, 1961, new edn 1968).
—— *Eichmann in Jerusalem* (New York: Viking Press, 1963, new edn 1965).
—— *On Revolution* (New York: Viking Press, 1963, new edn 1965).
—— *Men in Dark Times* (New York: Harcourt Brace Jovanovich, 1968).
—— *Crises of the Republic* (New York: Harcourt Brace Jovanovich, 1972).
—— *The Jew as Pariah* ed. R. Feldman (New York: Grove Press, 1978).
—— *The Life of the Mind*, vol. 1, *Thinking*; vol. 2, *Willing* (New York: Harcourt Brace Jovanovich, 1978).
—— *Lectures on Kant's Political Philosophy*, ed. R. Beiner (Chicago: University of Chicago Press, 1982).

## Books on Hannah Arendt

Barnouw, D. *Visible Spaces: Hannah Arendt and the German–Jewish Experience* (Baltimore: Johns Hopkins University Press, 1990).
Benhabib, S. *The Reluctant Modernism of Hannah Arendt* (London: Sage Publications, 1994).
Bowen-Moore, P. *Hannah Arendt's Philosophy of Natality* (London: Macmillan, 1989).
Bradshaw, L. *Acting and Thinking: The Political Thought of Hannah Arendt* (Toronto: University of Toronto Press, 1989).
Canovan, M. *The Political Thought of Hannah Arendt* (London: J. M. Dent, 1974).
—— *Hannah Arendt: A Reinterpretation of Her Political Thought* (Cambridge: Cambridge University Press, 1992).
Compenhausen, A., Shafer, G., and Ries, W. *Hannah Arendt zum Gedanken* (Hanover: Niedersächs, 1977).

Dossa, S. *The Public Realm and The Public Self: The Political Theory of Hannah Arendt* (Waterloo, Ontario: Wilfred Laurier University Press, 1988).

Enegrén, A. *La Pensée Politique de Hannah Arendt* (Paris: PUF, 1984).

Erler, H. *Hannah Arendt, Hegel und Marx* (Köln-Wien: Böhlaw, 1979).

Friedmann, F. *Hannah Arendt. Eine deutsche Jüdin im Zeitalter des Totalitarismus* (München: Piper, 1985).

Hansen, P. *Hannah Arendt* (Cambridge: Polity Press, 1993).

Isaac, J. C. *Arendt, Camus, and Modern Rebellion* (New Haven: Yale University Press, 1992).

Kateb, G. *Hannah Arendt: Politics, Conscience, Evil* (Oxford: Martin Robertson, 1984).

Lafer, C. *Hannah Arendt: Pensamiento, Persuaso, e Poder* (Rio de Janeiro: Paz e Terra, 1979).

May, D. *Hannah Arendt* (Harmondsworth: Penguin Books, 1986).

Parekh, B. *Hannah Arendt and the Search for a New Political Philosophy* (London: Macmillan, 1981).

Robinson, J. *And the Crooked Shall Be Made Straight: The Eichmann Trial, the Jewish Catastrophe, and Hannah Arendt's Narrative* (Philadelphia: Jewish Publication Society, 1965).

Tolle, G. J. *Human Nature Under Fire: The Political Philosophy of Hannah Arendt* (Lanham, Md.: University Press of America, 1982).

Watson, D. *Arendt* (London: Fontana Press, 1992).

Whitfield, S. *Into the Dark: Hannah Arendt and Totalitarianism* (Philadelphia: Temple University Press, 1980).

Young-Bruehl, E. *Hannah Arendt: For Love of the World* (New Haven: Yale University Press, 1982).

## Collections of articles on Hannah Arendt

Bernauer, J. W. (ed.) *Amor Mundi: Explorations in the Faith and Thought of Hannah Arendt* (Dordrecht: Martinus Nijhoff,1987).

Duso, G. (ed.) *Filosofia Politica e Pratica del Pensiero* (Milano: Franco Angeli, 1988).

Esposito, R. (ed.) *La Pluralità Irrappresentabile: Il pensiero politico di Hannah Arendt* (Urbino: Edizioni Quattro Venti, 1987).

Hill, M. A. (ed.) *Hannah Arendt: The Recovery of the Public World* (New York: St Martin's Press, 1979).

Kaplan, G. T. and Kessler, C. S. (eds) *Hannah Arendt: Thinking, Judging, Freedom* (Sydney: Allen & Unwin, 1989).

Krummacher, F. (ed.) *Die Kontroverse Hannah Arendt und die Juden* (München: Nymphenburger Verlagshandlung, 1964).

Reif, A. (ed.) *Hannah Arendt: Materialien Zu ihrem Werk* (Wien: Europa Verlag, 1979).

## Special issues of journals

*Aut-Aut, Il Pensiero Plurale di Hannah Arendt*, nos. 239–40, 1990.

*Cahiers de Philosophie, Hannah Arendt: Confrontations*, no. 4, 1987.

*Cahiers du Grif, Hannah Arendt*, no. 33, 1986.

*Comunità, Hannah Arendt,* no. 183, 1981.
*Esprit, Hannah Arendt,* no. 6, 1980.
*Études Phénoménologiques, Hannah Arendt,* no. 2, 1985.
*Merkur, Hannah Arendt,* no. 10, 1976.
*Il Mulino, La Filosofia Politica di Hannah Arendt,* no. 303, 1986.
*Praxis International, Symposium on Hannah Arendt's Political Thought,* vol. 9, no. 1–2, 1989.
*Response, Hannah Arendt,* no. 19, 1980.
*Salmagundi, Politics and the Social Contract* no. 60, 1983.
*Social Research, Hannah Arendt,* vol. 44, no. 1, 1977.
*Social Research, Philosophy and Politics II: Hannah Arendt,* vol. 57, no. 1, 1990.

## Selected articles on Hannah Arendt

Abel, L. "The Aesthetics of Evil: Hannah Arendt on Eichmann and the Jews," *Partisan Review,* vol. 30, no. 1, 1963.
Adamson, W. "Beyond Reform or Revolution: Notes on Political Education in Gramsci, Habermas, and Arendt," *Theory and Society,* vol. 6, no. 3, 1978.
Allen, W. "Hannah Arendt's Existential Phenomenology and Political Freedom," *Philosophy and Social Criticism,* vol. 9, no. 2, 1982.
—— "Homo Aristocus: Hannah Arendt's Elites," *Idealistic Studies,* vol. 13, 1983.
—— "A Novel Form of Government: Hannah Arendt on Totalitarianism," *The Political Science Reviewer,* vol. 16, 1986.
Aron, R. "L'essence du totalitarisme," *Critique,* vol. 10, no. 80, 1954.
Baccelli, L. "Critica della Modernità e Filosofia Politica. Nota sulla Riabilitazione di Arendt, Strauss, Voegelin," *Fenomenologia e Società,* vol. 12, no. 3, 1989.
Bakan, M. "Hannah Arendt's Concepts of Labor and Work," in M. Hill (ed.), *Hannah Arendt: The Recovery of the Public World* (New York: St Martin's Press, 1979).
—— "Hannah Arendt's Critical Appropriation of Heidegger's Thought as Political Philosophy," in D. Ihde and H. Silverman (eds), *Descriptions* (New York: SUNY, 1985).
—— "Arendt and Heidegger: The Episodic Intertwining of Life and Work," *Philosophy and Social Criticism,* vol. 12, no. 1, 1987.
Barnard, F. "Infinity and Finality: Hannah Arendt on Politics and Truth," *Canadian Journal of Political and Social Theory,* vol. 1, no. 3, 1977.
Beatty, J. "Thinking and Moral Considerations: Socrates and Arendt's Eichmann," *The Journal of Value Inquiry,* no. 10, 1976.
Beiner, R. "A Commentary on Hannah Arendt's Unwritten Finale," *History of Political Thought,* vol. 1, no. 1, 1980.
—— "The Importance of Storytelling," *The Times Higher Education Supplement,* 16 July 1982.
—— "Interpretive Essay: Hannah Arendt on Judging," in Hannah Arendt, *Lectures on Kant's Political Philosophy* (Chicago: University of Chicago Press, 1982).
—— "Action, Natality and Citizenship: Hannah Arendt's Concept of Freedom," in Z. Pelczynski and J. Gray (eds), *Conceptions of Liberty in Political Philosophy* (London: Athlone Press, 1984).
—— "Hannah Arendt and Leo Strauss: the Uncommenced Dialogue," *Political Theory,* vol. 18, no. 2, 1990.

Beiner, R. S. "Hannah Arendt on Capitalism and Socialism," *Government and Opposition*, vol. 25, no. 3, 1990.

Belardinelli, S. "Natalità e Azione in Hannah Arendt" (Parte Prima), *La Nottola*, vol. 3, no. 3, 1984

―― "Natalità e Azione in Hannah Arendt" (Parte Seconda), *La Nottola*, vol. 4, no. 1, 1985.

Bell, D. "The Alphabet of Justice: On Eichmann in Jerusalem," *Partisan Review*, vol. 30, no. 3, 1963.

Benhabib. S. "Judgment and the Moral Foundations of Politics in Arendt's Thought," *Political Theory*, vol. 16, no. 1, 1988, reprinted in *Situating the Self* (Cambridge: Polity Press, 1992).

―― "Hannah Arendt and the Redemptive Power of Narrative," *Social Research*, vol. 57, no. 1, 1990.

―― "Models of Public Space: Hannah Arendt, the Liberal Tradition and Jürgen Habermas," in *Situating the Self* (Cambridge: Polity Press, 1992).

―― "Feminist Theory and Hannah Arendt's Concept of Public Space," *History of the Human Sciences*, vol. 6, no. 2, 1993.

Berki, R. "The Idealism of Nostalgia," in *On Political Realism* (London: J. M. Dent, 1981).

Bernauer, J. "On Reading and Mis-Reading Hannah Arendt," *Philosophy and Social Criticism*, vol. 11, no. 1, 1985.

―― "The Faith of Hannah Arendt: Amor Mundi and its Critique-Assimilation of Religious Experience," in J. Bernauer (ed.), *Amor Mundi* (Dordrecht: Martinus Nijhoff, 1987).

Bernstein, R. "Hannah Arendt: The Ambiguities of Theory and Practice," in Terence Ball (ed.), *Political Theory and Praxis* (Minneapolis: University of Minnesota Press, 1977).

―― "Judging – the Actor and the Spectator," in *Philosophical Profiles* (Cambridge: Polity Press, 1986).

―― "Rethinking the Social and the Political," in *Philosophical Profiles* (Cambridge: Polity Press, 1986).

Bettelheim, B. Review of Hannah Arendt, *Eichmann in Jerusalem*, *New Republic*, no. 184, 15 June 1963.

Bettini, G. "Introduzione," to Hannah Arendt, *Ebraismo e Modernità* (Milano: Unicopli, 1986).

Bodei, R. "Hannah Arendt interprete di Agostino," in R. Esposito (ed.), *La Pluralità Irrappresentabile* (Urbino: Edizioni Quattro Venti, 1987).

Botstein, L. "Hannah Arendt: Opposing Views," *Partisan Review*, vol. 45, no. 3, 1978.

―― "Liberating the Pariah: Politics, the Jews, and Hannah Arendt," *Salmagundi*, no. 60, 1983.

―― "The Jew as Pariah: Hannah Arendt's Political Philosophy," *Dialectical Anthropology*, vol. 8, nos. 1–2, 1983.

Bowen-Moore, P. "Natality, Amor Mundi and Nuclearism in the Thought of Hannah Arendt," in J. Bernauer (ed.), *Amor Mundi* (Dordrecht: Martinus Nijhoff, 1987).

Boyle, P. "Elusive Neighborliness: Hannah Arendt's Interpretation of Saint Augustine," in J. Bernauer (ed.), *Amor Mundi* (Dordrecht: Martinus Nijhoff, 1987).

Burke, J. "Thinking in a World of Appearances. Hannah Arendt between Karl Jaspers and Martin Heidegger", *Analecta Husserliana*, vol. 21, 1986.

Burns, R. "Hannah Arendt's Constitutional Thought," in J. Bernauer (ed.), *Amor Mundi* (Dordrecht: Martinus Nijhoff, 1987).

Canovan, M. "The Contradictions of Hannah Arendt's Political Thought," *Political Theory*, vol. 6, no. 1, 1978.

—— "On Levin's 'Animal Laborans and Homo Politicus in Hannah Arendt,' " *Political Theory*, vol. 8, no. 3, 1980.

—— "On Pitkin's 'Justice,' " *Political Theory*, vol. 10, no. 3, 1982.

—— "A Case of Distorted Communication: A Note on Habermas and Arendt," *Political Theory*, vol. 11, no. 1, 1983.

—— "Arendt, Rousseau, and Human Plurality in Politics," *Journal of Politics*, vol. 45, no. 2, 1983.

—— "Politics as Culture: Hannah Arendt and the Public Realm," *History of Political Thought*, vol. 6, no. 3, 1985.

—— "Socrates or Heidegger? Hannah Arendt's Reflections on Philosophy and Politics," *Social Research*, vol. 57, no. 1, 1990.

Castoriadis, C. "The Destinies of Totalitarianism," *Salmagundi*, no. 60, 1983.

—— "The Greek Polis and the Creation of Democracy," *Graduate Faculty Philosophy Journal*, vol. 9, no. 2, 1983.

Clarke, B. "Beyond the Banality of Evil," *The British Journal of Political Science*, vol. 10, no. 4, 1980.

Cooper, B. "Action into Nature: Hannah Arendt's Reflections on Technology," in R. B. Day, R. Beiner, and J. Masciulli (eds), *Democratic Theory and Technological Society* (New York: M. E. Sharpe, 1988).

Cooper, L. "Hannah Arendt's Political Philosophy: An Interpretation," *Review of Politics*, vol. 38, no. 2, 1976.

Cotroneo, G. "Hannah Arendt, una filosofia per la libertà," *Libro Aperto*, vol. 3, no. 15, 1982.

Crick, B. "On Rereading The Origins of Totalitarianism," *Social Research*, vol. 44, no. 1, 1977; reprinted in M. Hill (ed.), *Hannah Arendt: The Recovery of the Public World* (New York: St Martin's Press, 1979).

Dal Lago, A. "Politeia: Cittadinanza ed Esilio nell'opera di Hannah Arendt," *Il Mulino*, no. 293, 1984.

—— "La difficile vittoria sul tempo. Pensiero e azione in Hannah Arendt," introduction to Hannah Arendt, *La Vita della Mente* (Bologna: Il Mulino, 1987).

—— "Una filosofia della presenza. Hannah Arendt, Heidegger e la possibilità dell'agire," in R. Esposito (ed.), *La Pluralità Irrappresentabile* (Urbino: Edizioni Quattro Venti, 1987).

Dallmayr, F. "Political Philosophy Today," in *Polis and Praxis* (Cambridge: MIT Press 1984).

—— "Praxis and Experience," in *Polis and Praxis* (Cambridge: MIT Press, 1984).

—— "Public or Private Freedom? Response to Kateb," *Social Research*, vol. 54, no. 3, 1987.

Denneny, M. "The Privilege of Ourselves: Hannah Arendt on Judgment," in M. Hill (ed.), *Hannah Arendt: The Recovery of the Public World* (New York: St Martin's Press, 1979).

d'Entrèves, M. P. "Il Concetto di Giudizio Politico nella Filosofia di Hannah Arendt," in R. Esposito (ed.), *La Pluralità Irrappresentabile* (Urbino: Edizioni Quattro Venti, 1987).

—— "Agency, Identity, and Culture: Hannah Arendt's Conception of Citizenship," *Praxis International*, vol. 9, nos. 1–2, 1989.

—— "Freedom, Plurality, Solidarity: Hannah Arendt's Theory of Action," *Philosophy and Social Criticism*, vol. 15, no. 4, 1989.

—— Review of Hannah Arendt, *The Origins of Totalitarianism, L'Indice dei Libri del Mese*, vol. 7, no. 6, 1990.

—— "Modernity and the Human Condition: Hannah Arendt's Conception of Modernity," *Thesis Eleven*, no. 30, 1991.

—— "Hannah Arendt and the Idea of Citizenship," in C. Mouffe (ed.), *Dimensions of Radical Democracy* (London: Verso, 1992).

Dietz, M. G. "Hannah Arendt and Feminist Politics," in M. L. Shanley and C. Pateman (eds), *Feminist Interpretations and Political Theory* (Cambridge: Polity Press, 1991).

Donoghue, D. "After Reading Hannah Arendt," *Poetry*, vol. 100, 1962.

Dossa, S. "Human Status and Politics: Hannah Arendt on the Holocaust," *Canadian Journal of Political Science*, vol. 13, no. 2, 1980.

—— "Hannah Arendt on Billy Budd and Robespierre: The Public Realm and The Private Self," *Philosophy and Social Criticism*, vol. 9, nos. 3–4, 1982.

—— "Hannah Arendt on Eichmann: The Public, the Private and Evil," *Review of Politics*, vol. 46, no. 2, 1984.

Dostal, R. "Judging Human Action: Arendt's Appropriation of Kant," *The Review of Metaphysics*, vol. 37, 1984.

Duffé, B. "Hannah Arendt: penser l'histoire en ses commencements. De la fondation à l'innovation," *Revue des Sciences Philosophiques et Theologiques*, vol. 67, no. 3, 1983.

Elevitch, B. "Arendt and Heidegger: The Illusion of Politics," *Boston University Journal*, vol. 20, nos. 1–2, 1972.

—— "Hannah Arendt's Testimony," *The Massachusetts Review*, vol. 20, no. 2, 1979.

Elshtain, J. "War and Political Discourse: From Machiavelli to Arendt," in *Meditations on Modern Political Thought: Masculine/Feminine Themes from Luther to Arendt* (New York: Praeger Publishers, 1986).

Enegrén, A. "Révolution et fondation," *Esprit*, vol. 4, no. 6, 1980.

—— "Hannah Arendt, lectrice de Merleau-Ponty," *Esprit*, vol. 6, no. 6, 1982.

—— "L'esprit au coeur du temps: itinéraire à travers la pensée de Hannah Arendt," *Esprit* , vol. 6, nos. 7–8, 1982.

—— "Pouvoir et liberté: une approche de la théorie politique de Hannah Arendt," *Etudes*, no. 4, 1983.

Eslin, J. "L'événement de penser"; "Un loi qui vaille pour l'humanité," *Esprit*, vol. 4, no. 6, 1980.

—— "Penser l'action. A propos de Hannah Arendt," *Esprit*, vol. 10, nos. 8–9, 1986.

Esposito, R. "Politica e Tradizione. Ad Hannah Arendt," *Il Centauro*, nos. 13–14, 1985.

—— "Hannah Arendt tra Volontà e Rappresentazione: Per una Critica del Decisionismo," *Il Mulino*, no. 303, 1986.

Ezorsky, G. "Hannah Arendt's View of Totalitarianism and the Holocaust," *The Philosophical Forum*, vol. 16, nos. 1–2, 1985.

Fehér, F. "The Pariah and the Citizen: On Arendt's Political Theory," *Thesis Eleven*, no. 15, 1986.

—— "Freedom and the Social Question: Hannah Arendt's Theory of the French Revolution," *Philosophy and Social Criticism*, vol. 12, no. 1, 1987.

Feldman, R. "The Jew as Pariah: The Case of Hannah Arendt," introduction to Hannah Arendt, *The Jew as Pariah* (New York: Grove Press, 1978).

Ferry, J. "Habermas critique de Hannah Arendt," *Esprit*, vol. 4, no. 6, 1980.

Fistetti, F. "Metafisica e Politica in *La Vita Della Mente* di Hannah Arendt," *Poleis*, no. 1, 1988.

—— "Scheherazade: La passione del racconto," *Poleis*, nos. 3–4, 1988.

—— "Hannah Arendt, l'inquietudine dell'apolide," *Micromega*, n. 3, 1989.

—— "Hannah Arendt: La Memoria come Spazio del Pensiero," Laicata Editore, n.d.

Flores D'Arcais, P. "L'esistenzialismo libertario di Hannah Arendt," introduction to Hannah Arendt, *Politica e Menzogna* (Milano: Sugarco, 1985).

Flynn, B. "The Question of an Ontology of the Political: Arendt, Merleau-Ponty, Lefort," *International Studies in Philosophy*, vol. 16, 1984.

Focher, F. "Sulla tradizione latina nel pensiero di Hannah Arendt," *Paideia*, vol. 41, nos. 3–6, 1986.

Frampton, K. "The Work of Hannah Arendt," in C. Jencks and G. Baird (eds), *Meaning and Architecture* (New York: Braziller, 1970).

—— "The Status of Man and the Status of His Objects: A Reading of The Human Condition," in M. Hill (ed.), *Hannah Arendt: The Recovery of the Public World* (New York: St Martin's Press, 1979).

Fuss, P. "Hannah Arendt's Conception of Political Community," *Idealistic Studies*, vol. 3, no. 3 1973; reprinted in. M. Hill (ed.), *Hannah Arendt: The Recovery of the Public World* (New York: St Martin's Press, 1979).

—— Review of Hannah Arendt, *The Life of the Mind*, in *The Independent Journal of Philosophy*, vol. 4, no. 4, 1983.

Galli, C. "Hannah Arendt e le categorie politiche della modernità," in R. Esposito (ed.), *La Pluralità Irrappresentabile* (Urbino: Edizioni Quattro Venti, 1987).

—— "Strauss, Voegelin, Arendt lettori di Thomas Hobbes," in G. Duso (ed.), *Filosofia Politica e Pratica del Pensiero* (Milano: Franco Angeli, 1988).

Germino, D. "The Contemporary Revival of Political Theory: Oakeshott, Arendt, Jouvenel, and Strauss," in *Beyond Ideology: The Revival of Political Theory* (Chicago: University of Chicago Press, 1976).

Glenn Gray, J. "The Winds of Thought," *Social Research*, vol. 44, no. 1, 1977.

—— "The Abyss of Freedom and Hannah Arendt," in M. Hill (ed.), *Hannah Arendt: The Recovery of the Public World* (New York: St Martin's Press, 1979).

Gray, S. "Hannah Arendt and the Solitariness of Thinking," *Philosophy Today*, no. 25, 1981.

Gunnell, J. "Hannah Arendt: The Decline of the Public Realm," in *Political Theory: Tradition and Interpretation* (Cambridge: Winthrop Publishers, 1979).

Habermas, J. Review of Hannah Arendt, *On Revolution*, in *Kultur und Kritik* (Frankfurt: Suhrkamp, 1973).

—— "Hannah Arendt's Communications Concept of Power," *Social Research*, vol. 44, no. 1, Spring 1977.

—— "On the German-Jewish Heritage," *Telos*, no. 44, 1980.

Heather, G. and Stolz, M. "Hannah Arendt and the Problem of Critical Theory," *The Journal of Politics*, vol. 41, 1979.

Heller, A. "Hannah Arendt on The Vita Contemplativa," *Philosophy and Social Criticism*, vol. 12, no. 4, 1987.

—— "An Imaginary Preface to the 1984 Edition of Hannah Arendt's *The Origins of Totalitarianism*" in F. Fehér and A. Heller, *Eastern Left, Western Left: Totalitarianism, Freedom and Democracy* (Cambridge: Polity Press, 1987).

Heller, E. "Hannah Arendt as a Critic of Literature," *Social Research*, vol. 44, no. 1, 1977.

Hill, M. "The Fictions of Mankind and the Stories of Men," in M. Hill (ed.), *Hannah Arendt: The Recovery of the Public World* (New York: St Martin's Press, 1979).

Hinchman, L. P. and Hinchman, S. K. "In Heidegger's Shadow: Hannah Arendt's Phenomenological Humanism," *The Review of Politics*, vol. 46, no. 2, 1984.

—— "Existentialism Politicized: Arendt's Debt to Jaspers," *Review of Politics*, vol. 53, no. 3, 1991.

Hinchman, S. K. "Common Sense and Political Barbarism in the Theory of Hannah Arendt," *Polity*, vol. 17, no. 2, 1984.

Hobsbawm, E. "Hannah Arendt on Revolution," in *Revolutionaries* (London: Quartet Books, 1977).

Honeywell, J. "Revolution: Its Potentialities and Its Degradations," *Ethics*, vol. 80, 1970.

Honig, B. "Arendt, Identity, and Difference," *Political Theory*, vol. 16, no. 1, 1988.

—— "Declarations of Independence: Arendt and Derrida on the Problem of Founding a Republic," *American Political Science Review*, vol. 85, no. 1, 1991.

—— "Toward an Agonistic Feminism: Hannah Arendt and the Politics of Identity," in J. Butler and J. W. Scott (eds), *Feminists Theorize the Political* (New York: Routledge, 1992).

Hughes, S. "Hannah Arendt and the Totalitarian Threat," in *The Sea Change: The Migration of Social Thought, 1930–1965* (New York: Harper & Row, 1975).

Ingram, D. "The Postmodern Kantianism of Arendt and Lyotard," *Review of Metaphysics*, vol. 42, 1988.

Isaac, J. C. "Arendt, Camus, and Postmodern Politics," *Praxis International*, vol. 9, nos. 1–2, 1989.

Jacobitti, S. "Hannah Arendt and the Will," *Political Theory*, vol. 16, no. 1, 1988.

—— "The Public, the Private, the Moral: Hannah Arendt and Political Morality," *International Political Science Review*, vol. 12, no. 4, 1991.

Jacobson, N. "Parable and Paradox: In Response to Arendt's *On Revolution*," *Salmagundi*, no. 60, 1983.

Jay, M. "Hannah Arendt: Opposing Views," *Partisan Review*, vol. 45, no. 3, 1978; reprinted in M. Jay, *Permanent Exiles* (New York: Columbia University Press, 1986).

Jonas, H. "Acting, Knowing, Thinking: Gleanings from Hannah Arendt's Philosophical Work," *Social Research*, vol. 44, no. 1, 1977.

Justman, S. "Hannah Arendt and the Idea of Disclosure," *Philosophy and Social Criticism*, vol. 8, no. 3, 1981.

Kateb, G. "Freedom and Worldliness in the Thought of Hannah Arendt," *Political Theory*, vol. 5, no. 2, 1977 .

—— "Hannah Arendt," in D. Sills (ed.), *International Encyclopedia of the Social Sciences: Biographical Supplement* (New York: Free Press, 1979).

—— "Hannah Arendt: Alienation and America," *Raritan*, vol. 3, no. 1, 1983.

—— "Arendt and Representative Democracy," *Salmagundi*, no. 60, 1983.

—— "Death and Politics: Hannah Arendt's Reflections on the American Constitution," *Social Research*, vol. 54, no. 3, 1987.

Kazin, A. "Woman in Dark Times," *The New York Review of Books*, 24 June 1982.

King, R. "Endings and Beginnings: Politics in Arendt's Early Thought," *Political Theory*, vol. 12, no. 2, 1984

Knauer, J. "Motive and Goal in Hannah Arendt's Concept of Political Action," *The American Political Science Review*, vol. 74, no. 3, 1980.

—— "On Canovan, Pitkin, Arendt, and Justice," *Political Theory*, vol. 11, no. 3, 1983.

—— Review of Hannah Arendt, *The Life of the Mind*, in *International Studies in Philosophy*, vol. 16, 1984.

—— "Rethinking Arendt's Vita Activa: Toward a Theory of Democratic Praxis," *Praxis International*, vol. 5, no. 2, 1985.

—— "Hannah Arendt on Judgment, Philosophy and Praxis," *International Studies in Philosophy*, vol. 21, no. 3, 1989.

Kohn, J. "Thinking/Acting," *Social Research*, vol. 57, no. 1, 1990.

Lafer, C. "O sopra do pensamiento, o peso da vontade, e o espaço publico do juizo. Dimensoes filosoficas da reflexao politica de Hannah Arendt," *Rivista Brasilera de Filosofia*, vol. 30, 1979.

Lane, A. "The Feminism of Hannah Arendt," *Democracy*, vol. 3, no. 3, 1983.

Laqueur, W. "Rereading Hannah Arendt," *Encounter*, vol. 52, no. 3, 1979.

Lasch, C. "Introduction," *Salmagundi*, no. 60, 1983.

Lefort, C. "Une interprétation politique de l'antisémitisme: Hannah Arendt" (I), *Commentaire*, vol. 6, no. 20, 1983

—— "Une interprétation politique de l'antisémitisme: Hannah Arendt" (II), *Commentaire*, vol. 6, no. 21, 1983.

—— "Hannah Arendt and the Question of the Political," in *Democracy and Political Theory* (Cambridge: Polity Press, 1988).

Levin, M. "On Animal Laborans and Homo Politicus in Hannah Arendt," *Political Theory*, vol. 7, no. 4, 1979.

Losurdo, D. "Hannah Arendt e l'analisi delle rivoluzioni," in R. Esposito (ed.), *La Pluralità Irrappresentabile* (Urbino: Edizioni Quattro Venti, 1987).

Lowell, R. "On Hannah Arendt," *The New York Review of Books*, 13 May 1976.

Luban, D. "On Habermas on Arendt on Power," *Philosophy and Social Criticism*, vol. 6, no. 1, 1979.

—— "Explaining Dark Times: Hannah Arendt's Theory of Theory," *Social Research*, vol. 50, no. 1, 1983.

McCarthy, M. "The Hue and Cry," *Partisan Review*, vol. 31, no. 1, 1964.

—— "Saying Good-Bye to Hannah," *The New York Review of Books*, 22 January 1976.

—— "Editor's Postface," in Hannah Arendt, *The Life of the Mind* (New York: Harcourt Brace Jovanovich, 1978).

—— "Hannah Arendt and Politics," *Partisan Review*, vol. 51, no. 4, 1984.

Macdonald, D. "A New Theory of Totalitarianism," *The New Leader*, vol. 34, 1951.

McKenna, G. "On Hannah Arendt: Politics: As It Is, Was, Might Be," *Salmagundi*, nos. 10–11, 1969–70.

—— "Bannisterless Politics: Hannah Arendt and Her Children," *History of Political Thought*, vol. 5, no. 2, 1984.

Magni, G. "Democrazia diretta, eguaglianza e diversità. Note di lettura su Hannah Arendt," *Classe*, nos. 2–3, 1988.

Major, R. "A Reading of Hannah Arendt's Unusual Distinction between Labor and Work," in M. Hill (ed.), *Hannah Arendt: The Recovery of the Public World* (New York: St Martin's Press, 1979).

Marcellan, A. "Uomo e tempo nel pensiero di Hannah Arendt," *Verifiche*, vol. 14, 1985.

Markus. G. "Praxis and Poiesis: Beyond the Dichotomy," *Thesis Eleven*, no. 15, 1986.

Markus, M. "The "Anti-Feminism" of Hannah Arendt," *Thesis Eleven*, no. 17, 1987.

Mason, T. "Loving the World and Changing It," *The Manchester Guardian*, 20 May 1982.

Mattei, J. "L'enracinement ontologique de la pensée politique chez Heidegger et Hannah Arendt," *Annales de la Faculté des Lettres et Sciences Humaine de Nice*, no. 49, 1985.

May, W. "Animal Laborans and Homo Faber," *The Thomist*, vol. 36, 1972.

Miller, J. "The Pathos of Novelty: Hannah Arendt's Image of Freedom in the Modern World," in M. Hill (ed.), *Hannah Arendt: The Recovery of the Public World* (New York: St Martin's Press, 1979).

Moors, K. "Modernity and Human Initiative: The Structure of Hannah Arendt's *Life of the Mind*," *The Political Science Reviewer*, vol. 10, 1980.

Morgenthau, H. "Hannah Arendt on Totalitarianism and Democracy," *Social Research*, vol. 44, no. 1, 1977.

Nelson, J. "Politics and Truth: Arendt's Problematic," *American Journal of Political Science*, vol. 22, no. 2, 1978.

Nisbet, R. "The American Revolution: Who were the People?," *The New York Review of Books*, 5 August 1976.

—— "Hannah Arendt and the American Revolution," *Social Research*, vol. 44, no. 1, 1977.

Oakeshott, M. Review of Hannah Arendt, *Between Past and Future*, *Political Science Quarterly*, vol. 77, 1962.

O'Sullivan, N. "Politics, Totalitarianism, and Freedom: The Political Thought of Hannah Arendt," *Political Studies*, vol. 21, no. 2, 1973.

—— "Hannah Arendt: Hellenic Nostalgia and Industrial Society," in A. de Crespigny and K. Minogue (eds), *Contemporary Political Philosophers* (London: Methuen, 1976).

Parekh, B. "Does Traditional Philosophy Rest on a Mistake?" *Political Studies*, vol. 27, no. 2, 1979.

—— "Hannah Arendt's Critique of Marx," in M. Hill (ed.), *Hannah Arendt: The Recovery of the Public World* (New York: St Martin's Press, 1979).

—— "Hannah Arendt," in *Contemporary Political Thinkers* (Oxford: Martin Robertson, 1982).

Pianciola, C. "La politica ridefinita di Hannah Arendt," *La Linea d'Ombra*, vol. 4, no. 13, 1986.

Pitkin, H. "Justice: On Relating Private and Public," *Political Theory*, vol. 9, no. 3, 1981.

Portinaro, P. "Hannah Arendt e l'Utopia della Polis," *Comunità*, no. 183, 1981.

—— "Il Problema di Hannah Arendt. La politica come cominciamento e la fine della politica," *Il Mulino*, no. 303, 1986.

—— "L'Azione, lo Spettatore e il Giudizio," *Teoria Politica*, vol. 5, no. 1, 1989.

Rametta, G. "Osservazioni su *Der Liebesbegriff bei Augustin* di Hannah Arendt," in R. Esposito (ed.), *La Pluralità Irrappresentabile* (Urbino: Edizioni Quattro Venti, 1987).

—— "Comunicazione, giudizio ed esperienza del pensiero in Hannah Arendt," in G. Duso (ed.), *Filosofia Politica e Pratica del Pensiero* (Milano: Franco Angeli, 1988).

Ratmore, L. and Bhati, P. "Hannah Arendt's Contribution to Contemporary Political Theory," *Indian Journal of Political Science*, vol. 40, no. 3, 1979.

Reshaur, K. "Concepts of Solidarity in the Political Theory of Hannah Arendt," *Canadian Journal of Political Science*, vol. 25, no. 4, 1992.

Richardson, W. "Contemplative in Action," in J. Bernauer (ed.), *Amor Mundi* (Dordrecht: Martinus Nijhoff, 1987).

Ricoeur, P. "Action, Story, and History: On Rereading *The Human Condition*," *Salmagundi*, no. 60, 1983.

—— "Liberté de l'esprit," introduction to Hannah Arendt, *Condition de l'homme moderne* (Paris: Calmann-Lévy, 1983).

—— "De la philosophie au politique," *Les Cahiers de Philosophie*, no. 4, 1987.

Riley, P. Review of Hannah Arendt, *Lectures on Kant's Political Philosophy*, *The Modern Schoolman*, vol. 62, 1984.

—— "On DeLue's Review of Arendt's *Lectures on Kant's Political Philosophy*," *Political Theory*, vol. 12, no. 3, 1984.

—— "Hannah Arendt on Kant, Truth and Politics," *Political Studies*, vol. 35, no. 3, 1987.

Ring, J. "On Needing both Marx and Arendt," *Political Theory*, vol. 17, no. 3, 1989.

—— "The Pariah as Hero," *Political Theory*, vol. 19, no. 3, 1991.

Ritter Santini, L. "La Passione di Capire. Hannah Arendt e il pensare letteratura," introduction to Hannah Arendt, *Il Futuro alle spalle* (Bologna: Il Mulino, 1981).

Roach, T. "Enspirited Words and Deeds: Christian Metaphors Implicit in Arendt's Concept of Personal Action," in J. Bernauer (ed.), *Amor Mundi* (Dordrecht: Martinus Nijhoff, 1987).

Roman, J. "Thinking Politics without a Philosophy of History: Arendt and Merleau-Ponty," *Philosophy and Social Criticism*, vol. 15, no. 4, 1989.

Rotenstreich, N. "Can Evil be Banal?" *The Philosophical Forum*, vol. 16, nos. 1–2, 1985.

Ryan, A. "A Thinker of Our Time," *New Society*, 10 June 1982.

Schürmann, R. "Le temps de l'esprit et l'histoire de la liberté," *Les Études Philosophiques*, no. 3, 1983.

—— Review of Hannah Arendt, *Lectures on Kant's Political Philosophy*, *Kant-Studien*, vol. 75, 1984.

Schwartz, B. "The Religion of Politics: Reflections on the Thought of Hannah Arendt," *Dissent*, vol. 17, no. 2, 1970.

Schwartz, J. M. "Arendt's Politics: The Elusive Search for Substance," *Praxis International*, vol. 9, nos. 1–2, 1989.

Schwartz, N. "Distinction Between Public and Private Life," *Political Theory*, vol. 7, no. 2, 1979.

Scott, J. V. "A Detour Through Pietism: Hannah Arendt on St. Augustines Concept of Freedom," *Polity*, vol. 20, 1988.

Serra, T. "Presentazione," to Hannah Arendt, *La disobbedienza civile e altri saggi* (Milano: Giuffrè Editore, 1985).

Shklar, J. Review of Hannah Arendt, *Between Past and Future, History and Theory*, vol. 2, no. 3, 1963.
—— "Hannah Arendt's Triumph," *The New Republic*, no. 173, 27 December 1975.
—— "Rethinking the Past," *Social Research*, vol. 44, no. 1, 1977.
—— "Hannah Arendt as Pariah," *Partisan Review*, vol. 50, no. 1, 1983.
—— Review of Hannah Arendt, *Lectures on Kant's Political Philosophy*, *Bulletin of the Hegel Society of Great Britain*, no. 9, 1984.
Sitton, J. F. "Hannah Arendt's Argument for Council Democracy," *Polity*, vol. 20, no. 1, 1987.
Smith, R. W. "Redemption and Politics," *Political Science Quarterly*, vol. 86, no. 2, 1971.
Spitz, D. "The Politics of Segregation," in *The Liberal Idea of Freedom* (Tucson: University of Arizona Press, 1964).
Springborg, P. "Arendt, Republicanism and Patriarchalism," *History of Political Thought*, vol. 10, no. 3, 1989.
—— "Hannah Arendt and the Classical Republican Tradition," in G. T. Kaplan and C. S. Kessler (eds), *Hannah Arendt: Thinking, Judging, Freedom* (Sydney: Allen & Unwin, 1989).
Spyros Draenos, S. "Thinking Without a Ground: Hannah Arendt and the Contemporary Situation of Understanding," in M. Hill (ed.), *Hannah Arendt: The Recovery of the Public World* (New York: St Martin's Press, 1979).
Stanley, J. L. "Is Totalitarianism a New Phenomenon? Reflections on Hannah Arendt's *The Origins of Totalitarianism*," *Review of Politics*, vol. 49, no. 2, 1987.
Steiner, G. "The Passionate Pilgrim," *The Sunday Times*, 23 May 1982.
Stern, P. and Yarbrough, J. "Hannah Arendt," *The American Scholar*, vol. 47, no. 3, 1978.
—— "Vita Activa and Vita Contemplativa: Reflections on Hannah Arendt's Political Thought in *The Life of the Mind*," *The Review of Politics*, vol. 43, no. 3, 1981.
Sternberger, D. "The Sunken City: Hannah Arendt's Idea of Politics," *Social Research*, vol. 44, no. 1, 1977.
—— "Hannah Arendt," in E. Nordhofen (ed.), *Physiognomien. Philosophen des 20. Jahrhunderts in Portraits* (Konigstein: Athenaeum Verlag, 1980).
—— "Politie und Leviathan. Ein Streit um den antiken und den modernen Staat," in H. Maier-Leibnitz (ed.), *Zeugen des Wissens* (Mainz: Hase & Koehler Verlag, 1986).
Stillman, P. "Freedom as Participation: The Revolutionary Theories of Hegel and Arendt," *The American Behavioural Scientist*, vol. 20, no. 4, 1977.
Stone, N. "Weimar in Partibus," *The London Review of Books*, 1–14 July 1982.
Suchting, W. "Marx and Hannah Arendt's *The Human Condition*," *Ethics*, vol. 73, no. 4, 1962.
Taminiaux, J. "Arendt, disciple de Heidegger?" *Études Phénoménologiques*, vol. 1, no. 2, 1985.
—— "La vie de quelqu'un," *Le Cahiers du Grif*, no. 33, 1986.
—— "Phenomenology and the Problem of Action," *Philosophy and Social Criticism*, vol. 11, no. 3, 1986.
—— "Heidegger et Arendt lecteurs d'Aristote," *Les Cahiers de Philosophie*, no. 4, 1987.
Thompson, K. "Constitutional Theory and Political Action," *The Journal of Politics*, vol. 31, no. 3, 1969.

Tolle, G. "Probing Arendt's Thought," *The Review of Politics*, vol. 47, no. 2, 1985.

Udovicki, J. "The Uses of Freedom and the Human Condition," *Praxis International*, vol. 3, no. 1, 1983.

Valadier, P. "La politique contre le totalitarisme. Ouverture à la pensée de Hannah Arendt," *Project* , no. 143, 1980.

—— Review of Hannah Arendt, *La Vie de l'Esprit I, Archives de Philosophie*, no. 46, 1983.

—— Review of Hannah Arendt, *La Vie de l'Esprit II, Archives de Philosophie*, no. 48, 1985.

Venco, L. "Il Concetto di Pubblico: Tre Interpretazioni," *Il Politico*, vol. 44, no. 3, 1979.

Veto, M. "Cohérence et terreur: introduction à la philosophie politique de Hannah Arendt," *Archives de Philosophie*, vol. 45, no. 4, 1982.

Villa, D. R. "Beyond Good and Evil," *Political Theory*, vol. 20, no. 2, 1992.

Voegelin, E. Review of Hannah Arendt, *The Origins of Totalitarianism, The Review of Politics*, vol. 15, no. 6, 1953 .

Vollrath, E. "Hannah Arendt and the Method of Political Thinking," *Social Research*, vol. 44, no. 1, 1977.

—— "Hannah Arendt über Meinung und Urteilskraft," in A. Reif (ed.), *Hannah Arendt: Materialien zu Ihrem Werk* (Wien: Europa Verlag, 1979).

—— "Associational versus Communicative Rationality of Politics," in B. Parekh and T. Pantham (eds), *Political Discourse: Explorations in Indian and Western Political Thought* (New Delhi: Sage Publications, 1987).

Volpi, F. "Il Pensiero Politico di Hannah Arendt e la Riabilitazione della Filosofia Pratica," *Il Mulino*, no. 303, 1986.

Wellmer, A. "Hannah Arendt on Judgment: The Unwritten Doctrine of Reason," unpublished manuscript, 1985.

Winter, G. "A Proposal for a Political Ethics," *Review of Religious Research*, vol. 21, no. 1, 1979.

Winters, F. "The Banality of Virtue: Reflections on Hannah Arendt's Reinterpretation of Political Ethics," in J. Bernauer (ed.), *Amor Mundi* (Dordrecht: Martinus Nijhoff, 1987).

Wolff, K. "On the Significance of Hannah Arendt's *The Human Condition* for Sociology," *Inquiry*, vol. 4, no. 2, 1961.

Wolff, R. "Notes for a Materialist Analysis of the Public and the Private Realms," *Graduate Faculty Philosophy Journal*, vol. 9, no. 1, 1982.

Wolin, S. "Hannah Arendt and the Ordinance of Time," *Social Research*, vol. 44, no. 1, Spring 1977.

—— "Stopping to Think," *The New York Review of Books*, 26 October 1978.

—— "Hannah Arendt: Democracy and the Political," *Salmagundi*, no. 60, 1983.

Young-Bruehl, Elizabeth "Hannah Arendt's Storytelling," *Social Research*, vol. 44, no. 1, 1977.

—— "From the Pariah's Point of View: Reflections on Hannah Arendt's Life and Work," in M. Hill (ed.), *Hannah Arendt: The Recovery of the Public World* (New York: St Martin's Press, 1979).

—— "Reflections on Hannah Arendt's *The Life of the Mind*," *Political Theory*, vol. 10, no. 2, 1982.

Zorzi, R. "Nota su Hannah Arendt," introduction to Hannah Arendt, *Sulla Rivoluzione* (Milano: Edizioni di Comunità, 1983).

# Index